GLOBAL SUPPLY CHAIN MANAGEMENT

LEVERAGING PROCESSES, MEASUREMENTS, AND TOOLS FOR STRATEGIC CORPORATE ADVANTAGE

TOMAS HULT • DAVID CLOSS • DAVID FRAYER

New York   Chicago   San Francisco   Athens   London
Madrid   Mexico City   Milan   New Delhi
Singapore   Sydney   Toronto

1 2 3 4 5 6 7 8 9 0 DOC/DOC 1 9 8 7 6 5 4 3

ISBN   978-0-07-182742-3
MHID   0-07-182742-0

e-ISBN 978-0-07-182743-0
e-MHID   0-07-182743-9

This publication is designed to provide accurate and authoritative information in regard to the subject matter covered. It is sold with the understanding that neither the author nor the publisher is engaged in rendering legal, accounting, securities trading, or other professional services. If legal advice or other expert assistance is required, the services of a competent professional person should be sought.
—*From a Declaration of Principles Jointly Adopted by a Committee of the American Bar Association and a Committee of Publishers and Associations*

Library of Congress Cataloging-in-Publication Data
Hult, G. Tomas M.
  Global supply chain management : leveraging processes, measurements, and tools for strategic corporate advantage / Tomas Hult, David Closs, and David Frayer.
    pages cm
  Includes bibliographical references and index.
  ISBN 978-0-07-182742-3 (alk. paper) — ISBN 0-07-182742-0 (alk. paper)
1. Business logistics. 2. International trade. 3. International business enterprises.
I. Closs, David J. II. Frayer, David. III. Title.
  HD38.5.H866   2014
  658.7—dc23

                                                                    2013024495

To the many supply chain management professionals whom we have interacted and dialogued with over decades of being engaged in global logistics, purchasing, operations, and market channels.

Contents

Preface

It was springtime in 2012, and the Eli Broad College of Business at Michigan State University (MSU) had recently entered into a partnership with Bisk Education, a worldwide leader in online education via its University Alliance platform. Since MSU had been a worldwide leader in supply chain management for more than half a century, it was looking strategically at the University Alliance platform as a global vehicle to take its supply chain management education and executive training across the globe. And naturally, *global* supply chain management had to be a critical portion of this global strategy.

But it had to be done in such a way that it was truly global supply chain management and not in any way skewed toward any of the core functions of the supply chain (logistics, purchasing, operations, and market channels). In effect, global supply chains have to be treated as an integrated and coordinated effort among global logistics, global purchasing, global operations, and global market channels based on a solid global strategy foundation. Often, books like ours are written by authors who have a particular view and perhaps a particular message to get across to the reader. We are the same. But our position is that logistics, purchasing, operations, and market channels should be treated equally when a firm is strategically developing and implementing global supply chains. Now, it may be that logistics should be stressed more than the other elements in certain situations, but the starting point is the same across all four elements of the global supply chain. The skewness toward one or more global supply chain functions depends on the industry globalization drivers and the worldwide infrastructure facing the company.

Another viewpoint we have is that global supply chain management is embedded in and part of corporate-based global strategy. Supply chain management is now an element of corporate strategy—at least, that is our strong belief and one that we stress throughout this book. Multinational corporations cannot run effective and efficient businesses without integrating supply chain management into their corporate strategy. The days when supply chains were treated as tactical, activity-based operations are long gone, and companies that still maintain such a view are falling behind, as we illustrate throughout the book. This means that global supply chains should be discussed at the same level and at the same time as what products or services to develop, how to go about creating global marketing strategies, what countries to enter, and how to strategically beat competitors in various global marketplaces. Corporate strategy does not drive global supply chains, and, by the same token, the corporate strategy that can be developed should not be constrained by global supply chains (although, of course, worldwide infrastructure issues do sometimes constrain what can be developed and implemented). A wealth of data and concepts in the book speak to this issue.

Overall, our book on global supply chain management incorporates topics related to leveraging processes, measurements, and tools for strategic corporate advantage. We provide an equal treatment of global logistics, global purchasing, global operations (management), and global market channels as well as a detailed discussion of the implications of industry globalization drivers for supply chains and the worldwide infrastructure that can facilitate global supply chain practices that exists. These and many related topics come together in eight chapters that culminate in a discussion of how to manage global supply chains. In the latter part of this book, we also use 16 diverse multinational corporations to illustrate their relative emphasis on global supply chain management vis-à-vis the other so-called global strategy levers.

Finally, we would like to thank David McDonald Yawn, Anne Hoekman, and Knox Huston for their dedicated assistance in helping us write the book in "conversational style" (David), for catching our idiosyncrasies in writing style (Anne), and for spearheading the promotion of this project (Knox). David is a long-standing business writer, journalist, and master communicator, and his input into the conversational style of the book was very valuable. Anne is a longstanding editor, copy editor, and master of the English language, and her input into the book ensured a clean read for everyone. Knox is senior editor and our point person at McGraw-Hill Professional, and his vision helped crystalize this project.

Happy reading, strategizing, and global supply chaining!

CHAPTER 1

Global Strategy and Global Supply Chain Management

Superior global supply chains are strategic total value systems.

WELCOME TO THE INTRIGUING WORLD OF GLOBAL SUPPLY CHAIN MANAGEMENT

No matter where in the world we are born and grow up, we are taught at a very young age to organize our daily lives into smaller pieces, often in a sequential way based upon time increments. This instruction is usually carried out in an informal manner over a considerable period, first by our parents and elementary school teachers, then perhaps by sports team coaches, music instructors, and other activity leaders. The idea is that breaking down projects and undertakings into their component parts or simple steps will make us focused, efficient, and effective in completing tasks. Sometimes we refer to this as *division of labor*. The desired result of creating these divisions is that each step is completed fully, with high quality and at high speed, to achieve an optimal outcome. In a way, we are all taught to be operational in our daily lives, whether we're focused on our family life or our work life. What about the bigger picture, though, where we can see and achieve vital business leverage?

Clearly, not all elements of a task, meetings in a day, or even morsels of food on a plate are equally important or interesting. So what do we do? We typically make either calculated or intuitive judgments that allow us to focus more heavily on one part of a major task. We make assumptions about a meeting's importance based on the number of people in attendance. And we eat the food on the plate that we like, although perhaps not the food that would give us the energy we need if we are to carry out the tasks we intend to do that day. In essence, we all develop a personal operational scheme for accomplishing things in our lives.

Whether we realize it or not, we intuitively develop a strategy for our lives through trial and error based on where we have been and what we hope to be involved in. This does not mean that we do not have bosses at work (or at home!). It simply means that we take all aspects of our lives into account—often indirectly and intuitively—and form a "strategy" for how to be global citizens, even in our small corner of the world. In contrast, people and organizations that are involved in global supply chains—all the linkages, resources, and connecting points—do not have the luxury of this level of daily oversight and cannot be involved in all aspects of the full supply chain. Rather, supply chain professionals are generally involved in just one or a few links and connecting nodes of the chain, although potentially having some influence over and input into other parts.

Like people, global supply chains are "total cost systems" that work best if all aspects of the chain (for example, links, resources, and connecting nodes) are strategically leveraged. For a global supply chain, the idea is to work toward helping the total chain to succeed, not toward maximizing the success of an individual element of the chain. Now, we still want the firms that are involved in global supply chains to maximize the value they receive from being a part of the chain. However, strategically, such efforts should be at the 30,000-foot level—where most commercial airplanes fly.

An airplane metaphor also works well in explaining the sophisticated and often delicate nature of global supply chains. Consider how to turn an aircraft; think of coordination and leverage points. That is, aircraft are typically steered by using an integrated system of ailerons on the wings, elevators at the rear, and a rudder at the tail, with all of these operating in combination with throttle adjustments to control the roll, pitch, and yaw of the aircraft. It sounds easy enough. In comparison to the aircraft, the ailerons, elevators, rudder, and throttle seem very small. But leverage allows the coordinated and integrated effort of these small pieces of the plane to steer the aircraft. In other words, putting the right combination of a little leverage on the right places through a coordinated effort leads to incredible maneuvering ability. Global supply chains are the same. We want the integrated and coordinated effort to yield optimum global results.

To yield optimum results, the tools and ideas covered in this book do away with the illusion that supply chain management in the global marketplace is purely a task-oriented, sequential chain of operational activities that are combined into a whole after the chain is completed. The best-value global supply chains are those that strategically leverage the inbound and outbound (or upstream and downstream) operations from raw material to finished products reaching end users. Thus, the use and study of critical leverage points, total cost analysis,[1] alignment with industry globalization drivers, and combination of global supply chain systems within corporate strategies become the emphasis.

Global supply chain management, then, is not the additive utility of its functions (for example, logistics, purchasing, operations, and market channels). Rather, it is the integration and coordination of the strategic leverage points embedded in those supply chain functions. In addition to the functions, we must consider the entities, activity links, and resources throughout the chain. Global supply chains have to be developed and implemented so that they are both operational and strategic. The corporate C-suite is as important as service personnel, and all organizational layers in between should be leveraged at all mission-critical points along the global supply chain.

While top management working alongside frontline service personnel is the starting point, we realize that there are constraining issues; for example, suppliers often develop a stronger relationship with corporate buyers than the corporate buyers have with the employees who actually use the products. Expressed from another angle, total cost analysis is interpreted to mean looking at the total cost of a shipment delivered to the ultimate location where it is consumed. What we need is better understanding, development, and implementation of the core leverage points throughout the complete global supply chain, involving all critical entities (including suppliers, partners, agents, buyers, and customers). In some cases, a second-tier supplier can be as critical to the total value offered in the chain as a retailer. Leverage points are leverage points for a reason; they need to be strategically identified, analyzed, and used.

In global supply chains, the starting point for determining global leverage and achieving maximum total value is to ask three basic questions:

> How global is our industry?
> How global should our strategy be?
> How global should our supply chains be?

These three questions provide the global strategy perspective on supply chains and the foundation for thinking strategically about global supply chains. The questions highlight a logical but often overlooked fact: virtually all industries have aspects that are global or potentially global. The same goes for strategy—it can be more or less global in its different strategy levers. In that context, an industry is global to the extent that intercountry connections exist within that industry. A strategy is global to the extent that a firm synthesizes its strategies across countries. Integration is the key. If a firm simply operates subsidiaries that design, produce, and market products within a country, then its focus is on being multinational or multilocal. A truly global firm is one that has at least the capability to do business in both the Eastern and Western Hemispheres and in both the Northern and Southern Hemispheres.

After all, global strategy explains 70 percent of a multinational firm's performance—a number that has remained steady over the past decade and is forecasted to stay the same for at least the next five years. More important, global supply chains, on average, explain about 20 percent of a multinational firm's strategic performance in the global marketplace today and are predicted to explain 25 percent in five years. Firms such as ABB (22 percent of ABB's strategy is based on supply chains), AB InBev (21 percent), Amex (16 percent), ArcelorMittal (21 percent), Cemex (15 percent), Daimler (13 percent), Dell (23 percent), FedEx (14 percent), Microsoft (19 percent), Nestlé (21 percent), Nokia (21 percent), OMV Group (17 percent), Siemens (22 percent), Skandia (19 percent), Swatch (18 percent), and Unilever (21 percent) are acutely aware of the importance of global strategic supply chains for the worldwide performance of their businesses.

In this opening chapter, we introduce a number of key concepts to help understand and position the global opportunity facing supply chain management in the modern business world. In essence, in Chapter 1 of the book, we broadly tackle a potpourri of reasons for strategic global supply chain management and provide a skeleton framework for it. Our journey begins with understanding global trade and global supply chains. Then we review the important role of emerging markets in supporting our global supply chains. The strategic nature of supply chain management drives how we leverage the location of global activities. We provide some important definitions and distinctions, discuss the internal and external integration of supply chain functions, and highlight some of the performance benefits of global supply chains. We conclude this discussion by highlighting the eight integrating processes that cut across all global supply chains.

Given all these topics to be covered, this opening chapter will have good reason to be a potpourri. But by the time we get through the book and to Chapter 8, "Managing Global Supply Chains," the structure should be clear in the best spirit of not only global supply chains, but *best-value strategic global supply chains*! Let's start by taking a look at global trade and global supply chains.

GLOBAL TRADE AND GLOBAL SUPPLY CHAINS

By some estimates, 90 percent of today's global demand is not fully met and satisfied by local supply. And as shown in Figure 1.1, international trade across countries' borders has increased dramatically in the last few decades. From a supply chain standpoint, this means that the global marketplace is highly dependent on global supply chains

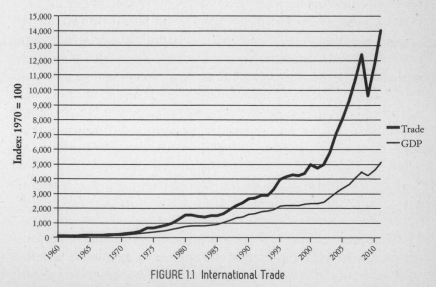

FIGURE 1.1 International Trade

World Bank, *World Development Indicators*

to provide the buying and supplying infrastructure that the world has come to depend on over the past several years. In essence, the incredible growth in world trade observed over the past decade has been driven largely by the effective development and implementation of global supply chains.

This begs the question: has your firm kept up with the globalization of supply chains, and will you be able to leverage your chains to increase their globalization by the predicted 25 percent in the next five years and 43 percent in the next ten years? If not, you are likely to fall behind, and your operation risks losing its competitive edge. What is even more important is strategically leveraging global supply chains; that is, you should incorporate your supply chains into your overall corporate strategies and leverage them as much as you do your products, market participation, marketing, and competitive moves to achieve global competitiveness.

Global supply chains are critical for the new breed of firms that are becoming major players in the global marketplace. The old blueprint of starting by serving one or a small set of countries using a diversified conglomerate approach is available to only a select few companies in each industry. Some say that no more than three firms can and will fit this "past reality" blueprint in the future.[2] Instead, the emerging reality is that firms will develop much more around focused businesses that go global soon after their inception or their reconfiguration and then thrive in a globally integrated economy.

As a result, the major competitors of the past—which could be seen from miles away because of their domestic and global footprint—are not the main threat anymore. The new threat is the firm that uses global supply chain strategies to get its products out effectively to a large number of customers in a globally integrated economy. This firm does so with more limited product lines and product assortments than the massive conglomerates we were accustomed to in the past.

This is all about what makes firms unique, and uniqueness comes in many forms. Consider this restaurant interaction: one minute you are surrounded by friends, and the next minute you are standing alone at the bar. A woman walks up and without hesitation asks, "What makes you unique?" The normal pattern of introductions or even a common icebreaker does not happen. Instead, "What makes you unique?" opens the dialogue. While this may be a true story, we will leave that bar interaction, but think about the question. "What makes you unique?" is really what it is all about in global supply chains. We take a number of people, working for a number of organizations, with access to a number of resources, and we create a global supply chain. The intention is to make the chain competitive in the marketplace, preferably emphasizing core competencies that can sustain the chain's value-added features and maintain the firm's competitiveness for some time.

In effect, it is like shifting views through a window. If we look out the window through the center of the glass, we are likely to see a lot of things outside. If we start moving toward the frame of the window, we are likely to still see some or even most of what is outside. But if we move our head to the left or right of the window frame, what do we see? Most likely, a wall and none of what's outside!

The same logic holds when it comes to stressing uniqueness and core competencies in multinational corporations. Firms that focus their efforts on the "middle of the window" by leveraging their core competencies to compete in the global marketplace are more likely to be successful than those that overly customize or veer to the left or the right. That is often caused by creating too much diversification of operations to satisfy the various needs of the global marketplace. Firms are at their best when they do what they are best at doing! Global supply chains are the same.

Being vertically integrated in order to exercise more control in global supply chains is not helpful if it results in reduced effectiveness. Similarly, involving additional firms in the chain without seeing a true value-added benefit leads to trouble not only in terms of providing total value from the full global supply chain, but also in terms of having extra layers and linkages that require coordination, integration, and investment. These result in additional cost centers. Every node, activity, and resource used in a global supply chain should result in value being added to the chain in the sense of a reduced total cost.

The total value analysis of global supply chains is a strategic, somewhat dynamic, and continuous process. A half century ago, the United States produced roughly 40 percent of the world's output. Today, that figure is about 20 percent. China has quadrupled its output in the past 50 years, while Europe is holding steady at about 20 percent. In addition, we know that the so-called BRIC countries— Brazil, Russia, India, and China—are important, in terms of both population and economic output.[3] For example, we know that many firms have sought out specific areas of expertise in these BRIC countries, such as call center operations in India. So the issue is not so much where we have found leverage points before or where they are now, but instead where they will be in the future.

Global supply chains thrive because they coordinate and integrate the best that the globe has to offer to provide the greatest value possible to the system. Firms demand this, supply chain members demand it, and customers demand it. This requires global competence on the part of firms, their employees, and their supply chain partners. Our customers are global, and they demand global solutions to their local and global needs. Most of all, they demand value. That value has to be sought in developed markets, newly industrialized countries, emerging markets, and even less developed markets. Most firms, though, see emerging markets as key to the next competitive landscape on the globe.

EMERGING MARKETS AND GLOBAL SUPPLY CHAINS _____

Various lists of the countries that are called "emerging markets" exist (based, for example, on classifications by Dow Jones, the *Financial Times*, Morgan Stanley, and the *Economist*), and in these various lists, the number of emerging markets generally varies between 21 and 35 (some reports even suggest that there are as many as 50 separate emerging markets). Therefore, there is no one definition or set of criteria for "emerging" markets, but these countries do have some commonalities. Very broadly, we will refer to emerging markets as countries where business activities or populations are rapidly growing and industrialization is taking place.

Based on a report by PricewaterhouseCoopers titled *Transportation and Logistics 2030*,[4] coupled with a scan of the global marketplace, a number of conclusions can be drawn regarding global supply chains and emerging markets. These include the notions of new trade corridors in the world, privatization in some countries, use of free trade zones, foreign direct investment, development of legal and regulatory infrastructure, and competition in the transportation and logistics industry.

With the emergence of countries that are engaging more and more in the global marketplace—whether newly industrialized countries or emerging markets—we will see new trade corridors being established, with significant implications for global supply chain management. We will also discover where and how to create global supply chain leverage. Some new trade corridors will develop between Africa and Asia, between South America and Asia, and within continental Asia. As firms look for opportunities to create more supply chain value and better value for the customer, while maintaining their cost structures, new trade routes will be used to create connecting nodes. Trade volume is likely to shift toward select emerging markets, especially in Asia, possibly in Latin America, and, later on, in Africa. Establishing such trade infrastructure will also make it much easier for less developed nations to engage in international trade. Multinational corporations that proactively and strategically plan their global supply chains for the next five to ten years to include such forecasted opportunities will have a leg up on the competition.

Social economies that are moving to become mixed or capitalist economies are likely to privatize previously untouchable aspects of their economies. Such privatization will also result in infrastructure changes that ultimately will have significant global supply chain implications. We are already seeing China's growth booming, although this growth rate will slow to about 8 percent during the next decade. Countries such as Brazil, India, Mexico, Russia, South Africa, Turkey, and Indonesia are already on our radar for production, economic engagement, and targeting of certain market segments. Each of these emerging markets is looking to benefit from increased efficiency and better access to capital, which is often tied to increased market privatization.

A unique connection to global supply chains will result from the increased establishment and use of free trade zones (FTZs) around the world, along with the increased foreign direct investment that often comes with increasing use of FTZs. Various aspects of the supply chain industry (for example, transportation and logistics) will have tremendous opportunities to provide their services around the globe. This is especially true for supply chain providers from developed countries, which can have a long-term advantage over their counterparts in emerging markets. Such emerging markets are growing rapidly in population and business activities, but for at least the near future, they are not well structured to increase the transportation and logistics services that they provide. That said, the competition for transportation and logistics (T&L) services in emerging markets will become increasingly tougher, with a large number of

T&L firms trying their business models in those markets. The long-term outlook, as in many industries that experience rapid growth and an influx of new players, is likely to be the consolidation of T&L providers into a smaller but capable set over the next few years.

While shipping routes—especially those involving Asia—will shift, the Asian-based emerging markets will not become the centers of gravity for global supply chains. For the near future, supply chain providers from developed countries have better infrastructure to use even in emerging markets than the emerging markets themselves do. Issues such as innovation, technology transfer, and standards setting will still rest with supply chain companies from mostly developed countries. This is also partly because of the lack of legal and regulatory infrastructure in emerging markets vis-à-vis developed countries when it comes to global supply chains. But, overall, countries like Brazil, China, India, Indonesia, Mexico, Russia, South Africa, Turkey, and Vietnam represent nodes in global supply chains that should be carefully evaluated and leveraged to add value across global supply chains.

Brazil

Brazil, with its $1.5 trillion economy (€1.2 trillion), has some $250 billion in exports and about $220 billion in imports, and a logistics market that is roughly $200 billion. About 195 million people live in the country. A unique supply chain opportunity in Brazil is its establishment of free trade zones and its involvement in the Mercosur agreement (a political and economic agreement among Brazil, Argentina, Paraguay, Uruguay, and Venezuela). However, as in India, the road infrastructure hampers transportation, and this is true of the air traffic portion of global supply chains as well. The road and air infrastructure are hard for a supply chain provider to influence, and solutions will probably have to come from privatization or from within Brazil itself.

China

China, with its $12 trillion economy (€9.6 trillion), has some $2 trillion in exports and about $1.8 trillion in imports, and a logistics market approaching $1 trillion. An estimated 1.3 billion people live in the country. China has been a production headquarters for a variety of firms for the last couple of decades. Now, the supply chain industry will have a crucial role in the country's development, continued economic growth, and broadening of its privatization measures. As closed as China typically appears to be, the country is ripe for foreign supply chain providers to become a part of the infrastructure and economic engine solution to maintain the country's growth at around the forecasted 8 percent area.

India

India, with its $4.5 trillion economy (€3.62 trillion), has some $300 billion in exports and about $450 billion in imports, and a logistics market that is roughly $125 billion. About 1.2 billion people inhabit this nation. India is unique in that the private sector of supply chain providers is the most likely infrastructure builder for India's supply chain system. The expectation is that government reforms—perhaps moving slowly and incrementally, but moving—will encourage a new breed of supply chain providers, especially foreign ones, to engage with India. Indian customers, perhaps more than those in many emerging markets, demand value, and that has significant implications and opportunities attached to it, especially for foreign supply chain providers.

Indonesia

Indonesia, with its $1.2 trillion economy (€1.0 trillion), has some $210 billion in exports and about $180 billion in imports, and a logistics market that is roughly $160 billion. About 240 million people live in the country. Indonesia's stable and predictable economic growth will have an effect on its supply chain industry, which is forecasted to grow at around 8 percent annually for some time. The projection is that there is still potential amounting to $1 trillion (€0.8 trillion) when more Indonesian companies begin to outsource their supply chain needs.

Mexico

Mexico, with its $1.7 trillion economy (€1.4 trillion), has some $340 billion in exports and about $340 billion in imports, and a logistics market that is incredibly hard to estimate but that we believe to be roughly $100 billion. About 115 million people reside in the country. As it is a more open market than many other emerging markets, multinational corporations dominate the marketplace within as well as into and out of Mexico. Still, Mexico is nowhere near the emerging markets within the BRIC framework (Brazil, Russia, India, and China) in terms of supply chain operations, and will not be until its legal and regulatory system makes these operations within the country easier to handle.

Russia

Russia, with its $2.5 trillion economy (€2.0 trillion), has some $500 billion in exports and about $320 billion in imports, and a logistics market that is roughly $75 billion (although, like Mexico's, the Russian logistics market is hard to estimate, it is likely to be somewhere between $60 billion and $100 billion, with the most logical estimate being about $75 billion). About 145 million people live in this vast country. It is reasonably easy to forecast that Russia's supply chain industry stands to benefit in the future from the corridor the country provides between East Asia and Europe. In addition, the establishment of port-based economic zones will help stimulate trade flows both inside the country and with, at least, Asia, Europe, and North America. In all, one can argue that Russia has too good an opportunity to be the corridor between these major trading areas of the world not to invest heavily in infrastructure to promote such trade.

South Africa

South Africa, with its $560 billion economy (€450 trillion), has some $100 billion in exports and about $100 billion in imports, and a logistics market that is estimated to be about $60 billion. It has a population of 50 million. South Africa has been and continues to be a logical supply chain link to Asia. While state-owned enterprises will continue to affect such explorations, we are cautiously optimistic that South Africa will develop the infrastructure to provide a corridor to Asia sooner rather than later. In that environment, it is hard to strategically plan too much simply from a supply chain provider standpoint, but some will find the risk-reward ratio strong enough to do so. The consolidation process involving supply chain providers, driven by the consumer goods sector, will open up unique opportunities.

Turkey

Turkey, with its $1.1 trillion economy (€0.8 trillion), has some $140 billion in exports and about $220 billion in imports, and a logistics market that is estimated to be about $95 billion. About 73 million people live there. Supply chain providers in Turkey are relatively advanced compared with their counterparts in other emerging markets. The country is also incredibly well positioned geographically, given its location between Europe, Asia, and the other Middle Eastern countries. Turkey has an energetic young population that relates to Europe in terms of technology and product trends and also has a mindset that facilitates entry into the Middle East and Asia. The supply chain industry, in particular, is experiencing and will continue to experience strong privatization efforts that should benefit Turkey, both as a trading partner and as a facilitator throughout the region.

Vietnam

Vietnam, with its $125 billion economy (€100 billion), has some $96 billion in exports and about $105 billion in imports, and a logistics market that is estimated to be about $25 billion. It has a population of 87 million. The systems of transportation, especially roads and bridges, are being developed fairly rapidly and are improving. However, ports and airports are at capacity. There are plans for several new airports, both domestic and international, in the next five years, and current planning calls for new ports and new railroads as well. Interestingly, the Vietnamese government is encouraging foreign direct investment and private capital to help build the supply chain infrastructure.

GLOBAL STRATEGIC SUPPLY CHAIN MANAGEMENT ⎯⎯⎯

Supply chains are increasingly becoming global and strategic. Sourcing near home and letting corporate strategy guide supply chain operations are becoming increasingly obsolete. At the same time, sourcing near home and performing supply chain tasks are part of the equation for leveraging the chain for value. However, firms that do not have the capability to strategically leverage their global supply chain options are likely to become stagnant and fall behind the competition. And it is not just about sourcing globally. Firms have to evaluate, develop, and strategically leverage their global coordination and integration of purchasing, logistics, operations, and market channels.

But global supply chain strategy can also be very different in its use of the core functions of purchasing (sourcing), logistics, operations, and market channels. In that context, a supply chain function is global to the extent that intercountry connections exist. The key, however, is gaining global leverage and ensuring that value is added. This is especially true when costs are added at each node and each activity in the chain. The aim is to have the capability to engage globally both in the Eastern and Western Hemispheres and in the Northern and Southern Hemispheres as needed.

While global supply chain operations continue to be critical to their effective implementation on a worldwide basis, the integrated coordination of supply chain management as part of corporate strategy emphasizes the leveraging and value-added features that make supply chains a global strategic weapon. This value must be strategic, not tactical, to provide a sustainable competitive advantage.

Let us clarify an important point regarding value and supply chains. We do not advocate going global for the sake of going global, diversifying, or decreasing labor cost. Instead, embedding supply chain management in corporate strategy means that optimizing global strategy entails evaluating for potential inclusion all plausible leverage points worldwide across the inbound and outbound parts of the chain. Leverage becomes strategic only when the quality received outweighs the cost endured. This leverage can be near or far from home. Coordination and integration of the internal (purchasing, logistics, operations, and market channel functions) and external (supply chain partners, activities, and resources) portions of the supply chain relative to the costs and benefits guide the strategic decision making on where to add value.

Value identification and achievement are important. Specifically, when they are incorporated into a global firm's strategy, supply chains account for about 20 percent of what makes such a firm perform successfully. Overall, global strategy considerations constitute about 70 percent of a global firm's performance (for example, return on investment, return on assets, and sales growth), with 30 percent being outside the firm's control. Adopting a global mindset and encouraging a platform that is centered on a "total global strategy" is critically important.[5] A firm's total global strategy goes through three basic stages that serve as the foundation for a set of global strategy levers, of which global supply chain management is one.[6] These stages are developing the core strategy, internationalizing the core strategy, and globalizing the international strategy.

Developing the core strategy means determining a firm's basis for sustainable strategic advantage. A typical scenario and progression would have the global firm develop the core strategy for its home country before moving into the global marketplace. Think back to the window example earlier. If we have several people looking out the window through the center of the glass, they are likely to see slightly different things, but the story line will be about the same. However, if they move toward the window frame or even to the side of the frame, the sight lines will be blurry at best. A firm's core strategy, core competencies, and core operations should leverage what it does best, at the center of the window. A core strategy includes several key elements: selection of the products offered, types of customers served, geographic markets served, sources of sustainable competitive advantage, functional strategy for important value-adding activities (for example, purchasing, logistics, operations, and market channels), competitive posture, and investment strategy.

Internationalizing the core strategy is the intermediate step that can potentially to derail the firm's globalization efforts. In effect, when a business expands outside its home markets, it sets out to internationalize its core strategy. This includes examining the firm's readiness to go international, the readiness of the product or service to be taken internationally, and channels for getting the product or service into the hands of end consumers while providing the level of value that they seek. Unfortunately, the end result is often that the firm winds up with strategies that are significantly different for different countries. The adaptations that are developed for each country's markets can actually weaken the firm's worldwide position in terms of cost, quality, customer preference, and competitive leverage—all issues that should in reality be benefits of operating as a global firm.

To overcome the potential disadvantages that are created by a business's adjusting to, customizing, and developing internationalization strategies for each country, firms need to be *globalizing the international strategy* in a way that coordinates and manages their uniqueness. This better achieves the desired global leverage and competitive advantages. Globalization strategy is multidimensional. Setting a strategy for a worldwide business requires choices along a number of strategic dimensions. Some of these dimensions determine whether the strategy lies toward the multilocal end of the continuum or toward the global end. The major implication for firms using a global strategy is that they actually do not need to be in the east and west, north and south; rather, they have the capability to engage anywhere. Not only that, but these firms may use any relevant strategic assets and access resources for any strategic purpose as they maximize profits on a global scale. The immediate implication for global supply chains within this scenario is that global supply chain management needs to be treated similarly. That is, global supply chains are based on the capability to leverage strategic supply chain nodes throughout the world, engage relevant supply chain assets, and access supply chain resources for strategic purposes. They maximize value on a chain basis through total cost analyses.

GLOBAL LOCATION OF VALUE-ADDED ACTIVITIES ⸻

Within the total global strategy framework, the global location of value-adding activities is a core lever, along with market participation, products and services, marketing, and competitive moves.[7] These five global strategy levers are illustrated in Figure 1.2. Importantly, as mentioned earlier, these five levers provide 70 percent of what drives the global firm's performance in the marketplace. Locating global activities represents the *global supply chain strategy lever* within this framework. It involves the choice of where to locate each of the activities that make up the entire global supply chain—from raw material to research to production to after-sales support—and the operations of connecting the nodes. On average, 20 percent of a global firm's performance can be directly attributed to the global location of value-added activities.

    Market participation involves the choice of country markets in which to conduct business and the level of activity (for example, market share) in each regional market. *Products and/or services* involve the extent to which a firm offers the same or different products in the countries in which it does business and the extent of product and/or service standardization across countries. *Marketing*

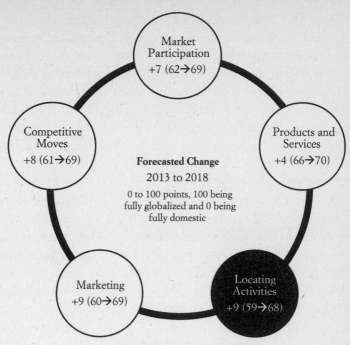

FIGURE 1.2 Global Strategy Levers

involves the extent to which a firm uses the same brand names, advertising, and other marketing elements in different countries. *Competitive moves* involve the extent to which a firm makes strategic and targeted marketplace moves in individual nations as part of a global competitive strategy either to make proactive moves or to reactively combat competitors.

Based on our benchmarking, we know that strategic supply chain management (along with marketing) will face the most pressure to increase globalization efforts in the next five years. This is within the context of the five global strategy levers that are central to a global firm's worldwide efforts. On a 0 to 100 scale, where 100 is fully globalized and 0 is fully domestic, we expect to see an increase from 59 to 68 for locating activities (market participation is expected to increase from 62 to 69, products and/or services from 66 to 70, marketing from 60 to 69, and competitive moves from 61 to 69). In essence, what used to be an operational component of global firms' efforts (that is, supply chains) now is expected to be as entrenched in global strategy as developing products and marketing them internationally.

In a perfect supply chain world, global firms would be able to develop and implement an extreme global supply chain in which each major activity (R&D, design, raw material sourcing, production, marketing, and so on) would be located in a different country where the comparative advantage was the greatest for that particular element of the chain. Perhaps in a perfect world for very domestic-centric consumers, each global firm would establish all operations in each nation in which it sold products, basically operating a fully constituted multilocal chain. Neither extreme, of course, is going to result in sustainable performance. Instead, what are the key issues that have to be considered when locating global activities to create a strategically oriented global supply chain?

The answer is to combine strategic (firm) and comparative (country) advantages when evaluating the global location of value-added activities. Reaching a logical decision that takes into consideration both strategic and comparative advantages requires careful attention to strategic alignment between industry globalization drivers and global supply chain strategy, along with careful integration of strategic advantages and knowledge of the firm. In effect, if a firm tries to globalize its supply chains more than the globalization drivers for its industry warrant, the firm's activities will have to include educating the marketplace about appropriate globalization efforts. On the other hand, if the firm does not globalize to the extent that the globalization drivers for the industry warrant, it is likely to fall behind, since it is not taking full advantage of the value-added advantages that can accrue through globalization.

Strategic alignment is fluid over time. What works today may not work tomorrow, and what is viewed as a position of strength in global supply chains today may be a position of weakness in a few years. Therefore, it is incredibly important that you put your finger on the right amount of globalization of supply chains so that you can leverage them effectively. It's all about the value-added identifiers at each step of the process relative to the cost incurred. Cost, in this sense, is also the expense resulting from not improving or changing through leveraging the global supply chain. For example, based on our benchmarking, we know that by 2018, firms will need to globalize their supply chains by 25 percent more than they are doing today to result in the same value leveraging as in 2013. The chains will need to be 43 percent more globalized by 2023 than they are in 2013 to achieve

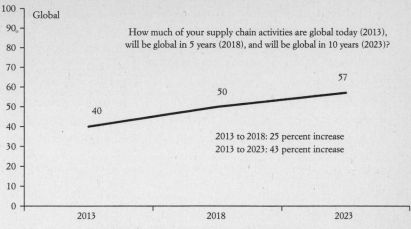

FIGURE 1.3 Forecasts of Supply Chain Globalization

the same value-added leverage from the perspective of a total chain analysis. These increased figures are illustrated in Figure 1.3.

Leverage, however, is a function of both a total chain perspective—from raw material to end consumer—and a fully coordinated effort within the firm with respect to the core supply chain functions of purchasing, logistics, operations, and market channels. It is mission-critical for the global supply chain to create a boundary-spanning role between the internal and external parts of the firm. This often involves serving in the main boundary-spanning role with external suppliers (inbound portion of the chain) and also serving in the main boundary-spanning role with external customers (outbound portion of the chain).[8]

The key functions of a global firm's internal (purchasing, logistics, operations, and market channels) and external boundary-spanning activities (suppliers and customers) can be illustrated (as in Figure 1.4) in a global supply chain framework that has purchasing as the critical link between suppliers and the manufacturer. This effectively starts at the very outbound portion of the chain and links manufacturers in the middle of the chain. Market channels link manufacturers to the end customers on the far outbound side of the chain. Meanwhile, logistics and operations function throughout the chain to support and provide added value. We will use this basic framework throughout the book.

FIGURE 1.4 Global Supply Chain Management

Importantly, as we said before, global supply chain strategy can be more or less global in each of its core functions of purchasing, logistics, operations, and market channels. The key, however, to gaining global leverage and to ensuring that value is added, especially when costs are added at each node or activity, is to be able to engage globally. This also means that the expectation is not that each core function in the global supply chain will be equally global or will contribute equally. Instead, we advocate alignment with the ideal degree of "globalness" supported by the structure that exists worldwide for each function. It's all about leveraging strategic advantage (the firm) with comparative advantage (the country) to assure achievement of the greatest total value in each cost scenario for the entire supply chain.

As with almost any business function, the expectation is that improvement, economies of scale, and better knowledge will be part of the timeline. What makes you successful today is probably not going to be sustainable in perpetuity. Therefore, you need to understand where you are today in terms of globalization efforts for each supply chain function and where you need to be in the future, and plan accordingly. Based on our benchmarking, the purchasing

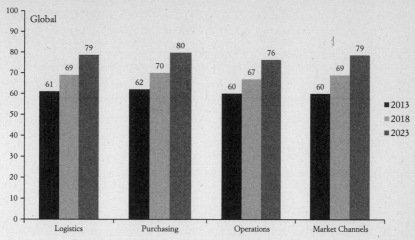

FIGURE 1.5 Globalization of Supply Chain Functions

function is slightly more globalized (most likely as a result of worldwide sourcing efforts that many companies engage in) than the other core (internal) supply chain functions. The 2013, 2018, and 2023 globalization statistics for the four supply chain functions are illustrated in Figure 1.5.

IMPORTANT DEFINITIONS AND DISTINCTIONS

Thus far, we have delved into several core elements of global strategy and supply chains, along with discussing a variety of "where we are now" and "where we need to go" issues. However, it is hard to know where to go if definitional boundaries are not clear. We need to measure everything that has the potential to serve as a leverage point in adding value in the global supply chain. At the same time, we cannot measure something if we cannot understand and define it. In the context of this book, we will use numerous terms and issues, most of which will be introduced and tackled in the context of their appropriate chapter. All the same, we have seven key terms that provide the platform for discussion throughout the book. For clarity, these need to be defined at this stage. They are global and globalize, global logistics, global purchasing, global operations, global market channels, global supply chain management, and global value chain.

- *Global and globalize.* Simply because it operates globally does not mean that a firm has a global strategy or uses
global supply chains. According to George Yip and Tomas
Hult in their book *Total Global Strategy*, "the global company does not have to be everywhere, but it must have the
capability to go anywhere, deploy any assets, and access
any resources as it maximizes profits on a global basis."[9] A
truly global firm is one that does business not only in the
Eastern and Western Hemispheres, but also in the Northern
and Southern Hemispheres. A fully integrated global supply chain has global activities in both the inbound/upstream
and outbound/downstream portions of the chain and has
the capability to leverage value-added points across all world
quadrants and hemispheres.
- *Global logistics.* Global logistics is the part of global supply
chain management that plans, implements, and controls the
effective forward and reverse flows and storage of goods, services, and related information between the worldwide point
of origin and the worldwide point of consumption to meet
global customers' requirements. Global logistics typically
involves the worldwide management of order processing,
inventory, transportation, and the combination of warehousing, materials handling, and packaging, all integrated
throughout a global network of facilities.
- *Global purchasing.* Global purchasing is the part of global
supply chain management that refers to the organization's
functions associated with the worldwide buying of goods,
services, and/or information required by the multinational
corporation. A number of terms can be used within the general context of "global purchasing"; consequently, the terms
purchasing, procurement, sourcing, strategic sourcing, and *supply management* are used interchangeably in this book (there
are technical and detailed differences among these terms;
however, the key here is to be strategic in using purchasing
globally). Order fulfillment and delivery and supplier selection are key areas.
- *Global operations.* Global operations is the part of global
supply chain management that refers to the systematic
design, direction, and control of domestic and global processes that transform inputs into services and products for

internal and external customers. Having a global operations strategy refers to the means by which operations implements the multinational firm's corporate strategy and facilitates the firm's being market driven. Global operations typically involves make-or-buy decisions, competitive priorities, total cost analysis, and process-based standards.

- *Global market channels.* Global market channels refers to the part of global supply chain management that includes all activities related to selling, service, and the development of relationships (preferably long-term relationships) with customers. A number of terms can be used within the general context of "global market channels." Consequently, the terms *market channels*, *marketing channels*, *channels of distribution*, and *distribution channel* are used interchangeably in this book. As with purchasing, there are technical and detailed differences among these terms, but the key for us is the strategic aspects of market channels that serve as a boundary spanner to external customers in the outbound portion of the strategic global supply chain. Global channel entities typically include some combination of producers, agents, brokers, wholesalers, retailers, and consumers.

- *Global supply chain management.* Global supply chain management involves being both proactive and responsive in managing the two-way movement, coordination, and control of products, services, and/or information from raw material through to the end user. This coordination, control, and integration within the global supply chain should center on a total cost analysis perspective that takes into account the values added throughout the chain. We strongly believe that maximizing value and cost effectiveness one node in the chain at a time is not the strategic, global way of conducting supply chain management. Instead, we believe that a full beginning-to-end perspective on the chain should be adopted. Global supply chain management typically involves logistics, purchasing, operations, and market channels as the core functions internally and several different entities externally (suppliers, customers, and many more).

- *Global value chain.* Global supply chains are a subset of the multinational corporation's global value chain (for example, all personnel in a firm are a part of the value chain, but they are not necessarily a part of every supply chain). Multiple levels of stakeholders are part of the multinational corporation's value chain, including employees, customers, suppliers, shareholders/investors, regulators, and local communities. Each of these (primary) stakeholders can have a role in adding value to the global supply chains. (This is most commonly done by employees, customers, suppliers, and shareholders/investors, but it can also be done by regulators and local communities.)

INTEGRATION OF GLOBAL SUPPLY CHAIN FUNCTIONS ____

How often do we run into a global supply chain issue, such as a quality standard not being met or a delivery not being made on time, that involves a first-tier supplier or perhaps even a second-tier supplier? Firms spend an incredible amount of time and energy trying to manage and control portions of their global supply chains that are critical to delivering unique value.

But what about integration of the firm's own supply chain functions? How often does purchasing strategically integrate its operations with logistics? In what ways are operations coordinated with market channels to leverage for value? Or, for that matter, how often are factors related to logistics, purchasing, operations, and market channels looked at? Yes, of course, we do coordinate at times, but are these functions really integrated throughout the firm's value chains to maximize value in the global marketplace?

Integration of global supply chain functions internal to the firm is as important as coordination across entities in the global supply chain from raw material to end customer. A global firm cannot be fully global, or at least cannot adopt a global strategy, without ongoing evaluation, development, and strategic alignment of its supply chain functions. This means that integration across the four functions and strategic alignment with what industry globalization drivers indicate (and allow) are the most effective global supply chain strategies.

Our benchmarking shows that purchasing is generally the most globalized of the supply chain functions today, followed by logistics, operations, and market channels. At the same time, purchasing is slightly lower than the other functions in ensuring that superior value is added in the complete chain. Specifically, our benchmarking indicates that the importance of purchasing for global supply chain strategy receives a score of 89 (with 0 being unimportant and 100 being the most important). This score is clearly an indication that purchasing contributes a tremendous amount to the value proposition, but not as much as the other three functions today. Market channels scores a 96, logistics scores a 94, and operations scores a 92. In reality, this means that the range from 89 to 96, where 100 is the most important, is rather narrow, with it being critically important that each supply chain function is leveraged for value (see Figure 1.6).

The results are rather interesting and indicate not only opportunities for improvement, but also opportunities for recalibrating leverage in many firms. Figure 1.6 shows the full picture of the scores. The top number in each oval represents the globalization of that function, and the bottom number in each oval represents the importance of the function to the overall global supply chain strategy. Both sets of figures are scored on a 0 to 100 scale, with 0 being fully domestic or unimportant and 100 being fully globalized or most important.

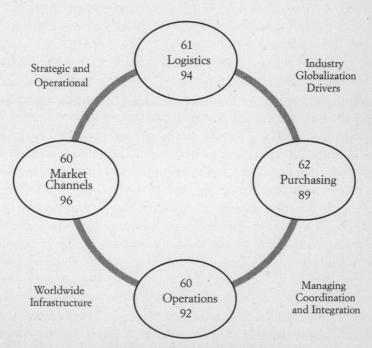

FIGURE 1.6 Global Supply Chain Levers

Of course, these are just numbers if they are not evaluated properly in the context of individual companies and their global supply chains. Therefore, assuming that your firm received the scores that are shown, where would you start your evaluation? What comes to mind in terms of possible changes that should be made? Intuitively, we can probably guess that purchasing, with its heavy emphasis on global sourcing of raw materials, component parts, and products, would be the most globalized of the four functions today. Will this hold true five years from now? Given that these scores represent the top multinational corporations today, can we expect that our firm looks like this? Well, the answer is no! The reason is that we are showing averages across all global companies in the benchmarking sample. Averages seldom tell the story of an individual firm.

What is more likely for any given firm, especially one that is below the top three in market share in any given industry, is that it has globalized much more in one area of its supply chain and much less in another area. For example, many companies have attempted to increase their global sourcing efforts during the last 20 years, basically because of cost factors. They have also tried to increase their global market presence by selling to customers in a larger number of countries and markets. Fewer companies have globalized their logistics and operations efforts to the same degree. But now we are talking mostly about companies that are below the top three in their industry. The larger companies, with greater market shares globally, really have put in serious efforts to become globalized across the supply chain—via logistics, purchasing, operations, and market channels. This is reflected in the average scores in our benchmark study.

What can we learn from benchmarks? A lot! This book was developed using materials across all core functions in the global supply chain (logistics, purchasing, operations, and market channels) and several benchmark studies that are not available in any other place. These benchmarking studies involve several thousand executive-level professionals (C-suite individuals) along with logistics, purchasing, operations, and market channels managers and professionals. In all, this book will provide a benchmark for where we have been, where we are now, and where we need to go in global supply chains to create superior value on a total cost basis and for the entire chain. This involves understanding coordination, integration, and managing of key internal functions of the multinational corporation's global supply chains as well as the strategic nodes, activity links, and resource ties in the external parts of the global supply chain.

In that context, as we stated earlier in this chapter, the tools and ideas covered in this book do away with the illusion that supply chain management in the global marketplace is a task-oriented, sequential "chain" of operational activities that are combined into a whole after the chain is completed. The best-value supply chains are those that strategically leverage the inbound and outbound operations, from raw material to finished products reaching the end users, through an integrated and strategic global supply chain system. Using critical leverage points, employing total cost analysis,[10] achieving alignment with industry globalization drivers, and embedding global supply chains into the corporate strategy remain our focus. This book will provide strategic insights along with technical details on the global aspects of supply chains.

This book certainly represents a tool kit that can be used and "leveraged" by individual logistics managers, purchasing managers, operations managers, and market channels managers. But, more important, the knowledge in this book should be used across those functions and across the hierarchical levels in the firm in an enterprisewide sense, especially by supply chain managers and executives in the firm (not just the top supply chain executive but all C-suite executives). With that in mind, let us take a look at the benefits that can be expected—at least in a broad sense—from leveraging global supply chain management for corporate strategic advantage.

HOW GLOBAL SUPPLY CHAIN MANAGEMENT ACHIEVES BENEFITS

There are a lot of benefits, both strategic and operational, that can result from global supply chain management. Table 1.1 summarizes the core benefits. The clear end result should be the achievement of the greatest value possible at the lowest cost possible. In essence, the global supply chain should deliver great, if not superior, quality at a reasonable price, since the ratio of quality to price determines the value attained. Therefore, from our perspective, achieving superior value is the key objective for the overall global supply chain. However, most firms also center their efforts on what they can achieve and attain from global supply chain management. Developing and

TABLE 1.1 How Global Supply Chains Achieve Benefits

Function	Cost Reduction	Improved Quality	Increased Customer Satisfaction	Competitive Leverage
Logistics	Creates a cost-efficient network of distribution centers, inventory management systems, and forward/reverse transportation options	Helps to improve quality (processes and products) via its globally maximized distribution, materials handling, and transportation efforts	Effective planning of inventory and forward and reverse transportation increases customer satisfaction with the overall global supply chain	Global inventory and transportation management help exploit economies of scale and differences in country factor costs
Purchasing	Integrates a strategic level of global purchasing given the customers and channels involved and the suppliers and supplier networks available	Effective use of core competencies, outsourcing, and global supplier selection result in quality improvements throughout the chain	Creates an order fulfillment and delivery system that maximizes global customer and channel needs	Global purchasing practices allow for maintenance of cost advantages independent of local conditions
Operations	Achieves cost reduction via a total cost analysis involving global options, competitive priorities, and process-based quality standards	Competitive priorities focused on quality, global production located to achieve quality, and process-based quality standards improve overall quality	The combination of a total cost analysis approach with process-based quality standards and production efficiencies creates greater value and satisfaction	Global operations allow for flexibility in where to base competitive advantage, whether it is speed, quality, cost, or flexibility based
Market Channels	Develops the strategically most optimal global market entry mode, online presence, and alignment with marketing mix variables	Maximizing efforts of the customer value–creating processes, alignment with the marketing mix, and understanding global customers' needs	Global channels are centered on creating satisfaction via value–value in the processes and value in the alignment with the marketing mix	A global market channel approach reduces design and production costs, focuses talents, and reinforces marketing

implementing global supply chain efforts can lead to numerous positive outcomes. Some of the strategic benefits include cost reductions, improved quality, increased customer satisfaction, and competitive leverage for each of the global supply chain functions of logistics, purchasing, operations, and market channels.

Cost Reductions

The cost reductions for logistics include creating cost-efficient networks of distribution centers, inventory management systems, and forward/reverse transportation options. For purchasing, the opportunities to reduce costs result from the integration of strategic-level global purchasing given the customers and channels involved and the suppliers and supplier networks available. The cost reductions involving operations are mission-critical for the overall global supply chain in that operations would be the best function in which to address the notion of a total cost analysis involving global options, competitive priorities, and process-based quality standards. Such an approach achieves cost reductions in the broader scope of the global supply chain via the development of the strategically optimal global market entry mode, online presence, and alignment with marketing mix variables.

Improved Quality

Logistics helps to improve quality across processes and products through its globally maximized distribution, materials handling, and transportation efforts. For purchasing, issues such as the effective use of core competencies, outsourcing, and global supplier selection result in quality improvements throughout the chain. Operations helps the value chain focus attention on the right leverage points. Competitive priorities focused on quality, global production locations, and process-based quality standards work together to improve overall quality. Market channels drive the notion of maximizing the efforts of the customer value–creating processes, alignment with the marketing mix, and understanding of global customers' needs.

Increased Customer Satisfaction

The use of logistics tools, effective planning of inventory, and forward and reverse transportation methods increases customer satisfaction with the overall supply chain. Purchasing's efforts to increase customer satisfaction are connected with the order fulfillment and delivery systems that maximize the satisfaction based on global customer and channel needs. For operations, the combination of a total cost analysis approach with process-based quality standards and production efficiencies creates greater value and satisfaction. The market channels are the center of attention when it comes to end-customer value and satisfaction. Specifically, global channels are centered on creating satisfaction through value—value in the processes and in the alignment with the marketing mix.

Competitive Leverage

Global inventory and transportation management help exploit economies of scale and differences in country factor costs. As a direct result, logistics contributes to the competitive leverage of the entire supply chain. Global purchasing practices allow for maintenance of cost advantages independent of local conditions. Global operations allow for flexibility in where to base competitive advantage, whether it is speed, quality, cost, or flexibility. A global market channel approach reduces design and production costs, focuses talents, and reinforces marketing.

SUPPLY CHAIN MANAGEMENT INTEGRATING PROCESSES

In order to achieve the benefits introduced in the previous section, we must begin to think in terms of processes, not just functions, in global supply chains. While supply chains can be organized in a variety of ways, there are generally eight integrating processes that all global supply chains perform to a greater or lesser extent.[11] These processes define the work of global supply chains, as illustrated in Table 1.2.

To help understand the importance of these integrating processes, let's consider one of the processes: product or service development and launch. Who in your organization is responsible for this vital activity? When we ask supply chain executives, we often hear functional responses: marketing, engineering, design, and so on. While each of these functions has a critical role to play in supporting the

TABLE 1.2 Integrating Processes in Supply Chains

Process	Description
Demand planning responsiveness	The assessment of demand and strategic design to achieve maximum responsiveness to customer requirements.
Customer relationship collaboration	The development and administration of relationships with customers to facilitate strategic information sharing, joint planning, and integrated operations.
Order fulfillment/service delivery	The ability to execute superior and sustainable order-to-delivery performance and related essential services.
Product or service development and launch	The participation in product or service development and lean launch.
Manufacturing customization	The support of manufacturing strategy and facilitation of postponement throughout the supply chain.
Supplier relationship collaboration	The development and administration of relationships with suppliers to facilitate strategic information sharing, joint planning, and integrated operations.
Life-cycle support	The repair and support of products during their life cycle. This includes warranties, maintenance, and repair.
Reverse logistics	The return and disposition of inventories in a cost-effective, secure, and responsible manner.

process, who actually leads the end-to-end process of product or service development and launch? Who makes the trade-offs between the needs of two different functions supporting this single process? If we put a function in charge of an end-to-end integrative process, we often see suboptimal decision making. We need leaders who can think and react in terms of processes, not just functions. This is the key to managing today's complex global supply chains. We need both strong functions and a strong process mindset.

The remainder of this book is organized around the more familiar functional groupings of global supply chain activities (such as logistics, purchasing, operations, and market channels). However, the eight core supply chain processes described in Table 1.2 cut across these functional groupings and are discussed at various points throughout these chapters. After all, strategic global supply chain management is the core focus of the book!

CHAPTER 2

Industry Implications for Global Supply Chains

Alignment of global supply chains and industry drivers generates leverage.

DIAGNOSING INDUSTRY GLOBALIZATION POTENTIAL ____

"This is not your father's Oldsmobile" was the advertising slogan that General Motors used in the 1980s for its Oldsmobile car brand. The firm was founded by Ransom E. Olds in 1897, and the brand lasted 107 years—longer than most car brands—before GM phased it out in 2004. Approximately 35 million Oldsmobile cars were produced in the century-long time span, some 14 million of them in Lansing, Michigan. Over the years, we have since seen hundreds of variations of the advertising slogan, such as, "It's not your father's America anymore," "It's not your father's newscast anymore," and "It's not your father's customer service anymore," to name just a few. The key point, though, is that the original ad slogan was what ultimately destroyed the Olds brand! As it turned out, the largest market for Oldsmobile cars at the time was actually people whose parents had owned one, and the automaker was using an ad that was not aligned with its many loyal customers. This created a mismatch in alignment between what the Olds brand stood for (or tried to portray) and what the customers expected, resulting in a collision course with Pontiac and Buick, other GM brands, and the ultimate downfall of Olds.

Alignment is the key. Having been around for 107 years, having a history as a remarkable success story, and being an icon meant very little in the end because alignment with the industry and its potential no longer existed for Olds. Global supply chains need to be nurtured to achieve this alignment. In this context, *industry globalization potential* refers to the likelihood that an industry will support and have the underlying conditions needed to facilitate the use of strategic global supply chain management. This is not your father's supply chain anymore. Supply chains today are global, strategic, and also operational. They are an important way to leverage value-added features in an industry by focusing on alignment with certain industry globalization drivers. If you have not noticed that your supply chains should be global and strategic, if you are still seeing them as an operational activity that is usually done close to your production facility, then you are probably too late in developing effective and efficient supply chains. Do not let the Olds example be repeated in your firm. If your supply chains are not global at all yet, there are potential major issues looming. Take action now to make sure that your supply chains are global, at least to some degree, and strategically plan for the chains to be much more global in the next five to ten years (as our data in Chapter 1 suggest will be needed to stay competitive).

In essence, industry globalization conditions dictate the starting point—what type of alignment should be created—for strategic implementation in the areas of logistics, purchasing, operations, and market channels. The industry conditions also provide a structure for how to coordinate and integrate the nodes in the global chain, how to link activity between the nodes (for example, firms, organizations, units, or individuals), and how to use resources between the nodes appropriately. The bottom line is that in order to achieve the benefits of globalization, supply chain managers and corporate executives need to recognize when industry conditions provide the opportunity to use strategic global supply chains as part of the multinational corporation's strategies. This does not mean that all chains should be global. Being more global than the industry warrants wastes resources (for example, your company may need to do part of the work of educating the marketplace), while being less global than the industry supports wastes opportunities (for example, your company may not be selling as much as it could). Alignment with each industry globalization driver is the key, and Figure 2.1 illustrates this alignment proposition.

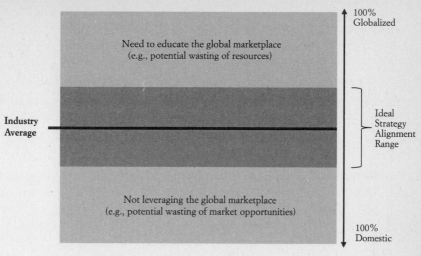

FIGURE 2.1 Global Alignment of Strategy and Industry

Based on work by George Yip and Tomas Hult,[1] we can divide the industry globalization drivers into market, cost, government, and competitive drivers. Market globalization drivers largely depend on customer behavior, the nature of the available distribution channels, and marketing practices in the industry. Cost drivers largely depend on the economics of the business and the primary industry in which it operates. Government drivers largely depend on the policies, regulations, and laws set by independent country governments. Finally, competitive drivers largely depend on the actions of competitors, the nature of the competitive landscape, and the expectations set by previous competitive actions in the industry. The appendix to this chapter includes details and measures of the industry globalization drivers.

Clearly, other industry drivers and other analytical industry frameworks are possible. However, our position is that these four types of drivers are the most critical categories of influencing conditions that affect global strategy development and implementation as well as strategic global supply chain management practices. Each of the four drivers (market, cost, government, and competitive) is time tested and has been used effectively for years by multinational corporations.

As a starting point for this chapter, we offer both a comparative ranking of the four industry globalization drivers and a forecast, based on data, covering where we are now and where we are

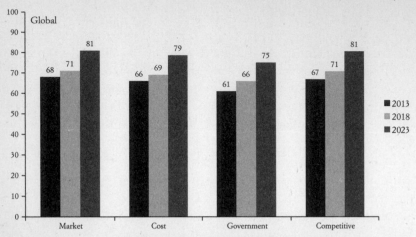

FIGURE 2.2 Industry Globalization Drivers

predicted to be in five and ten years, respectively. The data points are illustrated in Figure 2.2. These are discussed in terms of the likelihood of globalization based on a particular driver. The comparative analysis for the drivers is only approximate and will change over time, as indicated by the differences between the numbers for today and those forecasted for the next ten years. Each score is based on a 100-point scale, where a score of 100 represents a fully globalized driver and zero represents a fully domestic-oriented driver. As expected, none of the industry drivers falls near either end of the spectrum.

What we find is that the market globalization drivers exhibit the most globalization potential today (score = 68) and are also forecast to maintain that standing in five years (score = 71). Importantly, we will see an increase in globalization potential based on the market drivers (that is, the conditions for globalizing supply chains will be more favorable in five years than they are now for market drivers). The increase expected is 4.4 percent. The competitive drivers are also forecast to be at the same level (score = 71) in five years, an increase of 4 points from today, or 6.0 percent. In five years, we expect that the cost drivers will be slightly behind the market and competitive drivers in terms of globalization potential (score = 69, an increase from 66, which represents an improvement of 4.6 percent). However, the largest improvement will be seen, as forecast, in the government globalization drivers—from a score of 61 today to a score of 66 in five years (8.2 percent). Still, the government drivers remain the toughest aspect of globalizing supply chain efforts. This is true today, and it will continue to be true in five and ten years. Chapter 3, on infrastructure, will highlight some of these "bureaucratic" or government factors that sometimes hinder the globalization of supply chains even more.

The intention of this chapter on industry globalization drivers is to examine each of the four types of drivers—market, cost, government, and competitive—and highlight several implications associated with each that should be taken into account and planned for when developing global supply chains. We will also tackle each industry driver as it relates to 10 separate industries (air transportation, automobiles, cement, credit cards, computer software, computer hardware, electronic equipment, industrial machinery, insurance, and watches and clocks). These industry comparisons (based on real data) are for illustration only, since numerous additional industries exist in the marketplace. The objective of these analyses is to create a better understanding of each type of driver, key globalization conditions, and globalization scores for a select set of industries. The globalization conditions are presented as 10 key trends and implications pertaining to each type of driver. In essence, we see these 10 areas that we selected for each driver as being the "top 10" issues currently facing or forecast to influence the specific type of driver.

UNDERSTANDING MARKET GLOBALIZATION DRIVERS

The market globalization drivers are a function of worldwide consumer behavior, global distribution channels, and the nature of global marketing in the industry in which the firm operates. Issues such as the degree to which customers have relatively common needs, wants, interests, and tastes are critically important for a better understanding of market globalization drivers. In addition, the use of global marketing and the degree to which transferable marketing practices can be used are key determinants of the market drivers. The use of lead countries, how they change based upon industries and products, and how they are predicted to change based on the dynamics in the global marketplace affect the market drivers.

Taking all these issues into account, we offer both a comparative ranking of the 10 industries and a forecast, based on data, of where we are predicting them to be in five years in terms of the potential for global supply chains based on the pressure from market globalization drivers (see Figure 2.3). The comparative ranking for the market

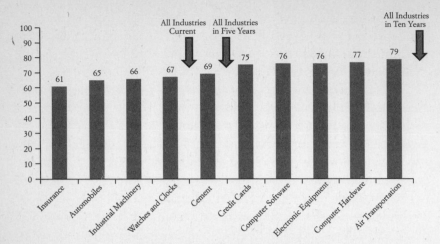

FIGURE 2.3   Market Globalization Drivers

drivers is approximate and will change over time, as indicated by the 4.4 percent change expected in market drivers, on average, for all industries over the next five years. This means that the expectation is that the market globalization drivers will be 4.4 percent more conducive to globalization efforts in five years. However, some industries will be more globalized and some will not experience the 4.4 percent positive change. For example, we forecast that there will not be much of a change in the worldwide market forces for industrial machinery, cement, and air transportation in the next five years. Ten years out, this gets harder to forecast and predict, but our data indicate that the market drivers across industries will become 19.1 percent more globalized (with a score of 81 on the 100-point scale).

MARKET GLOBALIZATION DRIVERS' IMPLICATIONS FOR SUPPLY CHAINS

The market globalization drivers influence global supply chains in various ways. Each industry has certain market forces that facilitate globalization and certain market forces that hinder globalization. Changing customer needs and tastes, infrastructure available for engaging customers, availability of global channels, applicability of transferable marketing, and the use of more diverse nations as so-called lead countries are determining the relative influence of market drivers on global supply chain management.

Regarding the supply chain functions of logistics, purchasing, operations, and market channels, it is logical to assume that market channels functions are most directly influenced by market globalization drivers. There is a unique and important overlap between the market drivers and market channels, such as satisfying customer needs and tastes, engaging customers, evaluating the availability of global channels, and using a program of transferable marketing. Logistics and purchasing have the least connection to the market globalization drivers, while operations will be moderately affected by these market drivers.

When striving for strategic alignment across entities in global supply chains and coordination of supply chain functions within a firm, there are some universal implications that can be drawn for market globalization drivers. We dig into a set of 10 factors—a top 10, if you will—that are leading to or predicted to experience changes in the market drivers. These changes are likely to have a significant effect on global supply chains. The factors are lifestyles, knowledge intensity, rising population, global e-commerce, global firms, infrastructure, world brands, global advertising, social networking, and sustainability.

Lifestyles

Younger adult consumers around the world are growing more alike. Worldwide brands, mass communications, increased travel, and multinational corporations are part of the "global village" that creates a convergence of lifestyles and tastes. This convergence is far more prominent among young customers, those up to roughly 40 years of age, than among older customers at this time. However, we predict that over the years, this convergence of lifestyles and tastes will become applicable to older people as well. This is a function of people staying with their "worldwide lifestyles" as they get older and their home areas becoming more global themselves. These lifestyle and taste changes are particularly important for market channels: consumers expect to have most, if not all, of the products that are available in other parts of the world available to them as well. Already, we have seen this pressure in the developed world and, to some degree, in emerging markets. The expectation is that all emerging markets, most newly industrialized countries, and all middle- to upper-income individuals in the less developed countries will have markedly increased expectations that market channels will be able to deliver on these converging lifestyles and tastes.

Knowledge Intensity

Consumers today have access to knowledge about products—such as quality, price, and most key features—almost everywhere and all the time. The most significant knowledge that they have today, and did not necessarily have yesterday, is that certain new products exist and are available. This knowledge was previously more locally based. Now, any product that comes into being is soon known throughout the world. Based on this knowledge, consumers expect products to be available to them wherever they are in the world. This increased "knowledge intensity" creates pressures on global supply chains, since 90 percent of what we buy locally is not made locally. The days when movies were introduced and launched in the United States months before their international launch are over. A week's delay, or even a few days, is often enough to create unhappy consumers, who then often look elsewhere for solutions. The same goes for product feature profiles. If a feature is available anywhere—whether as part of the base product or as an option—consumers expect that same feature to be available to them worldwide. New smartphone applications and computer software releases are examples. This increased knowledge intensity creates pressure on all aspects of the global supply chain system, but purchasing will face the most. Purchasing and sourcing operations have to ensure that enough raw material and component parts exist to satisfy a worldwide clientele.

Rising Population

Developing countries are growing at a faster rate than developed countries because diminishing returns are not as strong as in capital-rich countries. For example, developing (and poorer) countries can replicate the production methods, technologies, and supply chain infrastructures used in developed countries. These potential efficiencies will be coupled with the rising population in developing countries and the expected increase in prosperity. For example, the purchasing power of the middle class worldwide is estimated to double in the next two decades, with Asia accounting for about 80 percent of that growth. China, for example, has about 20 million people whom we can now classify as middle class by developed country standards. It will have approximately 200 million middle-class individuals in 2020. The outlook for India is very similar. Overall, this means that rising population and prosperity predictions have supply chain implications ranging from demand planning to inventory management to competitive priorities.

Global E-commerce

The world of e-commerce is booming. China's primary online marketplace, Taobao, sells more today than the top five brick-and-mortar retailers in the country combined. The marketplace now offers some 800 million different products online. Significant increases in online sales are expected in most parts of the world, but especially in developed countries and emerging markets. Forecasts have Latin America growing its e-commerce at more than 200 percent, Russia at more than 180 percent, North America and Oceania at about 100 percent, and Europe, Africa, and Asia at some 85 percent within the next two years, reaching a worldwide e-commerce total exceeding $500 billion annually. At the same time, the global infrastructure needed to deliver these products to meet customers' expectations is not yet ready in many countries, especially in emerging markets. Global supply chains will feel the pressure to be part of the value-added solution to these market channel needs.

Global Firms

Issues such as global sourcing, including sourcing from foreign markets for foreign markets, are becoming much more important. However, this is not global sourcing solely based on cheaper costs, as it frequently was in the past. Firms now source globally to achieve the best combination of quality, cost, and ultimately value. In this spirit, we also see increased tendencies among global firms to stress "glocalization"—meaning that they carry on business around the world based on both local and global considerations. It used to be that global firms largely standardized their operations for the worldwide marketplace. However, today's measures of effectiveness and efficiency allow global firms to integrate their worldwide operations while also allowing for operative customization in cases where that type of localization provides significant advantages. Glocalization means that global supply chains have to be flexible enough to incorporate both local and global raw materials, component parts, and products into the process while still strategically and operationally conducting business using a total global strategy. This creates increased pressure on global supply chains to conduct total cost analysis as a means of addressing the infusion of value-added elements at each step.

Infrastructure

Interestingly, the infrastructure for global supply chains is becoming much better, with numerous options for global and regional channels in most parts of the world. Shipping routes are being reconfigured, leverage points in the world are being reformulated, and value is being added to global supply chains. Products and services come from places and entities that many people did not even consider a few years ago. The forecast is that the infrastructure for global supply chains will improve by 11 percent in the next five years (more on that in Chapter 3). At the same time, worldwide annual employment growth is predicted to be less than 2 percent for years to come, but with significantly higher rates in the Middle East and Africa. This means that global supply chains will have to be staffed more with current people, retrained employees, or local resources than with new global employees.

World Brands

Companies around the world are spending incredible amounts of money—in any currency—to establish "world brands," sometimes also called "global brands," to achieve global sales productivity in targeting customers worldwide. Such world branding requires a sophisticated supply chain infrastructure and global networks, both inbound and outbound, to meet the demands of customers everywhere. World brands, in essence, will also require global supply chains that have relatively standardized leverage points throughout the chain to infuse value at almost the same stages of the chain, regardless of the countries involved. It used to be that if a product needed to be customized for the needs, regulations, or laws of a particular country, the customization often happened at a late stage in the supply chain. Such customization efforts may now happen at the middle or the beginning of the chain on a more standardized basis. This takes into account the connection between global supply chains and the requirements of world brands. Such brands have the potential to proactively create a want on the part of customers, but they also create a need on the part of global supply chains.

Global Advertising

Global advertising is a way to build valued connections with customers. A common platform and parallel campaigns that resonate with customers worldwide have spillover effects in terms of publicity, lifestyles, and tastes. We often act and behave the way our peers and neighbors do, and purchase what they purchase. Global advertising is a mechanism that allows global companies to build the world marketplace into a neighborhood. This new "global village" has wants and needs that are similar, based on peer behaviors and interests. At the same time, the more global an advertising campaign is, the greater the expectations on the outbound portion of the supply chain to meet customers' demands. Thankfully, we have developed mechanisms over the years to implement effective global advertising campaigns. The key for the future, though, is that more advertising campaigns will be global in scope. Fewer advertising campaigns will have detailed and unique customization for particular country markets, some because they are proactively building on the notion of a global village, and some because of the idea that cost efficiencies can be gained by global advertising.

Social Media

With the spread of global and regional media, an increased assortment of international retailing options, and the movement of people, products, and corporations across national borders, markets worldwide are becoming much more integrated. Most hotel rooms have CNN, BBC, and the mainstay channels from key countries. And there are thousands of online newspapers in English (and many other common languages) covering all parts of the world through a relatively common infrastructure. All of these global information sources are encapsulated more in the social media frenzy than through traditional media channels. We already know some of the impact of Facebook, LinkedIn, and Twitter (to name a few), but what about

China's Renren and other similar non-U.S.-based systems? Also important in this context is the need to provide engaging, interactive, and entertaining websites and social media platforms. Global customers worldwide prefer to be engaged, and typically not at the brand name's website, but instead at websites like Amazon and eBay, where they can find all brand-name products that interest them.

Sustainability at Customer Levels

An increasing number of customers are demanding that firms throughout the global supply chain engage in efforts to sustain the environment and offer "greener" products. Firms have felt these pressures for years, but the escalation in this area is likely to become a global supply chain phenomenon. In the past, consumers mostly held producers and/or retailers accountable for making sure that their products were "green." However, as consumers are becoming more knowledgeable, they are also becoming more engaged. This means that all entities and elements of global supply chains will be under increased pressure to offer green solutions at each stage of the process. This includes all steps in the forward portion of the supply chain as well as all steps in the reverse logistics portion of the chain. Customers and market forces are increasingly demanding this.

UNDERSTANDING COST GLOBALIZATION DRIVERS

The cost globalization drivers are generally a function of the economics of the environment. However, these economics are not always easy to detect and decipher, let alone accounting for achieving the value-added goals correctly at each step of the global supply chain. Issues such as global economies of scale, experiential curve effects, differences in country and regional costs, product development costs (especially those associated with complex but commodity-oriented products), and costs associated with each step and function of supply chains are critical components of the cost drivers.

Taking all these issues into account, we offer both a comparative ranking of the 10 industries and a forecast, based on data, of where we are predicted to be in five years (see Figure 2.4). These are expressed in terms of the globalization potential of supply chains based on the pressure from cost globalization drivers. The

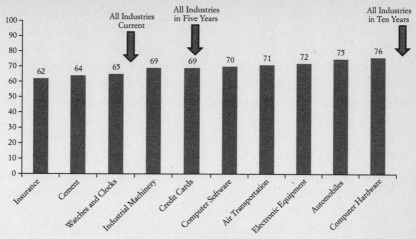

FIGURE 2.4 Cost Globalization Drivers

comparative ranking for the cost globalization drivers is approximate and will change over time, as indicated by the 4.6 percent change in cost drivers expected, on average, for all these industries in the next five years. This means that we expect cost globalization drivers to be 4.6 percent more conducive to globalization efforts in five years. However, some industries will be more globalized and some will not meet the 4.6 percent positive change. For example, we forecast that there will not be much of a change in the worldwide cost structure for insurance, credit cards, and automobiles in the next five years. Ten years out, it is more difficult to forecast; our benchmarking data suggest that the cost drivers across industries will become 19.6 percent more globalized (with a score of 79 on the 100-point scale).

COST GLOBALIZATION DRIVERS' IMPLICATIONS FOR SUPPLY CHAINS

The cost globalization drivers influence supply chains in specific ways that directly affect the value created at each step of the chain. Value is typically viewed as a function of the quality received in return for the price paid or cost expended. In that sense, the cost drivers can always have a significant effect on global supply chains. The cost drivers should be carefully evaluated on an ongoing basis to identify critical "cost bottlenecks" and to effectively create leverage throughout the chain that facilitates the realization of added value at each step.

Cost-prohibitive production in some countries, for example, led to an onslaught of outsourcing in the 1990s. Transportation costs and the costs of learning a new market also reduce some firms' interest in certain global market options, even when the cost really should not be prohibitive, given all the worldwide options today. In general, supply chains should be developed and implemented to achieve the best cost leverage, no matter where in the world such leverage is found, taking tangible and intangible inputs into account during the process. This is why we also advocated a total cost approach to global supply chains in Chapter 1 (and will add more on it throughout the book).

The purchasing function is the one that is most directly influenced by cost globalization drivers, since cost drivers in the industry environment are exceptionally well aligned with obtaining raw materials and component parts. The end portion of the market channel is also heavily influenced by the cost drivers, especially the "last mile" of the supply chain, which is structured to get the product or service to the end customers.[2] Logistics and operations are also affected moderately, especially transportation, but not as intensely as purchasing and the last mile of the chain. Overall, the most successful global companies are those that find ways to drive cost out of their global supply chains while still maintaining order fulfillment and customer service.

There are some general conclusions that can be drawn, based upon forecasting what will happen with the cost globalization drivers. The following top 10 factors for cost drivers are important enough for us to tackle in terms of their effects and potential effects on global supply chains: economies of scale, accelerating innovation, advances in logistics, newly industrialized countries, product development, resource scarcity, engaging locally, timing, costs of doing business, and security and risk.

Economies of Scale

Globalization has been driven in recent years by "connective" technologies in global supply chains. This means that global supply chains have increasingly been unbundled into finer stages of production to allow for economies of scale. We have also seen larger geographic dispersion of these unbundled activities. As a result, global supply chains are really the "connective tissue" that allows this fractionalization (unbundling) and geographic dispersion to operate effectively. This also puts a lot of pressure on global supply chains to ensure that the total value delivered is appropriate, given the many additive entities and links that are often missing from these chains after fractionalization. There is a risk that each entity, each link, and each resource in the chain will be evaluated independently of the others. Such evaluations often lead to effective and efficient performance at that node of the global supply chain. However, they seldom lead to value in the sense of a total cost analysis of the entire chain.

Accelerating Innovation

From Chapter 1, we know that globalization and increased international trade are two of the most important drivers of economic growth today, and they will continue to be among the most important drivers for years to come. Cross-border trade has gone up almost exponentially in the last 10 years. Add to that the 90 percent of what we buy locally that we do not produce locally, and the importance of global supply chains cannot be overstated. This is a powerful combination in which global supply chains drive the global marketplace, take advantage of accelerating technological innovation, and leverage comparative advantages around the world. Innovations in how we connect all nodes, activity links, and resources across a global supply chain will have a tremendous impact on the value being added. Equally important, global supply chains will be increasingly leveraged strategically, not only by the producers, but by all participants in the chain.

Advances in Logistics

Clearly, we have seen major advances in transportation and logistics solutions on a worldwide basis. Many large logistics service providers operate in more than 100 countries, and the largest express transportation companies, such as FedEx, UPS, and DHL, list as many as 200 or more countries as their global market space. Perhaps the most important advance in transportation and logistics is the transparency of information in the global supply chain. Knowing what is occurring across the entire supply chain at all times gives all parties and nodes in the chain a great advantage. At the same time, we predict that for the foreseeable future, logistics providers will mainly come from developed nations and serve all countries in the world. While emerging markets and newly industrialized countries are critically important for world development, there are unlikely to be too many firms from those countries starting up or reformulating to offer logistics services worldwide.

Newly Industrialized Countries

Newly industrialized countries (NICs) typically have a lower GDP than countries in the developed world, though they have a higher level of GDP growth. NICs are also characterized by a great deal of industry and/or international trade. We believe that global supply chain management drives the economic engine in these countries. NICs have productive capability and low labor costs, but they often lack the appropriate global supply chain infrastructure necessary to be efficient and effective. These countries need to be evaluated for low-cost sourcing, production opportunities, and target market segments. At the same time, the group of NICs is not as large as the group of emerging markets, and many people would classify NICs as emerging markets in any event. In sum, this means that the exposure that NICs have and the opportunities that they present for global supply chains are constantly being closely evaluated. A firm has to stay well astride of the NICs but cannot necessarily expect to outduel the competition in these markets.

Product Development

More and more products are requiring more financial and nonfinancial resources to develop and implement relative to their market lives. This means that the pressure is on firms to sell their products as widely and to as many customers as possible. The alternative—that is, to develop products with more limited features and perhaps lower quality levels—is not logical or even feasible today. Consumers are increasingly demanding the best at a good price. Global supply chains are a major part of the solution. Specifically, companies need to have a well-working global supply chain infrastructure available to them to push out their products to a larger number of potential customers than ever before. Customers want new products with more features and better quality—all costly propositions. Using global supply chains helps offset these costs through potentially larger market coverage involving more customers.

Resource Scarcity

The trend toward a more homogenized world, creating global consumers and the need for inbound and outbound global supply chains, has potentially serious implications for resources. In some cases, the demand for certain products cannot be fully met because of resource constraints (for example, a lack of raw materials, component parts, or supply chain infrastructure). These constraints also have direct value implications. When the quantity of raw materials, component parts, or finished products employed to make other products becomes limited, quality standards are likely to drop in many cases. Alternatively, creative resource solutions have to be developed to offset the lack of resources in some areas. Global companies that are trying to satisfy customers' demands and are under pressure to deliver will engage with a larger assortment of suppliers. This undoubtedly will result in a drop-off in quality standards. In some industries, we will also see resource constraints to such an extent that projects will have to be delayed or even eliminated (for example, high-quality processed steel is a resource that is limited today).

Engaging Locally

A lack of understanding and knowledge of the global markets is a huge potential cost driver. Global supply chains are considered to be at the market level because they engage companies in different parts of the world and draw on the experience and expertise of those firms. Global supply chains are not global just because they source from different parts of the world. Value in the chain is a function of integrating firms and individuals with local knowledge into the supply chain. The trick is finding the right firms for the right scenario. Even in large countries such as China and India, skilled labor is getting tougher to identify. This is especially true with the cost structures that we have grown accustomed to in the last two decades. Careful evaluation of talent, leverage points in the world, and how best to integrate the critical (local) knowledge are important features of global supply chains.

Timing

The old adage that "time is money" has been around in business circles for years. Now we often talk about speed, cycle time,

time for delivery, and timing. What all these things really mean is straightforward: customers want products when they want them, not necessarily when companies want to sell them to the customers. Many times these do coincide, even though this was not always planned. Instead, companies operating global supply chains need to strategically plan for the cycle time costs associated with production and delivery in different parts of the world. Additionally, they must create scenarios in which cycle time serves as an input into the value-added results that go into the products. We have implemented just-in-time systems in many industries for a reason! However, while these worldwide cycle-time costs are becoming more predictable in certain areas (such as China and India), they are still not predictable for many emerging markets, newly industrialized countries, and less developed countries. The outlook, though, is positive. As more and more of the world's countries become engaged and even entrenched in the global marketplace, global supply chain cycle time should become more predictable and more ingrained into the chain's total cost structure.

Costs of Doing Business

One would think that the costs of doing business should be rather universal, but we know better. The World Bank's "ease of doing business index" is calculated as a function of 10 subindexes: starting a business, dealing with construction permits, getting electricity, registering property, getting credit, protecting investors, paying taxes, trading across borders, enforcing contracts, and resolving insolvency. Many trade specialists think of these as the intangible costs of doing business globally. However, they become incredibly tangible when, for example, bureaucracy slows down global supply chains or costs are added to the product via taxes. They also become tangible when getting paid is an issue. As economic freedom is improving globally and as more countries are promoting their locations for business operations, the regulations and laws associated with the costs of doing business will become better for global supply chains. But the time horizon for improvement around the world is vastly different depending on where you are, and quite different, too, depending on the part of the global supply chain in which you are engaged.

Security and Risk

Piracy is still alive and well, and we are not just talking about copying products. Piracy on the world's waterways presents a security risk that has cost implications for global supply chains. The cost comes in the form of lost raw material, component parts, and products as well as the need for increased insurance, not to mention different shipping routes and even different shipping modes. But the security and risks go far beyond those cost measures. Supply chain risk combines three elements. It starts with a potential threat and then combines the probability of that threat with its potential severity (more on this in Chapter 3 as well). Costs are associated with each issue (that is, threat, probability, and severity), and allocation of a potential or even probable cost is not likely to become easier even though the worldwide marketplace is becoming more global.

UNDERSTANDING GOVERNMENT GLOBALIZATION DRIVERS

The government globalization drivers generally involve the laws and regulations imposed by governments in the world's countries. Some of the laws are enacted with protectionism in mind, and others are intended to encourage trade. Issues such as trade policies, technical standards, marketing regulations, government-owned competitors, government-owned customers, and government concerns with the entrance of global companies into their economy are critical components of the government globalization drivers.

Taking all these issues into account, we offer a comparative ranking of 10 industries and a forecast, based on data, of where we are predicting them to be in five years in terms of the globalization potential of supply chains (see Figure 2.5). These are based on pressures from government globalization drivers. The comparative ranking for the government globalization drivers is approximate and will change over time, as indicated by the 8.2 percent change expected in government drivers, on average, for all these industries over the next five years. The expectation is that the government globalization drivers will be 8.2 percent more conducive to globalization efforts in five years. However, some industries will be more globalized and some will not meet the 8.2 percent positive change. For example, we

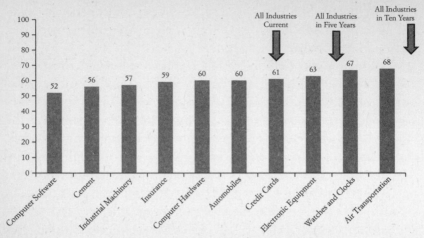

FIGURE 2.5 Government Globalization Drivers

forecast that there will not be much of a change in government regulations and policies for computer software, computer hardware, and air transportation in the next five years. Ten years out, it gets more difficult to forecast, but our data indicate that the government drivers across industries will become 23.0 percent more globalized and approach the globalization of the other industry drivers (with a score of 75 on the 100-point scale).

GOVERNMENT GLOBALIZATION DRIVERS' IMPLICATIONS FOR SUPPLY CHAINS

Government globalization drivers influence global supply chains in direct ways that affect value creation at all stages of the chain. These government drivers are somewhat unpredictable, especially in emerging markets and less developed countries, where government protectionism and laws can be imposed on the marketplace at sometimes unpredictable times. This unpredictability stems from governments often not being rational in terms of implementing laws and regulations on a universal basis. Instead, governments of all kinds have a tendency to focus more narrowly on certain industries for various reasons. Alternatively, when governments should be focusing on single issues, they sometimes create sweeping changes and regulations that affect a plethora of trade issues, even though the main issues that had to be dealt with initially had nothing to do with a given industry. Strategic supply chain plans, contingency analysis, and constant evaluation of feasible alternatives are a must in creating value across global supply chains.

All four industry globalization drivers are heavily affected by government globalization. Governments generally would have the most direct and critical effect on the market channels. This is, after all, where the true competition with home-country companies is the most obvious and perhaps the most severe. Purchasing raw materials and component parts, for example, can be more strategically assigned to countries that facilitate trade. The assumption is that the raw materials and component parts are available from multiple countries and are cost-effective. Logistics and operations facilitate purchasing's connection with the producer in the chain, which means that they should be affected less by government restrictions than purchasing and market channels are. However, the unpredictability of (some) governments warrants constant monitoring, evaluation, and strategic planning with regard to all the steps in the global supply chain. This, in effect, maximizes a global environment that facilitates the trade needed in any given chain. Overall, the most successful global companies find ways to work with host-country governments to infuse value into the chain while offering high-quality order fulfillment, customer service, and products.

There are some general implications that can be drawn from forecasting what will happen with the government globalization drivers. We have developed a top 10 set of government drivers that are important for global supply chains: policies and regulations, tariff barriers, nontariff barriers, government buying and selling, privatization, emerging markets, prevention of security breaches, sustainability at government levels, trading blocs, and world trade organizations.

Policies and Regulations

Government policies can have unique and even unintended consequences for global supply chains. The most obvious is that government policies can impose costs on supply chains in ways that suppress business activity. In the worst cases, government policies can lead to artificial breaks in activity links between chain nodes that really are intended to work together. The most normal, albeit usually negative, policies involve governments creating regulations that lead to increased costs or that reduce global companies' ability to improve efficiency in the chain. These may include a myriad of regulations such as transportation standards, size of retail stores, and policies directly associated with supply chain operations. In fact, in many cases, policies that are directly tied to the operation of different nodes and activity links in the chain are often more constraining than normal trade policies. At the same time, the increase in global supply chains in the last 20 years means that at least many governments have less of an incentive to negatively affect chains and/or are more positively inclined toward being a part of the worldwide solution of adding value to products via these chains.

Tariff Barriers

Tariffs have declined steadily since the 1940s. With supply chain decomposition, firms can identify where the greatest value is and then identify policy priorities that fit their global supply chain. At the same time, today's global supply chains are complex, often involving production in different countries and bringing together components from several countries for final assembly. Markups via tariffs across the global supply chain range from just a few percentage points to some 900 percent previously for Barbie dolls produced in China and sold in the United States, for example. The typical tariff markup going from a developed country to another developed country is about 170 percent. As a result, value creation for the total supply chain has to take tariff barriers into account for each country-to-country link and each node-to-node link in the chain.

Nontariff Barriers

The effects of nontariff measures, which are compounded with the addition of each node and link in global supply chains, need to be monitored as well. This means that nontariff barriers to trade can have a discontinuous effect on global supply chains. Understanding such nontariff barriers is critical, since production often takes place in different countries. This entails strategic planning and coordination of inventories of intermediate goods, delivery of final goods, and return of defective products (through a well-operating reverse logistics system). In fact, while the way product standards interact with international trade is complex, harmonized standards can promote trade and also make supply chains more efficient.

Government Buying and Selling

Governments clearly need to exist in order to provide infrastructure. However, situations that occurred in the past in which governments were both large producers and large customers are unlikely to emerge again. Governments may be more facilitators than producers, although they will maintain some of their role as customers. Obviously, in some cases, governments also hinder the process, as we have seen with, for example, tariff and nontariff barriers, laws, and regulations. In the facilitator role, however, governments have a direct connection to global supply chains—both from an infrastructure standpoint and from the standpoint of how to add value and sell into a market.

Privatization

Privatization refers to an ownership shift of assets in a country from the government to private entities. It can also refer to shifting the way public services are provided from the government to private entities. Generally, increased privatization of a country's economy and public services leads to an increase in consumer choices, improvement in operational efficiency and effectiveness, and heightened competition. These are all technically good outcomes of privatization, but they also put different types of pressures on global supply chains. In essence, after privatization, negotiations and leverage points in the global supply chain are done at the firm level, not the state level, and competition to provide these value-added services will probably increase drastically, especially in commodity-oriented industries. So, while the overall result is a more open market, increased opportunities, and added know-how on how to operate optimally, global supply chains face negotiations with more firms rather than with what used to be state-run entities.

Emerging Markets

Broadening the idea of the BRIC countries, nine emerging markets—Brazil, China, India, Indonesia, Mexico, Russia, South Africa, Turkey, and Vietnam—are expected to contribute about 50 percent of global GDP growth in the coming decade. These nine countries were also covered in detail in Chapter 1. Emerging markets will represent an even larger share of the growth in product categories that are highly mature in developed economies (for example, automobiles). These are fantastically high numbers that create a real sense of urgency among many multinational corporations. In fact, many companies realize that they are likely to fall behind in the years to come simply by not being strategic and planning effectively for the integration of these emerging markets into their value chains. Many supply chain analysts also recognize that the growing global middle class in these emerging markets could significantly affect supply chains in the future. The middle class is growing significantly in all emerging markets and represents the "hidden" economy in most of these markets. That is, a large portion of the economy in emerging markets is not accounted for, since it is virtually impossible to predict accurately, much less account for objectively, and people in the low- and middle-income brackets in these emerging markets are driving this hidden but often large portion of the economy.

Preventing Security Breaches

Recently, the United States released a National Strategy for Global Supply Chain Security to focus on the protection of supply chains. This is in direct response to the staggering amount of trade that takes place every day between nations (millions of tons of cargo). The world and the United States have realized that world trade is driven by global supply chains. The national strategy developed by the United States was created over a two-year period with input from hundreds of supply chain stakeholders. The United States also has the Container Security Initiative and the Customs-Trade Partnership Against Terrorism, to mention just a few examples. In addition to individual governments, other organizations and programs are also addressing the security and risk issues facing global supply chains, beyond the specific industries and companies involved. ISO 28000 deals specifically with managing security and risks and is covered in detail in Chapter 3. Other examples include the International Maritime Organization, which administers the International Ship and Port Facility Security Code, and the World Customs Organization, the only organization focused exclusively on customs matters. These are also covered in Chapter 3.

Sustainability at Government Levels

Earlier, we described scenarios in which customers demand sustainability and "greening" of the products that they buy. The higher levels of governments are doing the same thing. They are also starting to demand green products, placing the burden on firms in global supply chains in particular. These sustainability efforts have also been elevated to the United Nations. The United Nations Global Compact, a corporate social responsibility initiative, states that "supply chain sustainability is the management of environmental, social and economic impacts, and the encouragement of good governance practices, throughout the lifecycles of goods and services. The objective of supply chain sustainability is to create, protect and grow long-term environmental, social and economic value for all stakeholders involved in bringing products and services to market."[3] The UN Global Compact was launched in the year 2000 and has now been signed by some 8,000 entities in more than 135 countries. This response across the world demonstrates that sustainability is clearly permeating government ranks and will be a key area for future governmental scrutiny and guidance.

Trading Blocs

Interestingly, we have far fewer operational barriers today than ever before. In terms of infrastructure, aspects of getting from point A to point B have improved over the years in almost all countries. This does not mean that it is easy to get to some less developed nations or even emerging markets, but it does mean that the transportation infrastructure allows firms to be anywhere in the world that they want to be within a day or so. In parallel with this better transportation infrastructure, however, we have also seen a drastic increase in trade agreements around the world, from almost none being in existence in the early 1970s and fewer than 50 in the early 1990s to there now being more than 300 throughout the world. Many countries are part of many trade agreements, making the trade complexity even more severe at times. Clearly there are global supply chain implications resulting from these trading bloc structures that many, if not most, firms face. Planning and accounting for potential trading bloc obstacles is a must in global supply chain strategy.

World Trade Organizations

Following World War II, the United States, working with its allies overseas, built institutions that it hoped would secure a peaceful, prosperous world for the future. The United Nations, the International Monetary Fund, the World Bank, and other international associations and councils were founded with these high hopes. Unfortunately, none of these lofty plans has succeeded as well as the institutions created to foster and expand global trade: the General Agreement on Tariffs and Trade (GATT) and its successor, the World Trade Organization (WTO). Nine multilateral negotiating rounds have increased world trade from $80 billion in 1947 to some $20 trillion in 2012, allowing incomes to rise in country after country. In fact, many of the trading bloc issues that we discussed earlier are reinforcing the WTO agreement to facilitate the promotion of trade. In many cases, we do have common platforms, although not common processes, for issues that facilitate trade (such as patents, copyrights, and contracts) that also involve many of the world's countries.

UNDERSTANDING COMPETITIVE GLOBALIZATION DRIVERS

The competitive globalization drivers generally depend on the actions of competitors. Issues that relate to the competitive drivers include the degree to which an industry has major competitors from different countries. They also encompass whether an industry has a lot of imports and exports across countries, the degree of interdependence among countries involved in an industry or with a competitor, the degree to which competitors are globalized in their industries, and whether major competitors have a transferable competitive advantage that relates to their core competencies.

Taking all these issues into account, we offer both a comparative ranking of 10 industries and a forecast, based on data, of where we are predicting them to be in five years in terms of the globalization potential of supply chains based on the pressure from competitive globalization drivers (see Figure 2.6). The comparative ranking for the competitive globalization drivers is approximate and will change over time, as indicated by the 6.0 percent change expected in competitive drivers, on average, for all these industries in the next five years. This means that we expect the competitive globalization

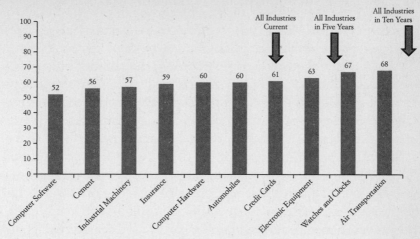

FIGURE 2.6 Competitive Globalization Drivers

drivers to be 6.0 percent more conducive to globalization efforts in five years. However, some industries will be more globalized and some will not reach the 6.0 percent positive change. For example, we forecast that there will not be much of a change in the competitive forces for insurance, watches and clocks, and cement in the next five years. Ten years from now, the forecast is less certain but still rather predictable. Our data indicate that the competitive drivers across industries will become 20.9 percent more globalized (with a score of 81 on the 100-point scale).

COMPETITIVE GLOBALIZATION DRIVERS' IMPLICATIONS FOR SUPPLY CHAINS

The competitive globalization drivers influence global supply chains directly through the actions of the major competitors in an industry. In effect, having several major competitors will result in an industry environment that can facilitate global supply chains through the networks of first-, second-, and third-tier suppliers that are created to support an industry. Competition can also hinder global supply chains if one or a select few firms create monopoly-like tendencies in an industry. However, this type of situation is rare. Most of the time, competition helps build infrastructure and helps facilitate effective global supply chain operations throughout the world.

Logistics and operations are directly and significantly affected by competitive globalization drivers. Related issues such as speed, quality, cost, and flexibility in supply chains all relate to the competitive drivers and the end products. In addition, the number of logistics service providers is increasing internationally, to the extent that we forecast some consolidation in emerging markets in the near future. Competitiveness in an industry is also directly connected with purchasing and market channels. Clearly, customers want to receive the most value possible in return for the price that they pay for a product. These pressures on firms increase as more major competitors become part of an industry. Likewise, the expectation is that firms purchasing on the inbound side of the chain will be able to find high-quality raw materials and component parts to satisfy end consumers who interact with the supply chain at the market channels level.

There are some topics and general conclusions that can be drawn from forecasts of what will happen with the competitive globalization drivers. We have developed a set of top 10 competitive globalization drivers that pertain to global supply chains: increased world trade, competitive battlegrounds, foreign acquirers, new competitors, born globals, interdependent countries, global centering, strategic alliances, commoditization, and talent.

Increased World Trade

Trade across countries has dominated worldwide production for some time. Whereas international trade used to be about double the production that takes place inside a country, now there is about a three-to-one ratio in favor of trade. More broadly, since 1980, world trade has seen about an 800 percent increase, whereas world output in the form of production has only quadrupled. The reasons for this increased trade are numerous, but some of the more prominent ones include decreases in the costs of trading (such as transportation, communication, information search, and tariffs), development of a more globalized and homogeneous world population, increases in incomes and purchasing power in more countries, and, perhaps most important, increases in the similarity of interests and needs across the world's customers. More recently, the last 10 years have seen even more remarkable increases in international trade, largely driven by global supply chains. And, given that global supply chains are predicted to become 25 percent of a firm's global strategy in five years (versus 20 percent now), global supply chains will be even more prominently featured in international trade.

Competitive Battlegrounds

The so-called triad markets—North America, Western Europe, and Japan—plus the newly industrialized countries in Southeast Asia are still the key battleground markets in the world. Even so, more of the competitive battlegrounds will involve emerging markets such as Brazil, China, India, Indonesia, Mexico, Russia, South Africa, Turkey, and Vietnam (see Chapter 1). These countries are expected to contribute more than 50 percent of global GDP growth in the coming decade. The purchasing power of the middle class worldwide is estimated to double in the next two decades, with Asia accounting for about 80 percent. This will establish parts of Asia, including Southeast Asia, as fruitful and important battlegrounds for global firms.

Foreign Acquirers

Foreign acquisitions of firms that were traditionally owned by local entrepreneurs and investors leads, over time, to an increased global mindset within the corporate culture in such firms. A more globally oriented fabric of companies typically leads to more global exposure, engagement, and international trade activity. The end result is that global supply chains are pressured to perform because of the shift in corporate cultures and also because firms are seeking market opportunities worldwide on a more proactive basis. For all the soccer enthusiasts who are reading this book, think about the unheard-of possibility that any English, Italian, or Spanish soccer club, for example, would be owned by a noncitizen of those countries, and yet that is now an enormous reality.

New Competitors

With the world's wide-ranging economies increasingly becoming integrated into one global economy, and with the Internet providing the infrastructure for more firms to go after customers in worldwide markets, the competitive pressures and increased motivation to establish a global presence have taken on greater importance for many firms. The Internet can solve the information gap that previously held firms back from addressing global customers' wants and needs. Global supply chains have to solve the integration of chains into "value networks" and the reaching of these global customers.

Born Globals

Born global firms are those that conduct business across borders from the inception of their firm or close to it (academically, we often say from within two years of inception). Despite the limited resources that typically characterize new businesses, born globals have substantial international sales early on. These types of companies are being created in very significant numbers worldwide, and they have been observed in all major trading countries and across all industries. The born globals put pressure on their global supply chain partners and expect them to bring full-service solutions for reaching those customers in the global markets that are most likely to buy the firm's products at an early stage. Vertical integration of global supply chain activities worldwide is the key—companies expect it, and more and more companies, such as third-party logistics providers, are delivering it.

Interdependent Countries

In the span of one generation, global economic interdependence has grown extraordinarily as a consequence of enormous technological progress and policies aimed at opening national economies to competition, internally and externally. Global supply chains are the solution to this interdependence among countries. Firms operate across interdependent countries to create value in the supply chain, but value cannot be achieved without effective coordination and integration among chain entities and countries. Leveraging the interdependence, then, becomes the role of global supply chains and their partners. As a result, countries cannot be interdependent without supply chains that solve the complexity that results from this interdependence, identifying nodes that are part of the chain and identifying and leveraging the value-added components to be gained from interdependence among countries. This is very much like the way supply chain partners are often interdependent.

Global Centering

In 2006, Sam Palmisano, then CEO of IBM, defined a globally cen-tered firm as "a company that fashions its strategy, its management, and its operations in pursuit of a new goal: the integration of pro-duction and value delivery worldwide." National headquarters are still the norm, but global companies—firms with no obvious attach-ment to a home country, such as Asea Brown Boveri (ABB)—are on the rise. Integration of production and value delivery worldwide requires effective and efficient global supply chains to take advan-tage of absolute and comparative advantages worldwide, given the typically lower levels of control and coordination of these globally centered companies compared with those that are nationally or even regionally centered.

Strategic Alliances

A global strategic alliance is usually established when a firm wants to enter into a related or even new business or geographic market. For example, in the last couple of decades, many companies have established partnerships in Europe so that they could be treated as European Union firms within the EU borders (assuming more than 50 percent ownership by the EU partner). This could also be true in countries like China, where the foreign government prohibits imports in certain cases in order to protect the domestic industry. One eye-opening point is that you might be surprised to find that you can build mutually advantageous alliances with some unlikely allies. Many companies make conscious decisions to form partnerships with complementary or even competing companies that can offer them opportunities in new countries. BMW, Mercedes, and Porsche having joint dealerships in the United States is an example of relatively fierce competitors joining forces in some parts of the world and maintain-ing their competitiveness in other parts.

Commoditization

With the increase in trade in the last 10 years, we have also seen a drastic increase in the commoditization of products. Whereas some products had economic value and a distinguishable unique-ness in terms of attributes in the past, customers now treat them as commodities. The market differentiation that these products enjoyed at one time has been replaced by price competition as the central factor that customers use when deciding which products to buy. Global supply chains have facilitated the commoditization of products by being able to get them into almost all corners of the world, something that could not be done in the past. This has resulted in customers treating the products as commodities. The days of low-cost, everyday products being the only goods likely to be treated as commodities are over. Many high-tech, high-complexity products have also been commoditized, such as memory chips, laptop components, transportation services, auto parts, floor polishers, and certain construction materials.

Talent

It seems improbable to say that we lack qualified talent in the world marketplace, but this really is the case in many industries and for many jobs. Worldwide annual employment growth is predicted to be less than 2 percent for years to come. The exceptions are in the Middle East and Africa, where the rates are expected to be much higher. For global supply chains, some of the implications include the fact that supply chains may have to be staffed more with current people, retrained employees, and local resources than with local or global employees. It may also mean that certain industries will have a shortage of qualified people who can do the job, resulting in increased pressures on global supply chains to deliver products and even services where value-to-cost can be best utilized.

GUIDELINES FOR DIAGNOSING INDUSTRY GLOBALIZATION POTENTIAL

The issue of alignment between industry globalization drivers and global supply chain efforts in the areas of logistics, purchasing, operations, and market channels is one of the most critical aspects of implementing strategic global supply chains. If the industry is more globalized than your chains, your firm is probably losing out on opportunities, efficiencies, and leverage points. If the industry is less globalized than your chains, your firm is probably spending extra on efforts to educate the marketplace. Neither scenario is necessarily a weak position in the global marketplace, but each does raise a "red flag" and is a cause for concern and careful evaluation of opportunities.

The starting point for globalizing supply chains should be determining the degree to which the industry is globalized. Next, the firm's global strategy should be evaluated in the context of current and planned future global supply chain efforts. Supply chain management is a part of corporate strategy and should be leveraged within the context and alignment of other global strategy levers (market participation, products and services, marketing, and competitive moves). After these two critical stages, global supply chains should be evaluated both holistically (from raw material to delivery of a product to an end customer) and within each supply chain function within a firm (that is, logistics, purchasing, operations, and market channels). Total cost analysis is the key. Each of these three steps is dependent on understanding, evaluating, and taking action vis-à-vis the industry globalization drivers. In diagnosing industry globalization potential, these guidelines and observations are applicable to all industries and companies:

- All industries are global to some degree and probably not global in some areas. There is not a single industry that is either fully domestic or fully global at this time. There is globalization potential in every industry represented by the approximately 5,000 commodity groups in the so-called Harmonized System (covered in Chapter 3).
- Different supply chain functions can operate in different directions in the same industry. Some may favor globalization, such as global sourcing in the case of purchasing, for example, while others may not favor globalization, as may be the case with operations when it comes to opening production facilities in foreign locations.
- Multinational corporations should respond selectively to industry globalization drivers. They should typically globalize only those supply chain functions (logistics, purchasing, operations, or market channels) and those activity links that are favored by globalization.
- Firms should keep in mind that an industry's globalization potential changes over time, as our data have shown, and that each industry driver operates independently in terms of both changes over time and strength in an industry.

- Corporations should use industry globalization drivers as a starting point for globalizing strategy and supply chains, using the world, a region of the world, or a select set of countries as the marketplace. Global supply chain efforts can be leveraged at multiple levels and with different complexities.

APPENDIX: MEASURES OF INDUSTRY GLOBALIZATION DRIVERS

Yip and Hult (2012) provide an extensive discussion of measures of each of the industry globalization drivers (market, cost, government, and competitive drivers) in Chapter 10 of their book *Total Global Strategy*.[4] In assessing the industry globalization drivers as they are in 2013 and using statistical methods to forecast what the state of these industry drivers will be in 2018 and 2023, we base our results on the extensive battery of measures that Yip and Hult detail in their book. A listing of the core drivers and measures are included in this appendix in Tables 2.1 through 2.4. We encourage the reader to consult *Total Global Strategy* for more detail.

TABLE 2.1 Market Drivers and Methods

Market Driver	Measure
Common customer needs and tastes	Extent to which customer needs and tastes are common around the world; percentage (by cost) of the components of a global product or service that can be common worldwide
National global customers	Share of worldwide market sales to customers who search the world for vendors
Multinational global customers	Share of worldwide volume accounted for by customers who purchase or select centrally
Global channels	Share of worldwide volume accounted for by channels that purchase centrally
Transferable marketing	For each element, share of world market accounted for by countries where foreign element is acceptable
Lead countries	Number of countries that account for the most important product/service innovations

TABLE 2.2 Cost Drivers and Methods

Cost Driver	Measure
Global scale economies	Percentage of world market needed for minimum efficient scale production or service operation
Steep experience effects	Percentage decrease in unit production costs with each doubling of accumulated capacity
Sourcing efficiencies	Potential percentage savings in purchase expenditures from making all purchases centrally
Favorable logistics	Transportation cost over a standard intercontinental route, excluding customs and duties, as a percentage of the selling price
Differences in country costs	Ratio of lowest- to highest-cost countries in the industry for (1) fully loaded hourly cost of the most common form of production labor and (2) total unit production cost
High product development costs	Total cost of developing (but not marketing) a major new product or service, as a percentage of the expected lifetime sales of the product or service
Fast-changing technology	Market life of typical new product

TABLE 2.3 Government Drivers and Methods

Government Driver	Measure
Tariffs	Percentage of the pretariff selling price, averaged globally
Subsidies	Percentage of the presubsidy selling price, averaged globally; net percentage effect on selling prices of subsidized competitors
Nontariff barriers	Percentage of the world market that is blocked from imports
Compatible technical standards	Percentage, in cost, of the typical product that is in components that are technically compatible worldwide
Common marketing regulations	Proportion of the industry's worldwide marketing expenditures that are in activities allowed in every country
Government-owned competitors	Combined global market share of all government-owned competitors
Government-owned customers	Combined share of global industry purchases made by government-owned customers

TABLE 2.4 Competitive Drivers and Methods

Competitive Driver	Measure
Exports	Exports as a percentage of the world market
Imports	Imports as a percentage of the world market
Competitors from different continents	Number of continents that are the home of global competitors from different continents
Interdependent countries	Amount of volume sold in each country that is dependent on production facilities that supply more than one country, averaged across competitors
Competitors globalized	Extent to which competitors use global strategy levers
Transferable competitive advantage	Extent to which competitive advantages in the industry are transferable globally

CHAPTER 3

Global Supply Chain Infrastructure

The world's infrastructure is the facilitator of global supply chains.

BASIC WORLDWIDE INFRASTRUCTURE ISSUES

The worldwide infrastructure for global supply chains involves transportation, communication, utilities, and technology, but there are lots of tangents and important issues that accompany those basic elements (for example, security, risks, value, legal considerations, contracts, insurance, customs, and payment). Clearly, the world's infrastructure planning can, and maybe should, include a plethora of infrastructure issues that have effects on global supply chains—whether in the area of logistics, purchasing, operations, or market channels. However, we will focus on transportation, communication, utilities, and technology as having critical and direct effects on many aspects of the functioning of global supply chains, and use them as the starting point for incorporating other important infrastructure issues. In a way, these four infrastructure domains serve as the facilitators or inhibitors of the operations of global supply chains. They also serve as the structures for how global supply chains at any given point in time have been operating worldwide.

Think tennis! Well, some more specificity may be warranted. For a century, all tennis players used a one-handed backhand to go along with their one-handed forehand. But in the 1970s and 1980s, Björn Borg and Jimmy Connors came along with two-handed backhands. Connors in essence used a hybrid of a one- and two-handed backhand, with a "push stroke," as opposed to Borg's more free-swinging two-handed backhand. In any event, Borg, who has the best winning percentage of all professional tennis players, and Connors, who has the third best winning percentage of professional tennis players (Ivan Lendl is second), started a trend that is very much alive today. Two-handed backhands came into vogue and have retained their significance for the game. But whereas Borg played with a heavy topspin on his backhand and Connors preferred a flat, heavy ball, a few years later, Mats Wilander came along with a nice hybrid of the two, using a two-handed topspin backhand, but also a one-handed slice backhand. After he won four of the top five tournaments in 1988 and four Grand Slams before the age of 20, Wilander's approach to tennis provided a new method for being successful in the game. And players of all calibers started copying Wilander's way of playing.

At the same time, the throwback approaches of John McEnroe and to some degree Ivan Lendl were used very effectively. Now, amateur players had multiple choices for how to hit the ball and even multiple materials to use in their tennis rackets. That led to other players (such as Michael Chang) using longer graphite rackets to their advantage, narrowly focused players (such as Boris Becker) playing power games, and finesse players (such as Stefan Edberg) using power. So, while there was a time when everyone played with wooden rackets and used one-handed backhands (think of some of the greats such as Rod Laver and Ken Rosewall), more recently, we have a diverse assortment of players, games, and approaches, from the delicate and finesse-oriented ways of Roger Federer, to the heavy topspin power game of Rafael Nadal, to the all-around games of Novack Djokovic and Andy Murray. And this is only on the men's side of the game. Women have made even greater strides in diversifying their games from pure elegance, almost beauty, to now also having numerous power hitters and varied approaches.

All of this is really a function of the "tennis infrastructure" that exists in the game. A few decades ago, tennis players of all calibers used wooden rackets, one-handed backhands, and a relatively flat continental grip. Today, the game has many coaches teaching a wide variety of ways to play and be successful—in essence, customizing the approach to playing the game to suit each player so that he or she can achieve the most from it (if your tennis coach uses a one-size-fits-all approach in teaching you how to play, you may want to switch coaches!).

The tennis infrastructure and its evolution correlate well with the evolution of global supply chains over the last decade. Who would have thought that call centers in India were feasible, production facilities in China were thinkable, and transportation of certain heavy bulk products by air was a possibility? Phrases such as "global economies of scale" and "demand for local responsiveness" are now mainstays in global supply chain practice. In essence, we have gone from a global culture in which speed, quality, cost, and flexibility were truly competing priorities to one in which we want to have (almost) all of them at the same time. Competing priorities have given way to developing the right "mix" of features (very similar to the established idea of the "marketing mix" of product, place, price, and promotion—covered in Chapter 7—in the field of marketing).

Well, as the new saying goes, you *can* have your cake and eat it too! Before, the saying used to be that you can't have your cake and eat it too. But we think you can. The global supply chain infrastructure not only allows for this but demands it. While we do not have superstar athletes like those in professional tennis, we do have superstar firms operating incredible global supply chain networks. Amazon, Apple, Dell, McDonald's, Procter & Gamble, Walmart, and the like have demonstrated an incredible ability to put the right amount of leverage on the right places at the right time to run quite efficient and effective global supply chains. These chains not only support the firms' corporate strategies but are also embedded in their total global strategy. These firms are using the best of the global infrastructure that exists for supply chains and overcoming the inhibitors in the infrastructure so that they can do well. They are growing their global supply chains, offering resilient systems, and building enough redundancy into the supply chains via multilocal operations to allow for contingencies.

Infrastructure, by its nature, involves a lot of basic organizational and physical structures and operating procedures that support or hinder global supply chains. In essence, we are talking about all the publicly or privately owned elements that are in place to facilitate operating supply chains throughout the world. In this chapter, we will address issues such as transportation, communication, utilities, technology, security, risks, legal considerations, commercial documents, customs, terms of payment, International commerce terms (Incoterms), harmonized codes, and the like. Of the many infrastructure issues listed, some may be viewed as helping to run global supply chains, while others, at times, may be perceived as hindering the work of global supply chains.

What we do know, however, is that infrastructure scores a 61 on a 100-point scale today (where 100 is fully globalized and zero is fully domestic), but the expectation is that global supply chains' infrastructure "facilitators" will become better for global operations. These scores are illustrated in Figure 3.1. We expect improvements of 11 percent in the global supply chain infrastructure in the next five years and another 15 percent in the following five years, or an expected globalization of the infrastructure supporting the operating of global supply chains of 28 percent in the next ten years (by 2023).

This does not suggest that there will be less bureaucracy and red tape. What it does suggest is that countries, firms, and individuals will be more likely to work through the issues associated with global supply chains. We will still have security and risk issues in global supply chains. Legal considerations are still going to be there, especially across country borders. Commercial documents will continue to exist (although hopefully there will be fewer of them), and they will also maintain their importance in terms of transparency and clarity concerning shipments. Incoterms are likely to continue to be defined as they are now, since the most recent revision was published on January 1, 2011 (Incoterms were started in 1936, and they have been amended and revised roughly every decade in the last 30 years).

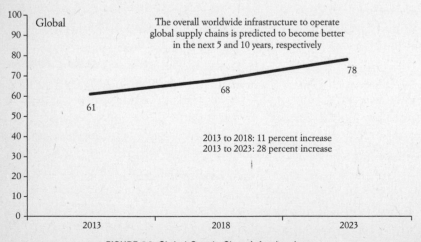

FIGURE 3.1 Global Supply Chain Infrastructure

Terms of payment and currency of payment may be an area where we will see some more options and flexibility.

TRANSPORTATION, COMMUNICATION, UTILITIES, AND TECHNOLOGY INFRASTRUCTURE

Addressing various infrastructure issues is important because global supply chains depend on worldwide infrastructure in order to operate well. One illustration of this is FedEx in China. FedEx entered mainland China in 1984 and has been committed to increasing its access points in the country and the region ever since. Recently FedEx began tripling its capacity of operations in Shanghai through the development of a new hub to be completed in 2017. Working with the Shanghai Airport Company Limited, FedEx plans to establish a new international express and cargo hub at Shanghai Pudong International Airport.

This development reinforces FedEx's commitment to China, where it has an intense set of flights daily to and from various places such as Beijing, Shanghai, Guangzhou, Shenzhen, and Chengdu. But landing a Boeing 777 freighter in Shanghai takes a great airport infrastructure such as that at Shanghai Pudong International Airport, delivering the large number of packages carried onboard the 777 takes trucks, driving those trucks to customized destinations takes roads and gasoline, knowing where the packages are and where they need to go takes communication and technology, and so on. It requires a coordinated and strategic effort integrating transportation, utilities, communication, and technology to operate FedEx's and most other organizations' global supply chains.[1]

To illustrate how dynamic this picture is, consider FedEx's announcement on March 21, 2013, of a capacity cut to and from Asia. The third quarter was very challenging because of continued weakness in international airfreight markets, pressure on yields as a result of industry overcapacity, and customers selecting less expensive and slower transit services. Beginning April 1, FedEx decreased capacity to and from Asia and began to manage traffic flows to place low-yielding traffic through lower-cost networks, in the process assessing how the actions might allow FedEx to retire more of its older, less efficient aircraft as part of the fleet modernization program it had begun several years earlier. The Asia capacity cut points to a need for constant diligence in matching supply to demand. Contingencies and flexibility are strategies that this firm has refined to the utmost, allowing for elasticity in operations.

Transportation Infrastructure

The most obvious infrastructure-related issue for global supply chains is transportation. How many nodes are there in a specific supply chain that spans some portion of the globe? What transportation do you expect to use between each pair of nodes, and is that type of transportation supported by the appropriate infrastructure (for example, roads for trucks, railways for trains, and waterways for ships)? What type of packaging needs to be used to carry the goods from one mode of transportation in the chain to another? And where in the chain can delays be expected? These are just a few of the many transportation-related items that warrant strategic and tactical planning.

Perhaps a closer-to-home example is this. Where do you live? What does the place where you live look like? Do you have a nice driveway? What about the street to which your driveway connects? You would take all these things into account if you were to move, right? Well, perhaps a better question is this: can a semitrailer get close enough to your house to load your furniture directly, or will you need a smaller truck or vehicle to transport your furniture to a location where it can be transferred to the larger truck? Now, let's say that you currently live in the Lansing area in Michigan (coincidentally, where the three authors of this book live), and you have decided to take a job in Stockholm. The starting point may be your house in Lansing, and the ending point may be your new apartment in Stockholm. But what will it take to transport your furniture from Lansing to Stockholm? These are global supply chain issues on a micro scale for one family and one house. Now think about the transportation infrastructure needed for FedEx again, and its deliveries of small packages from the 400,000 or so people living in the metro area of Lansing to the 1.5 million people in the metro area of Stockholm.

Global supply chains depend on transportation infrastructure in the form of roads, railways, airports and air space, waterways, ports, and warehousing. Does your firm have a handle on each of these transportation issues? For example, we know that roads are a critical component of the transportation infrastructure worldwide.

Roads become even more important in the "last mile" of the global supply chain.[2] In that sense, roads support ports, airports, and railroads, which are typically used prior to roads (with notable exceptions being the United States and other countries that are heavily dependent on trucks). The general quality of roads and the road infrastructure in strategically located areas is usually pretty easy to figure out with some basic research. What matters for the road infrastructure—beyond the quality of the roads—are issues such as congestion, networks and connections, and signage on the roads, including highways, roads outside cities and towns, and streets in very populated areas.

Railroads have become more viable as a way to transport raw materials, parts, and finished products in light of the increased congestion on highways and roads, the increased concerns about pollution around the world, and the creation of effective and efficient multimodal containers. The multimodal containers, in particular, eliminate the need to load and unload products into and from traditional boxcars and have made the transportation much more efficient and logical. That said, railway transportation is still very much a world region issue. For example, in the United States, cargo has priority over passenger transportation, but the opposite is true in Europe and most of the rest of the world. In Europe, passenger transportation on trains is very popular, and it usually takes precedence over cargo. Strategic planning is the key, but the multimodal options have significantly helped in making the best choices.

Naturally, we can assume that airports are a critical part of the infrastructure for global supply chains. At the same time, we have to realize that the kind of cargo carried by airplanes usually has a high cost. This means that it will be a long time before air transportation will be dominant as a cargo transportation vehicle, if that ever happens. Ships, trains, and trucks are just too good an option vis-à-vis air. Now, for companies like FedEx, UPS, and DHL, and for component parts and finished goods that lend themselves to air transportation, air is a natural complement to the transportation infrastructure and has an important place in getting things shipped around the world. Memphis and Hong Kong have competed for the busiest cargo airport in the world for a few years, with Shanghai predicted to become a challenger soon, especially when the new FedEx hub is completed around 2017. The basics to consider when evaluating air transportation include the length of the runways, which determines the size of the aircraft that can land at and take off from an airport, and the number of runways.

Waterways around the world are perhaps the most critical aspect of the global supply chain infrastructure. We have vast amounts of seawater on the globe, and lots of raw materials, component parts, and finished goods are carried on various types of ships. Beyond the ocean waters, which are relatively uncongested compared with other forms of transportation, we also need to consider the depth and width of canals and other waterways that make up the beginning and ending portions of ocean travels. For example, the size of the locks associated with waterways is incredibly important. At this time, some of the internationally strategic waterways and canals include the Bosphorus in Turkey, the Suez Canal in Egypt, the Panama Canal in Panama, the Saint Lawrence Seaway in North America, and the Corinth Canal in the Mediterranean. The Panama Canal in particular has received a lot of attention over the years; it's a superb connection between the Pacific and Atlantic Oceans. After the construction of two new sets of locks (each new lock will have three water chambers, and each chamber will have three water reutilization basins) and the widening and deepening of existing channels in Gatun Lake and the Culebra Cut, the Panama Canal is set to become an even more strategic global supply chain node for larger ships in 2014 and beyond.

Waterways would be marginalized if we didn't have the necessary ports where small, medium, and usually large ships can dock. It is not just the ports themselves, though. They need cranes and other infrastructure items to load and unload cargo onto and from the ships. For example, can the port cranes load the maximum number of containers a ship can carry? Ships typically carry 13 containers side by side, but there is a possibility to carry as many as 18 containers in the post-Panamax era (Panamax measures refer to the maximum specifications allowed since the opening of the Panama Canal in 1914; ships that fall outside of the Panamax sizes are called post-Panamax; in 2015, the "New Panamax" specifications will be in effect when the canal's third set of larger locks becomes operational). Other typical issues that come into play at ports are unionized workforces with strict hours of operation and constrained port capacity, as many worldwide ports are operating at maximum capacity already. The starting point for evaluating ports should be the depth of the water leading to the port. We also have to take into account the maximum clearance under bridges on the way to the port. Hopefully, the planning can be more strategic than it was for the *Oasis of the Seas*: after departing from Finland on her maiden voyage to be delivered to the Royal Caribbean, the *Oasis of the Seas* had to have her telescoping funnels retracted and also use the "squat effect" technique (travel at a high speed in shallow water to lower the ship by being drawn deeper into the water) to clear under the Great Belt Fixed Link (Storebæltsforbindelsen) outside Denmark.

The final transportation infrastructure issue appears to have nothing to do with transportation at all, but it's a transportation-related matter that needs to be taken into account. Have you thought about why there are so many warehouses in Memphis and Louisville? Louisville is an easy starting point; that's where UPS has a stronghold. Memphis is both the same and different; Memphis is where FedEx has a stronghold, but the I-40 highway that runs across the state also runs through it, and lots of trucks go by every day. And, of course, Memphis is where the Mississippi River passes by, with lots of different types of ships. In addition, it has a number of Class I railroads and many trucking terminals. Warehousing infrastructure is important for global supply chains and the multiple nodes in the chain. Products are very likely to be stationary for certain periods of time, and warehouses are natural holding locations during these layovers and transitions to multimodal operations. In this spirit, Memphis, Tennessee, has become known as "North America's Logistics Center," with FedEx as a major client and the enormous web of warehouses to support the firm's cargo operations.

Communication Infrastructure

iPhones, iPads, Microsoft Surface computers, and the like have created a very sophisticated communication infrastructure for most individuals worldwide. It used to be that few people in the emerging markets and less developed nations could afford phones. The mobile phone changed that landscape, and now there is a cell phone in nearly every hand in every country. Obviously, there are a myriad of options. Apple's iPhone, along with competitors such as Samsung's Galaxy, Motorola's Droid, and Nokia's Lumia, give customers options that provide fantastic communication opportunities. There are even lots of "apps" to tackle supply chain management issues—who would have thought it! Broader than personalized apps, though, telecommunication and mail services are the backbone of our communication infrastructure worldwide.

Telecommunication networks serve as the foundation of our global society, especially the information society. By some accounts, telecommunications accounts for about 3 percent of the gross domestic product (GDP) of industrialized nations. In the last decade, however, voice telecommunications has increased by about 10 percent, whereas data transfers via telecommunications networks have roughly doubled every year. This data transfer is critically important for effective operation of global supply chains—it has changed the game from the agent's being the gatekeeper of information to global supply chains operating with maximum transparency. Now we know where our shipments are at all times (or at least we should), and we have more control and involvement in where and how those shipments flow from node to node and to the end customers. So, strategic development of the information infrastructure to go along with the transportation of products is as critical as any component of the chain.

Utilities Infrastructure

An argument might be made that utilities are not really a global supply chain issue, and we can agree that utilities have an effect on many different aspects of global business, but these aspects also include global supply chain management. In some way, we take it for granted that utilities such as electricity, water, sewer, and gas exist and are available to support global supply chain operations. Is this really true? Where have you traveled? Was the utilities infrastructure the same as the one at home? Probably not! Our guess is that, at a minimum, you had a hard time figuring out where to adjust the temperature in your hotel room, you may have had a hard time adjusting the water in the shower so that it was perfect for you, and the food may not have been cooked to your liking. These are fairly minor issues in the broad scheme of things. Now think of the bullwhip effect when it comes to supply chains and utilities. A small item at the beginning of the global supply chain (or at any early point in the chain, for that matter) can ultimately have a large effect down the line.

This bullwhip problem escalates if we move beyond the developed nations and focus our attention on the other 150 or so countries in the world. We are not trying to downgrade or put a negative spin on the countries that are not as developed as those in North America, Western Europe, and the like, but we do need to highlight concerns that should be taken into account. In India, for example, why aren't Indian electricity blackouts having an effect on the country's technology centers? The answer is strategic, easy, and predictable: Indian businesses know how to get things done and plan accordingly. They need their call center operations to work, and so diesel generators keep their cell towers running and their technology operations such as call centers working even during blackouts where hundreds of millions of people may have no power. We are talking billions of gallons of diesel fuel, but the utilities need to be on if India is to thrive commercially. A contradiction or at least a comparison can be made to the United States, where the electrical grid has sometimes been called a "patchwork quilt" that has been stitched together to cover the country.

Water and sewer systems can be a concern in many countries. Do you readily drink the water in every hotel room? What about swimming in the pool, river, or even ocean where you are planning to vacation—do you always assume that you can? Water interruptions, rationing, and shortages are not uncommon. For example, by most accounts, there are 54 countries in Africa. Are they all the same when it comes to water supply and sewer services? No. What about a large-scale city such as Atlanta, with its top-ranked (in terms of numbers of passengers) airport traffic? Lake Lanier is the main water reservoir in the northern portion of the state of Georgia that supplies the city of Atlanta with water. In July 2009, however, a federal judge from Minnesota (selected as a neutral judge in a "water lawsuit" involving Lake Lanier) ruled that Congress had never authorized the use of Lake Lanier to provide water to Atlanta. Civic leaders in Atlanta said that if the ruling were followed, they would see a 75 percent cut in drinking water to the region, which, ultimately, would result in disaster. Similar water shortages exist in many places, such as California (http://www.calwatercrisis.org), and they have potentially severe effects on global supply chains. At this time, the World Bank estimates that 80 percent of the world's population has access to clean water within one kilometer (about 0.62 mile) of their home.

Switching to another form of utilities, think of energy. Energy pipelines allow the fuel required to meet the world's energy needs to be increasingly transported by pipelines instead of by ships, trucks, and trains. Pipelines are typically the most economical way to transport large quantities of oil, refined oil, oil products, and natural gas on land. These pipelines include gathering pipelines (inbound supply chain pipelines), transportation pipelines (long pipelines with a large diameter), and distribution pipelines (outbound supply chain pipelines). Think of the pipelines that may transport gas to your house as the smallest and most distribution-oriented pipelines. So, while we often forget the pipeline option, it is becoming more common throughout the world, and perhaps your shipment (even if it is not oil derivatives) should be thought of in this context.

Technology Infrastructure

Technology infrastructure is a component of the communication infrastructure discussed earlier, but also, to some degree, a component of the related utilities infrastructure. In fact, technology is all around us in various forms. As it relates to infrastructure and global supply chains, however, we will center our attention on software and hardware that allow a firm to manage supply chain operations effectively. In that context, we can broadly talk about e-commerce being integral to international trade. E-commerce helps break down the barriers of geographic distance, supports information exchanges across all inbound/upstream and outbound/downstream nodes, and supports just-in-time information exchanges. That typically happens before the products (raw material, component parts, or finished products) arrive at the next node in the supply chain. There's now an array of options and systems for integration that you can at least consider, depending on the size of your operations globally. These include electronic data interchange (EDI); enterprise resource planning (ERP); collaborative planning, forecasting, and replenishment (CPFR); vendor-managed inventory (VMI); warehouse management system (WMS); and radio frequency identification (RFID), to mention a few of the most critical ones.

EDI refers to the electronic interchange of data between two or more companies. Transmission of data via EDI is usually automated, meaning that no employees are required to administer the system. Most often, it is displayed in a real-time format for accurate access and decision making. Data transferred via EDI typically includes purchase orders, invoices for payment, payment instructions, and delivery schedules. On a broader scale, ERP has made it easier for the right hand to know what the left hand is doing within firms. ERP is a wide-ranging business planning and control system that includes supply chain–related subsystems (for example, materials requirements planning, or MRP). It requires a significant commit- ment of financial and nonfinancial resources both to implement and to maintain it. Large companies such as multinational corporations often implement an ERP system, whereas small and medium-sized enterprises (SMEs) often implement some smaller version of an ERP. WMSs often operate in concert with ERP systems; for example, an ERP system defines material requirements, and these are transmitted to a distribution center for a WMS. Increased complexities in global supply chains create increased complexities in the warehouse. WMS manages this complexity to ensure that the right work is done at the right time to meet demand.

CPFR was developed to fill the interorganizational connections that ERP cannot fill within a supply chain context. In fact, CPFR is mainly a collaborative method for scheduling logistics between suppliers and customers. It can include few to many supply chain partners, few to many data exchanges, forecasting of various activ- ities, planning (for example, marketing, product development, and transportation), and coordination of replenishment processes. Building on the notion of a CPFR, a VMI typically involves a retailer outsourcing its inventory management to a supplier. In that sense, a VMI allows for a holistic overview of the supply chain, with a single point of control for all inventory management. It helps predict sup- ply and demand relationships more accurately, and it can include different related formulations: replenishment only; replenishment and forecasting; replenishment, forecasting, and customer inven- tory management; or replenishment, forecasting, customer inventory management, and distribution planning.

Finally, when applied in global supply chains, RFID technologies identify and locate tangible products that are in freight. RFID tags can be placed on individual product items, batches of freight, con- tainers, or almost anything involved in global supply chains. Remote communication capabilities set RFID apart from other traceable technologies (such as bar codes, which need to be read or scanned).

SUPPLY CHAIN SECURITY, RISKS, AND VALUE

In the year of this book's publication, the History Channel on TV in the United States is finding success with two shows that are outside the normal scope of TV entertainment; one show is called *Big Rig Bounty Hunters*, and the other is called *Ice Road Truckers*. Both are about truck driving, and they highlight many issues related to security, risks, and value that supply chains face. In the supply chain context, security refers to the application of policies, procedures, and technology to protect supply chain assets (products, facilities, equipment, information, and personnel) from theft, damage, or terrorism and to prevent the introduction of unauthorized contraband, people, or weapons of mass destruction.[3]

Big Rig Bounty Hunters highlights a unique but important security and risk component of the trucking business. Specifically, each year, thousands of trucks carrying important and valuable cargo across North America go missing for one reason or another. Generally, these trucks disappear because of piratelike occurrences. If you think about it, trucks can easily carry hundreds of thousands of dollars' worth of valuables inside, such as raw materials, component parts, and/or finished products, so they might seem to be a great target for criminals. On the TV show, the big rig bounty hunters literally hunt down the missing trucks and sometimes even the people who took them, and they haul the cargo to a preplanned destination so that the trucking firms do not take a loss. Interestingly, the truck-hunting business is pretty lucrative for these unique bounty hunters, but the value of the cargo on the trucks clearly warrants the trucking firms' business model.

Ice Road Truckers highlights another risk and value proposition that supply chains encounter with truck transportation. These truck drivers and their cargo do not usually come across the kind of security issues faced by the truckers in *Big Rig Bounty Hunters*, although that also sometimes happens. Instead, in *Ice Road Truckers*, drivers face the risks of the iciest and most treacherous roads in North America—those at the farthest reaches of the continent. Think of Siberia in Russia, and you can imagine what these truckers face in the far north of North America. Prudhoe Bay, North Slope, Manitoba, Dempster Highway, and even ice roads on the Arctic Ocean have become familiar names and places for those who drive these treacherous lanes and those who follow the show.

These brief TV show examples illustrate some of the risks we are talking about—driving large trucks that are fully loaded with expensive and very valuable cargo, and driving on ice roads that cross rivers, ponds, lakes, and even parts of the Arctic Ocean. Though the work is risky, these truckers do fill an important link in global supply chains.

Security Management Systems

The International Organization for Standardization (ISO) is a world-wide leader in developing and publishing international standards for a variety of business and operating activities. In fact, the ISO is the largest developer of voluntary international standards in the world today. Its international standards provide up-to-date specifications for products, services, and practices, helping to make industries more efficient, effective, transparent, and predictable. Developed through global consensus (from broad industry input), the ISO's standards help break down barriers to international trade. Founded in 1946, the ISO today has members in more than 160 countries and some 3,400 technical bodies to take care of the development of international standards. One such standard is directly connected to supply chain security and is labeled ISO 28000.

ISO 28000 is titled "Specification for Security Management Systems for the Supply Chain" and includes ISO 28000 (specifications), ISO 28001 (best practices), ISO 28002 (development of resilience in the supply chain), ISO 28003 (requirements for bodies providing audit and certification of supply chain security management systems), ISO 28004 (guidelines for the implementation of ISO 28000), and ISO 28005 (electronic port clearance). Broadly, this collection of ISO 28000 documents establishes a supply chain security system that works to protect people, products, infrastructure, equipment, and transportation against security incidents. The ISO 28000 packet specifies requirements for establishing, implementing, maintaining, improving, and auditing a supply chain security management system. Guidelines for creating a supply chain security plan, developing supply chain security training programs, and implementing the related management system are also an integral part of ISO 28000.

Supply chain risk combines three elements (see Figure 3.2). It starts with a potential *threat* and then combines the *probability* of that threat with its potential *severity* to arrive at the likelihood of a significant supply chain risk. In the context of ISO 28000, the concept of risk encompasses two future-oriented and important questions: first, what is the probability that a potential security threat will actually occur in the future, and second, how severe would the impact be if

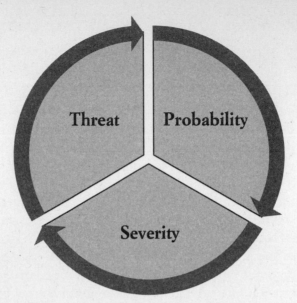

FIGURE 3.2 Supply Chain Risk Combines Three Elements

the potential security threat were to become an actual security incident? With that in mind, for a high security risk, the threat would have a high probability of occurring and would have a severe impact if it actually occurred. But there are numerous examples of security and risk issues, along with the value (lost or not achieved value) attached to them, that fall on a continuum. Thus, firms need to continuously evaluate this in the context of their global supply chains.

The risks associated with multinational corporations (MNCs) in the marketplace can be categorized into those risks that pertain directly to an MNC and those that pertain to the international environment in which the MNC operates (see Figure 3.3). This framework allows for a direct connection between the different components that we discuss and those risks that MNCs face on a day-to-day basis. The framework also allows for an easy identification mechanism for the areas of risk—at the broad level—that can become problematic if they are not identified and tackled appropriately. If a risk appears or can be predicted in the future in any of these areas, a closer analysis and identification of risk possibilities (threat, probability, and severity) should be undertaken.

As Figure 3.3 illustrates, the risk framework can be divided into those issues that the multinational corporation faces directly and those

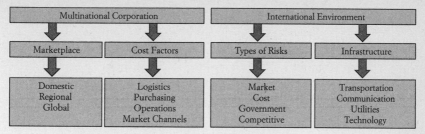

FIGURE 3.3 Basic Supply Chain Risks

that the MNC faces as a result of the risk components in the international environment. The MNC operates within a marketplace consisting of market segments that can be domestic (for example, American firms marketing products in the United States), regional (for example, Italian firms marketing products in the Scandinavian countries of Sweden, Norway, Denmark, Finland, and Iceland), or global (for example, Japanese firms marketing products throughout the six main continents of the world). There are risks associated with certain countries and regions, and also with being fully global in marketing efforts.

For the MNC, global supply chain management represents an integrated and coordinated effort by logistics, purchasing, operations, and market channels. Sometimes these are called "functions" within the firm, and sometimes (usually in smaller firms) they are all located in a supply chain department. In many cases, they are considered strategic to the firm's globalization efforts, while at the same time being also tactical and operational in terms of getting supply chain things done. Each element of the global supply chain has associated risks—for example, logistics in the areas of distribution, transportation, and inventory management; purchasing in the areas of order fulfillment and delivery, supplier selection, outsourcing, and offshoring; operations in the areas of buying decisions, competitive priorities, quality standards, and total cost issues; and market channels in the areas of entry modes and customer value creation. Strategic and tactical elements of logistics will be addressed in Chapter 4, purchasing will be covered in Chapter 5, operations in Chapter 6, and market channels in Chapter 7.

Going back to Figure 3.3, we know from Chapter 2 that industry globalization drivers are made up of market, cost, government, and competitive drivers (see Figure 3.4). Each of these globalization drivers is associated with risks that should be taken into account when addressing the threat, probability, and severity of global supply

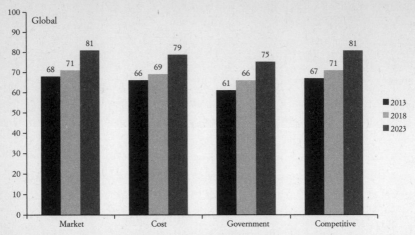

FIGURE 3.4   Industry Globalization Drivers

chain breakdowns. What we know from the framework introduced in Chapter 2 is that globalization efforts will be markedly different in five and ten years, respectively, for each of the industry globalization drivers. It will be easier to operate global supply chains, but it will also be important that you actually further globalize your supply chains. If your chains are not globalized more—at the level of what Figures 1.3 and 1.5 show—your firm is likely to fall behind the competition, since it is not leveraging the opportunities in its industry.

Earlier in this chapter, we introduced four basic infrastructure issues in the environment: transportation infrastructure, communication infrastructure, utilities infrastructure, and technology infrastructure. Each is associated with a set of risks: both risks that relate to a breakdown in transportation, communication, utilities, or technology and risks associated with the infrastructure needed to support the transportation, communication, utilities, and technology required to run a global supply chain being weak or not there. Obviously, each firm should evaluate all these risks in concert with countries, suppliers, and other potential interorganizational partners as a way to minimize the threat, probability, and severity factors.

A number of security, risk, and value organizations and initiatives exist to help companies address these issues beyond the ISO 28000 guidelines. They include:

- **International Maritime Organization (IMO).** The IMO is the United Nations' specialized agency with responsibility for the safety and security of shipping and the prevention of marine pollution by ships (www.imo.org).

- **International Ship and Port Facility Security Code (ISPS Code).** The ISPS Code is a comprehensive set of measures to enhance the security of ships and port facilities, administered by the IMO.
- **World Customs Organization (WCO).** The WCO is the only intergovernmental organization that is exclusively focused on customs matters (www.wcoomd.org).
- **Container Security Initiative (CSI).** CSI is a program that is intended to help increase security for maritime containerized cargo being shipped to the United States from around the world; it is administered by U.S. Customs and Border Protection (www.cbp.gov).
- **Customs-Trade Partnership Against Terrorism (C-TPAT).** C-TPAT seeks to safeguard the world's trade industry from terrorists, maintaining the economic health of the United States and its neighbors; it is administered by U.S. Customs and Border Protection (www.cbp.gov).

Managing security and risks within the guidelines of ISO 28000 and in adherence with the standards of most security, risk, and value organizations and initiatives in the world marketplace includes eight different, complementary, and important steps. They are:

1. Establish a security management system (SMS).
2. Document your organization's security management policy.
3. Identify security threats and assess global supply chain risks.
4. Identify security management control measures and objectives.
5. Create a security management structure (roles, responsibilities, and authorities).
6. Implement an operational SMS.
7. Prepare emergency SMS plans and procedures.
8. Monitor and measure security performance.

Kraljic Portfolio Model

In the context of security and risks, it is always important to address the value of the raw material, component parts, and/or products.

One easy-to-understand method is the so-called Kraljic portfolio model. It centers mainly on the purchasing element of global supply chains, but we think it serves us well in addressing risk and value issues in global supply chains in general.[4]

The Kraljic model is represented as a two-by-two matrix defined by the dimensions of risk (low and high) and value (low and high), as represented in Figure 3.5. The matrix is sometimes called the portfolio method by Peter Kraljic and dates from the 1960s, but it became popular in the 1980s after Kraljic published the portfolio matrix in the *Harvard Business Review*. The model is rather simplistic and relatively easy to incorporate into global supply chains. It uses the risks to the availability of a product on the *y* axis and the financial value of the products on the *x* axis. The *x* axis is also sometimes identified as the volume of purchasing, but that assumes that value is equal to high volume, so we prefer to use value as the generic label on the *x* axis.

We'll return to FedEx as our example firm, and put it into the Kraljic model as an illustration. Again, FedEx is a transportation firm that has its headquarters in Memphis, Tennessee, but that operates worldwide in more than 200 countries. Fred Smith founded Federal Express in 1971 with his $4 million inheritance and $91 million raised in venture capital (fedex.com). For

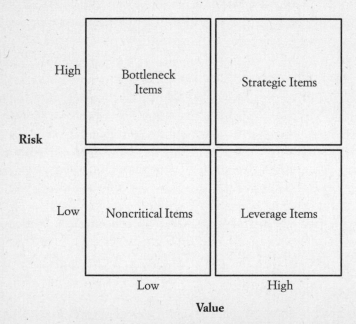

FIGURE 3.5 Managing Supplier Risk and Value

illustration purposes, let's see what the model in Figure 3.5 might look like in the case of FedEx.

The bottom left quadrant in the Kraljic matrix (low value and low risk) represents an area where the firm should try to aggregate and consolidate global supply chain initiatives (such as purchasing) and use substitute products, suppliers, or supply chain partners. The reason for this approach is that we are talking about products with low purchasing value and low purchasing risk (that is, commodity products). This quadrant could include FedEx purchasing office stationery for its headquarters in Memphis: the options for such purchases are probably great, and the per-item cost is relatively low.

Moving to the quadrant represented by the low value and high risk characteristics, we are guiding the firm to look for ways to control and/or manage suppliers and consider possibly overordering to ensure supply. In essence, we are dealing with bottleneck items in this case—items that are critically needed even though they are of low value. This quadrant could include FedEx purchasing uniforms for its truck drivers in the more than 200 countries where it operates.

The strategy for the high value and low risk quadrant involves increasing the number of sources and maintaining competition among suppliers. These are tactical items that are operationally needed to carry out critical tasks in the global supply chain. For FedEx, a situation in which this may apply is purchasing jet fuel for its fleet of more than 400 airplanes.

The high-high quadrant (high value and high risk) is characterized by collaboration and developing strong relationships with global supply chain partners—in particular, global suppliers. Given the high-high situation, this quadrant also warrants strategic thinking that involves contingency plans and ongoing analysis of risks. One possible example for FedEx in this quadrant is purchasing cargo airplanes to maintain its fleet of more than 400 airplanes in good working order (replacing planes when they become obsolete).

LEGAL CONSIDERATIONS, INTERNATIONAL CONTRACTS, AND INSURANCE

Some may think that we are venturing a bit off the topic of global supply chains when we include legal considerations, contracts, and insurance issues in this infrastructure chapter. But the reality is that legal considerations (including legal systems, patents, trademarks, and copyrights), international contracts, and insurance issues are very much a part of a well-functioning (or not) global supply chain. The key is to take advantage of the existing infrastructure as much as possible or, better yet, figure out a way to operate effectively and efficiently within the existing (and forecasted) legal, contractual, and insurance constraints. Today, we do have some great legal, contractual, and insurance avenues for our global supply chains. At the same time, this is not a book on legal issues, contract issues, or insurance issues—we are merely identifying them from a strategic standpoint so that they are not lost in the process of developing and implementing global supply chains.

The easiest starting point for this discussion is a look at the world's legal systems (see Figure 3.6). They can be effectively grouped into four main systems: civil law, common law, dual-jurisdiction-based (known as bijuridical, encompassing civil and common law), and Islamic law. The two most common are the common law system and the civil law system. Common law originated in England. It is also known as case law or precedent because it is based on tradition, precedent, and custom. Civil law is based on a detailed set of laws organized into codes, with its origin in Western Europe.

While legal systems around the world are not always easy to deal with, they are relatively easy to spot. The map shows where each is

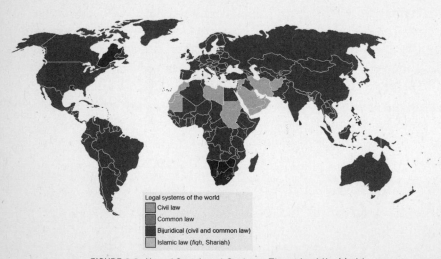

FIGURE 3.6 Use of Core Legal Systems Throughout the World

Source: Hton1 at en.wikipedia.

prominent. What is not necessarily so easy to spot is how and where to invoke patent protection. But the interesting story line here is that the Patent Cooperation Treaty (PCT) helps with this and should be leveraged throughout the global supply chain wherever such protection is needed. For example, this can be for component parts or for products flowing through the chain. The PCT is an international patent law treaty that provides a unified procedure for filing patent applications. Keep in mind, though, that to obtain international protection, patent applications must be made in each country or to each regional authority where protection is desired. The PCT just helps the process work better and be more standardized. See Figure 3.7 for the worldwide coverage of the PCT.

Copyright (©) is a legal concept, endorsed by most countries' governments, giving the creator of an original work exclusive rights to it, usually for a limited time period of some number of years. The Berne Convention for the Protection of Literary and Artistic Works covers copyrights involving some 165 parties (see Figure 3.8). In that respect, the Berne Convention is a great starting point to figure out the often mazelike process for obtaining copyrights in each country.

Another form of protection is to use a trademark in the international marketplaces where you operate global supply chains or where you have supply chain partners. There are three different forms of trademarks to be aware of in this context: "TM" represents an unregistered trademark, "SM" represents an unregistered service mark, and the symbol ® represents a registered trademark.

FIGURE 3.7 Areas Covered by the Patent Cooperation Treaty

Source: Japindereum at en.wikipedia.

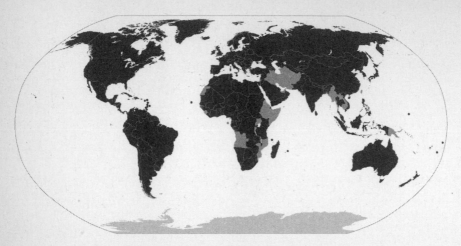

FIGURE 3.8   Areas Covered by the Berne Convention for
the Protection of Literary and Artistic Works

Source: cflm at en.wikipedia.

One of the most legalistic and valuable pieces of paper in international trade (or in any form of trade, for that matter), especially between companies, is a signed contract. Naturally, we know that in some parts of the world (for example, several Asian countries), contracts are viewed as a starting point for dialogue, whereas in other countries (for example, several Western European countries), the contract serves as the be-all and end-all. The most obvious advice is to get expert assistance with international contracts. A firm can do a lot of things and have many in-house experts, but the ultimate breaking point is to try to develop and implement a contract without professional legal assistance (unless, of course, you are a large multinational corporation with a very astute legal team). Helping out with contracts overall is the United Nations Convention on Contracts for the International Sale of Goods (see Figure 3.9). This is a treaty offering a uniform international sales law that has been ratified by 77 countries. Clearly, we have to take into account that there are some 150 more countries in the world, but these 77 countries are responsible for a lot of the world's wealth and trade.

In general, it is possible to obtain insurance for almost anything within the global supply chain, including perils associated with the ocean, air, land, and multimodal transportation. Lloyd's of London (www.lloyds.com) is the oldest insurance market in shipping, acting

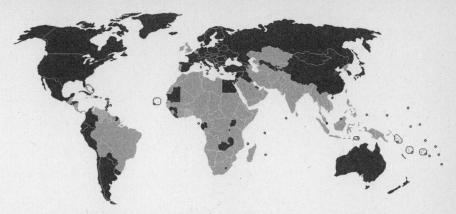

FIGURE 3.9 Areas Covered by the United Nations Convention on Contracts

Source: Alinor at en.wikipedia.

as an intermediary between those who want insurance and those who offer it. Lloyd's writes a diverse range of policies, both direct insurance and reinsurance, covering casualty, property, marine, energy, motor, aviation, and many other types of risk. We are not advocating the use of Lloyd's of London per se, but it does represent a fascinating part of the insurance business for global supply chains and it has been around for a long time.

COMMERCIAL DOCUMENTS AND CUSTOMS CLEARANCE

Most international trade transactions require the filling out of several commercial documents, usually in a very specific way that is based on the country of destination for the products, the type of products, the method of transportation, the method of payment, and so on. The most popular method is still to fill out paper forms and provide multiple "original" copies. The result is that the average international transaction has a stack of documents about 0.5 inch (1.3 cm) thick. And it gets worse. Look at the oval chart we have included in Figure 3.10. These are some of the forms you may potentially have to fill out when you operate in global supply chains. We can all agree that the number of forms seems excessive, but they do create transparency, some protection, and commitment throughout the global supply chain.

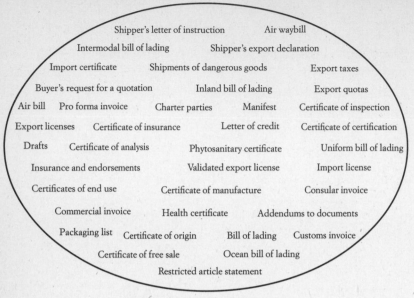

FIGURE 3.10 Commercial Documents

Instead of being overwhelmed, let's try to make sense of these documents and pare them down to the basics. Along the path of the global supply chain, commercial documentation passes nodes in the chain, such as seller, freight companies, import country government, and buyer. The key information included in these documents should be a description of the product, the mode of transportation, the terms of sale, the origin of the product, the identity of the seller/shipper, the identity of the buyer, the terms of payment, shipping instructions, and evidence of shipping. In most cases, these are documents that most companies are familiar with when shipping domestically.

But what about the actual forms and necessities? Let's make this even more direct and look at the most common and most important documents for a universally applicable "gadget." In this case, we are talking about nine different forms that should be attended to when participating in global supply chains and/or sales across borders. They are quotations, pro forma invoice, commercial invoice, packaging list, declaration, bill of lading, certificate of origin, insurance certificate, and customs clearance.[5]

The start of an international transaction is typically a quotation giving the basic parameters for sale. The main reasons to prepare a quotation are to confirm the selling price and to clarify the various costs, if any, that the buyer has to pay in addition to the selling price (such as packaging, freight, insurance, and documentation charges). A pro forma invoice serves many of the same functions as the initial quotation, but some buyers may prefer the pro forma invoice instead of or as well as a quotation to be more formal at the beginning of the process. In essence, the pro forma invoice is a formal document, whereas the quotation can be more informal (for example, a fax, e-mail, or basic letter).

After an order has been formally received and the seller is ready to ship the products, it is time to prepare a commercial invoice. Most buyers will accept the seller's domestic format for the commercial invoice (as long as proper notations concerning the international transaction can be added to the form). Along with the commercial invoice that goes along with the shipment, most international shipments should also have a packaging list included. A packaging list is especially needed when a letter of credit is being used as part of the transaction. More practically, a packaging list really should be included with all shipments as a normal practice for any transaction (domestic and international).

If a freight forwarder is used, the freight forwarder often completes the shipment (export) declaration with information obtained from the seller. That said, the agent (the freight forwarder) is not legally responsible for the declaration—the seller is. Keep in mind that a shipment typically has to use the internationally established Harmonized System of industry codes (not the SIC or NAICS, for example). As well as providing transportation, the transportation firm (for example, a trucking, railroad, or shipping line) issues bills of lading. They serve three main purposes: a receipt for the shipment, a contract for the transportation, and a document declaring ownership (title). When the transportation firm is an airline, the bill of lading is called an "air waybill." Similarly, certificates of origin have several functions, with perhaps the most important being the determination of import tariffs, taxes, or duties. Some countries require only that the country of origin be stated on another document, while other countries require extensive documentation.

As a practical matter, all international shipments should have adequate insurance to cover product loss, damage, and any other potential liability that may arise. A rule of thumb is to have insurance amounting to CIF (cost, insurance, and freight) plus 10 percent—that is, the product invoice value plus insurance plus freight plus an additional 10 percent.

Finally, each and every document mentioned so far, and those listed in the oval in Figure 3.10, can be asked for when clearing customs, but typically that does not happen. At a basic level, three information documents are required in virtually every country in the world: (1) a form designated for entry based on the specification of the requirements of the importing country; (2) a certificate of origin to verify and identify the country of origin; and (3) a commercial invoice with enough information to assess the value of the shipment and its harmonized code classification.

TERMS OF PAYMENT AND CURRENCY OF PAYMENT _____

Getting paid, preferably when you want it and in the way you want it, is a must if you are to stay in business. Broadly, we are talking about terms of payment and currency of payment. For the former, we have to deal with issues such as cash in advance (that would be nice!), letter of credit, documentary collection, open account, and/or a so-called TradeCard. For the latter, at the very basic level, we make choices with respect to seller's currency, buyer's currency, and/or a third country's currency.

As the name would suggest, a cash-in-advance transaction requires the buyer to provide payment up front, before the shipment of the products has been made. Bank transfers of money using the so-called SWIFT code system (Society for Worldwide Interbank Financial Telecommunication, www.swift.com) are typical and preferred. Cash-in-advance transactions are typical in less developed and developing countries and less common in developed countries.

A letter of credit refers to a transaction in which the buyer's bank promises to pay the seller if the buyer does not pay. The seller is then, de facto, relying on the creditworthiness of the bank instead of that of the buyer. The letter of credit is a contractual arrangement between the buyer's bank and the seller, all spelled out clearly in the transaction documents.

Documentary collection is a process in which the seller asks a bank in the buyer's home country to "safeguard" the seller's interests. The bank, in essence, acts as a passive intermediary in that it will not release the title to the products (bill of lading) until the buyer has paid for them.

The open account approach is very similar to what we can expect in most developed countries today. That is, the seller ships the products and sends an invoice requesting payment within a certain time period (often stated as 30 days, 60 days, or 90 days). This is, of course, a way of showing complete trust in the relationship between the seller and the buyer, which from a relationship standpoint is great if the risks are low.

TradeCard is a low-risk payment system for international transactions, with a low fee and largely electronic processing of documents. The system has more than 10,000 members and 45,000 individual users in 78 countries (www.tradecard.com), but it has not caught on as quickly as was perhaps expected. It was created by the World Trade Centers Association in 1994. As a few examples, Guess, Levi Strauss, and Adidas use TradeCard to transact with worldwide partners.

Switching to the issue of currency of payment, here we can deal with three forms: the seller's currency, the buyer's currency, and/ or a third country's currency. When international transactions use the seller's currency, this means that the seller is taking no currency fluctuation risks. An example could be a seller from Sweden transacting with a buyer in Italy and using the Swedish currency, the krona (crown). When international transactions use the buyer's currency, this means that the buyer is taking no currency fluctuation risks. An example could be a seller from Sweden transacting with a buyer in Italy and using the euro as the currency (since Italy uses the European Union–based euro). When international transactions use a third country's currency, this means that the buyer and the seller are both taking currency fluctuation risks. An example could be a seller from Sweden transacting with a buyer in Italy and using the U.S. dollar as the currency.

INTERNATIONAL COMMERCE TERMS (INCOTERMS) ───────

In 1936, the International Chamber of Commerce (www.iccwbo.org) developed a set of standardized terms of domestic and international trade to facilitate trade around the world. The ICC itself has been around since 1919, when a handful of entrepreneurs got together and decided to create an organization that would facilitate and represent business everywhere on the globe—a lofty goal, perhaps, but worthwhile.

This small group of industrialists, financiers, and international traders from five countries set out to bring economic prosperity to a world that was feeling the aftermath of the devastation caused by World War I. These professionals founded the International Chamber of Commerce and designated themselves as "the merchants of peace." The ICC was important to the infrastructure of trade, since the world had few working international structures following the first of the twentieth century's global conflicts. In fact, there was no world system of rules to govern trade, investment, finance, or commercial relations. The ICC provided that infrastructure early on.

The ICC's so-called Incoterms are now categorized into 11 international commerce terms. These Incoterms, along with their former iterations, have long been the worldwide trading norms. Revisions to the Incoterms took place in 1953, 1967, 1976, 1980, 1990, 2000, and 2010 (iccwbo.org/products-and-services/trade-facilitation/incoterms-2010). Based on the latest set of terms, from the 2010 revision, there are 11 Incoterms divided broadly into two groupings: rules for any mode or modes of transport, and rules for sea and inland waterway transport. The rules for any mode or modes of transport include the abbreviated terms of Ex Works (EXW), Free Carrier (FCA), Carriage Paid To (CPT), Carriage and Insurance Paid To (CIP), Delivered at Terminal (DAT), Delivered at Place (DAP), and Delivered Duty Paid (DDP). The rules for sea and inland waterway transport include Free Alongside Ship (FAS), Free on Board (FOB), Cost and Freight (CFR), and Cost, Insurance, and Freight (CIF).

Ex Works (EXW). EXW refers to the seller's fulfilling its obligations by having the products available for the buyer to pick up at its premises or another named place (such as a factory or a warehouse). The buyer bears all risks and costs starting when it picks up the products at the seller's location and continuing until the products are delivered to the buyer's location. The seller has no obligation to load the goods or clear them for export.

Free Carrier (FCA). FCA refers to the seller's delivering the products, cleared for export, to the carrier stipulated by the buyer or another party authorized to pick up products at the seller's premises or another named place. The buyer assumes all risks and costs associated with delivery of the products to their final destination, including transportation after delivery to the carrier and any customs fees required to import the product into a foreign country.

Carriage Paid To (CPT). CPT refers to the seller's clearing the products for export and delivering them to the carrier or another person stipulated by the seller at a named place of shipment. The seller is responsible for the transportation costs associated with delivering the products to the named place but is not responsible for procuring insurance.

Carriage and Insurance Paid To (CIP). CIP refers to the seller's clearing the products for export and delivering them to the carrier or another person stipulated by the seller at a named place of shipment. The seller is responsible both for the transportation costs associated with delivering the products and for procuring minimum insurance coverage to the named place.

Delivered at Terminal (DAT). DAT refers to the seller's clearing the products for export and bearing all risks and costs associated with delivering the products and unloading them at the terminal at the named port or destination. The buyer is responsible for all costs and risks from this point forward, including clearing the products for import into the named destination country.

Delivered at Place (DAP). DAP refers to the seller's clearing the products for export and bearing all risks and costs associated with delivering the products to the named destination, but not unloading them. The buyer is responsible for all costs and risks associated with unloading the products and clearing customs to import the products into the named destination country.

Delivered Duty Paid (DDP). DDP refers to the seller's bearing all risks and costs associated with delivering the products to the named destination ready for unloading and cleared for import.

Free Alongside Ship (FAS). FAS refers to the seller's clearing the products for export, delivering them to the named port of shipment, and placing them alongside the vessel. The buyer assumes all risks and costs regarding the products from this point forward.

Free on Board (FOB). FOB refers to the seller's clearing the products for export, delivering them to the named port of shipment, and placing them on board the vessel. The buyer assumes all risks and costs regarding the products from this point forward.

Cost and Freight (CFR). CFR refers to the seller's clearing the products for export, delivering them to the named port of shipment, and placing them on board the vessel at the port of shipment. The seller also bears the cost of freight to the named destination port. The buyer assumes all risks for the products from the time the products have been delivered on board the vessel at the port of shipment.

Cost, Insurance, and Freight (CIF). CIF refers to the seller's clearing the products for export, delivering them to the named port of shipment, and placing them on board the vessel. The seller also bears the cost of freight and insurance to the named destination port. The seller's insurance requirement is only for minimum coverage. The buyer is responsible for all costs associated with unloading the products at the named destination port and clearing the products for import. Risk passes from the seller to the buyer once the products are on board the vessel at the port of shipment.

WORLD CUSTOMS ORGANIZATION AND THE HARMONIZED SYSTEM

The Harmonized Commodity Description and Coding System (HS) of tariff nomenclature is an internationally standardized system of names and numbers for classifying traded products. It was developed in 1983 and is maintained by the World Customs Organization (WCO, formerly the Customs Co-operation Council), an independent intergovernmental organization based in Brussels, Belgium, with more than 170 member countries. The harmonized codes came into force in 1988.

Established in 1952, the World Customs Organization (www .wcoomd.org) is the only intergovernmental organization exclusively focused on customs matters. With its worldwide membership, the

WCO is now recognized as the voice of the global customs community. It is particularly noted for its work in global standards, simplification and harmonization of customs procedures, trade supply chain security, and international trade. The WCO also administers the technical aspects of the WTO Agreement on Customs Valuation and Agreement on Rules of Origin. Overall, the WCO's mission is to improve the effectiveness and efficiency of its member customs administrations across the globe. While three-quarters of its members are developing countries, the WCO's combined membership is collectively responsible for managing and processing more than 98 percent of world trade around the globe today.

Global challenges transcend borders and call for worldwide responses. Securing trade and combating illegal trafficking and commercial fraud without disrupting legal trade requires a high degree of cooperation among countries and the application of uniform methods and standards that are recognized and applied by all. As a frontline border agency dealing primarily with the cross-border movement of goods, people, and means of transport, the WCO creates policies to ensure the security of international trade, promoting national economic prosperity and social development. In this spirit, the World Customs Organization serves a critical role in standardizing many of the operations and services that we have come to rely on in global supply chains.

The key activities of the WCO include four areas: harmonization and simplification (the WCO develops and promotes harmonized and simplified customs procedures), security and enforcement (the WCO strengthens the security of the international trade supply chain through the WCO SAFE Framework of Standards), partnerships and cooperation (the WCO fosters cooperation, exchange of information and intelligence, and mutual assistance among customs administrations), and modernization and capacity building (the WCO devises capacity-building programs and encourages customs modernization projects). Directly tied to global supply chains, WCO has developed a SAFE Framework with four core elements that are illustrated in Figure 3.11.

The WCO's Harmonized Commodity Description and Coding System is governed by the International Convention on the Harmonized Commodity Description and Coding System. The Harmonized System, or simply HS, is a multipurpose international product nomenclature. It comprises about 5,000 commodity groups;

First, it harmonizes the advance electronic cargo information requirements on inbound, outbound, and transit shipments.	*Second*, each country that joins the SAFE Framework commits to employing a consistent risk management approach to address security threats.
Third, it requires that at the reasonable request of the receiving nation, based upon a comparable risk targeting methodology, the sending nation's Customs administration will perform an outbound inspection of high-risk containers and cargo.	*Fourth*, the SAFE Framework defines benefits that Customs will provide to businesses that meet minimal supply chain security standards and best practices.

FIGURE 3.11 WCO SAFE Framework: Four Core Elements

each is identified by a six-digit code, arranged in a legal and logical structure that is supported by well-defined rules to achieve uniform classification. The system is used by more than 200 countries and economies as a basis for their customs tariffs and the collection of international trade statistics. More than 98 percent of the merchandise in international trade is classified in terms of the Harmonized System. The HS has 21 sections and 97 chapters (Figure 3.12).

Section I (Chapters 1–5), live animals and animal products	Section XII (Chapters 64–67), footwear, umbrellas, artificial flowers
Section II (Chapters 6–14), vegetable products	Section XIII (Chapters 68–70), stone, cement, ceramic, glass
Section III (Chapter 15), animal or vegetable fats and oils	Section XIV (Chapter 71), pearls, precious metals
Section IV (Chapters 16–24), prepared foodstuffs, beverages and spirits, tobacco	Section XV (Chapters 72–83), base metals
Section V (Chapters 25–27), mineral products	Section XVI (Chapters 84–85), electrical machinery
Section VI (Chapters 28–38), chemical products	Section XVII (Chapters 86–89), vehicles, aircraft, vessels
Section VII (Chapters 39–40), plastics and rubber	Section XVIII (Chapters 90–92), optical instruments, clocks and watches, musical instruments
Section VIII (Chapters 41–43), leather and travel goods	Section XIX (Chapter 93), arms and ammunition
Section IX (Chapters 44–46), wood, charcoal, cork	Section XX (Chapters 94–96), furniture, toys, miscellaneous manufactured articles
Section X (Chapters 47–49), wood pulp, paper and paperboard articles	Section XXI (Chapter 97), works of art, antiques
Section XI (Chapters 50–63), textiles and textile products	

FIGURE 3.12 HS Nomenclature, 2012 Edition: 21 Sections Covering 97 Chapters

GLOBALEDGE™: YOUR SOURCE FOR GLOBAL BUSINESS KNOWLEDGE

Since 2004, globalEDGE has been the top-ranked website in the world for "international business resources" on Google. Businesspeople, public policy makers, academics, and college students have been using globalEDGE (globalEDGE.msu.edu) since 1994, when it first started as International Business Resources on the World Wide Web. The site has always been free. We hope you take advantage of the incredible wealth of information and data that globalEDGE offers on almost everything involving international business and trade. The globalEDGE logo is shown in Figure 3.13 for ease of identification.

We include a section on globalEDGE.msu.edu in this book on global supply chain management for two main reasons. First, the site was developed and is maintained by Michigan State University— the home university of all the authors of this book. Its intention and design is to serve as a knowledge web resource that connects international business professionals worldwide to a wealth of information, insights, and learning resources on global business activities. Specifically, globalEDGE is intended to offer the latest and most comprehensive international business and trade content for a wide range of topics. Whether you are conducting extensive market research, looking to improve your international knowledge, or simply browsing, you're sure to find what you need on globalEDGE to sharpen your competitive edge in today's rapidly changing global marketplace. The start-up page for globalEDGE is shown in Figure 3.14 to capture some of the story line around the site.

The tagline for globalEDGE is "your source for global business knowledge," and it functions as a one-stop website for everything involving international business and trade. With millions of users and

FIGURE 3.13 globalEDGE Logo

FIGURE 3.14 globalEDGE Screen Shot (Main Page)

thousands of firms linking to globalEDGE, the site has unique traction in the global marketplace. In fact, our tracking data show that globalEDGE has users every hour in all but a handful of countries (located mostly in central Africa). That means that globalEDGE is used in more than 200 countries every hour of every day! We are not selling subscriptions here, just highlighting a resource that millions of people use and that fits the context of global supply chain management incredibly well.

The second reason why globalEDGE is worth exploring is that we have taken great care to offer lots of information and data on global supply chain management—topics and issues in the areas of logistics, purchasing, operations, and market channels are covered. We also cover strategic issues that can help elevate supply chain management to "strategic supply chain management" and a place at the corporate strategy table. Importantly, we build on unique expertise in doing so. Michigan State University's supply chain management programs (undergraduate and graduate) have been ranked either number one or number two among education programs in the United States for decades (for example, by *US News & World Report*). This is backed up by the most prominent training and consulting unit focused on supply chains in the United States. Overall, globalEDGE incorporates this expertise with a dedicated team to provide state-of-the-art information and data on global supply chains.

As of 2013, globalEDGE has five main sections or menu items(Global Insights, Reference Desk, Knowledge Tools, Get Connected, and Academy), and their usefulness is highlighted in the testimonials in Figure 3.15.

Global Insights is further organized into four subsections. The trade bloc section is a submenu where the analysis and resources are organized by major global trade blocs. It covers the major ones that currently exist in the world, and it keeps adding more as they become prominent. The country section includes statistics, history, politics, demographics, and everything else that may be needed to understand all aspects of doing business in a country. More than 200 countries are covered in great detail. The state section includes international business and trade information for the 50 U.S. states. As a major international business center and university in the United

---

globalEDGE provides a wealth of information on corporations, industries, and countries that assists us as we conduct research for our international customer satisfaction indices.

—Claes Fornell, Chairman, CFI Group Worldwide

globalEDGE is a very valuable partner for the U.S. Commercial Service in our mission to assist U.S. companies to be competitive in global markets.

—Doug Barry, Director, U.S. Department of Commerce

globalEDGE is an essential tool for students, executives, and researchers. It is a magnificent source and resource, continuously updated; its diagnostic tools are true interactive learning opportunities for all users.

—John McIntyre, Professor, Georgia Tech University

FIGURE 3.15 globalEDGE Testimonials

States, we feel compelled to cover each U.S. state and its business and international trade activities. States are often uniquely different, and doing business from and with a U.S. state may also be different; we cover those unique aspects. In the industry section, we delve into news, events, and statistics for 20 distinct industry sectors. The global marketplace has about 450 different main industries (or some 5,000 commodity groups in the Harmonized System), and globalEDGE covers each by grouping them into industry sectors.

Reference Desk is organized into four subsections. The glossary section offers a comprehensive list of international business terms accompanied by definitions. The online course modules provide an easy, straightforward approach to learning about international business using case studies, quizzes, and narrated slides. The global resource subsection consists of a directory that takes a broad approach to international business research by providing relevant and applicable resources across a wide range of topics. The expert tutorials guide users through international business topics in order to sharpen, refine, or build their current knowledge.

Knowledge Tools are organized into five subsections. The Market Potential Index (MPI) is an index designed to help business professionals evaluate emerging markets across the globe. The Database of International Business Statistics (DIBS) is a robust database that simplifies and synthesizes complex international business data. The diagnostic tools can help your business grow. These self-assessment tools can help you identify your exporting potential and find the right freight forwarder, international distributor, and/or international partner (this section does ask for a nominal fee). The comparator tool allows for a comparison of countries across the globe. The test-your-knowledge component of the site is a fun game that measures your international business prowess.

Get Connected is the site's smallest section in terms of content but also one of the most popular for staying in the know. In this section, the globalEDGE blog is a very popular and active portion of the site that covers opinions and views on important international business events—just what you would expect of a blog on globalEDGE! The globalEDGE Business Review (gBR) has short articles (typically fewer than 1,000 words) that provide a major learning experience for international business professionals. The gBR is mainly targeted at business executives, but also, to some degree, to public policy makers, academics, and college students. Some 30,000 people get gBR in their inbox every month at no charge. The globalEDGE Newsletter is a monthly newsletter sharing global trends and insights with more than 80,000 business professionals.

The Academy portion of the site targets mainly college students, faculty members, and teachers. It includes five different subsections. The course content subsection provides international business curriculum resources for educators. The research component has publication and research resources for academics. The community colleges section is focused on two-year colleges offering associate degrees in the United States, and it includes international business resources that community college students and teachers can use to support their learning activities. The announcements section has calls for papers, conference announcements, and grant opportunities. Finally, the program resources section includes international internships and academic program directories. The internship directory is fantastic, listing and describing international internships that are available around the globe (your firm should look into being included for free if it is not already listed).

GUIDELINES FOR ASSESSING GLOBAL SUPPLY CHAIN INFRASTRUCTURE

There are numerous infrastructure issues that should continually be evaluated and decided upon in global supply chain management. Some of these are major items that you can easily see, and some are intricate details of doing global business that are not readily obvious or understood. But given the web of relationships in global supply chains and the many actors, activity links, and resource ties involved in the worldwide infrastructure, certain issues need to be seriously taken into account and strategically integrated into global supply chain operations. In assessing the global supply chain infrastructure in the worldwide marketplace, these guidelines are applicable to all industries and companies:

- Strategic global supply chain management involves the continual evaluation and development of chains that incorporate the most logical, efficient, and effective network of transportation, communication, utilities, and technology infrastructure. Many countries and world regions have solid transportation, communication, utilities, and technology infrastructure, but many also have poorly developed infrastructure in these areas. Firms need to carefully assess and then implement their global supply chains to leverage the appropriate infrastructure items while diminishing the effect of poor infrastructure.

- Risk and reward scenarios should always be evaluated when developing global supply chain efforts. An increasing amount of attention is being given to security issues in global supply chains, risks in global supply chains, and the value of different parts (for example, raw materials, component parts, and finished products). Such security, risks, and value analysis needs to be part of the strategic evaluation of how to structure global supply chains and manage the chains.

- Legal considerations, international contracts, and insurance policies are critical for each actor (that is, firm) involved in a global supply chain, the linkages between those actors, and the resource ties that the actors have in the chain. Firms should use worldwide standards and organizations to facilitate the enforcement of laws, patents, copyrights, and trademarks as much as possible, at least in the countries that belong to multicountry arrangements in these areas.

- The varieties of commercial documents and customs clearance paperwork in the global supply chain are almost endless. But there are some basics that should be followed, with the idea that many documents can be treated as extras at times. Documents related to the following nine topics and areas are the basic starting point, and they are usually enough for many scenarios: quotations, pro forma invoice, commercial invoice, packaging list, declaration, bill of lading, certificate of origin, insurance certificate, and customs clearance.

- Firms should use the available standards for industries and commodities, called international commerce terms (Incoterms), along with the Harmonized System to identify industries and commodities. These standards are worldwide and are very helpful at each step in the global supply chain. While SIC and NAICS industry codes work reasonably well, the Harmonized System is strongly preferred in the global marketplace.

APPENDIX: LOGISTICS PERFORMANCE INDEX 2012 _____

The World Bank established a "logistics performance index" (LPI) in 2007 that centers on trade logistics in the global economy.[6] The most recent iteration available at the time of this book was the 2012 index (third installment of the report and index). The LPI measures on-the-ground trade logistics performance, with 155 countries being rated and ranked in the 2012 edition. The World Bank's idea is that the LPI should help national leaders, policy makers, and private sector traders understand the challenges faced in international logistics. This appendix provides a summary of the LPI scores for a select set of the 155 countries rated as an illustration of these rankings (we use the top 20 countries ranked in 2012), as summarized in Table 3.1.

TABLE 3.1 Logistics Performance Index 2012

Economy	Rank	Score	% of Highest Performer
Singapore	1	4.13	100.0
Hong Kong	2	4.12	99.9
Finland	3	4.05	97.6
Germany	4	4.03	97.0
Netherlands	5	4.02	96.7
Denmark	6	4.02	96.6
Belgium	7	3.98	95.3
Japan	8	3.93	93.8
United States	9	3.93	93.7
United Kingdom	10	3.90	92.7
Austria	11	3.89	92.5
France	12	3.85	91.2
Sweden	13	3.85	91.2
Canada	14	3.85	91.1

(continued on next page)

TABLE 3.1 Logistics Performance Index 2012 (*continued*)

Economy	Rank	Score	% of Highest Performer
Luxembourg	15	3.82	90.3
Switzerland	16	3.80	89.7
United Arab Emirates	17	3.78	88.9
Australia	18	3.73	87.2
Taiwan	19	3.71	86.6
Spain	20	3.70	86.4

CHAPTER 4

Logistics in Global Supply Chains

Logistics is the driver of global supply chains.

GLOBAL LOGISTICS STRATEGY

This chapter begins a discussion of the four critical functions of global supply chain management: logistics, purchasing, operations, and market channels. We start with global logistics. Interestingly, logistics is also where North American supply chain management meets European supply chain management. Since the early 1980s, North Americans have used the term *supply chain management* as an all-encompassing descriptor for a variety of activities that include not just logistics, but also purchasing (procurement, sourcing, and supply management), operations, and market channels (or marketing channels). Meanwhile, Europeans often refer to supply chain management as simply *logistics*, while Asians have a tendency to use the term *operations* in the same context.

This discussion of global supply chain management and each core function describes how the strategic initiatives and tactical activities must be integrated. With that in mind, it is appropriate to trace the origins of the term *supply chain*. In 1982, Keith Oliver, a consultant at Booz Allen Hamilton, was the first person to use the phrase "supply chain management" in an interview with Arnold Kransdorff for a June 4, 1982, article in the *Financial Times*. Oliver defined supply chain management (SCM) as the "process of planning, implementing, and controlling the operations of the supply chain with the purpose to satisfy customer requirements as efficiently as possible. Supply chain management spans all movement and storage of raw materials, work-in-process inventory, and finished goods from point-of-origin to point-of-consumption."

A few years earlier, Oliver had been pushed on his supply chain ideas and his concept of "integrated inventory management" (or I2M, as he called it) by Mr. Van t'Hoff of the Dutch electronics giant Philips. While Oliver thought that I2M indicated a set of integrated events—a chain of supply—Van t'Hoff argued for a more precise term to identify the phenomenon of a set of linked connections rather than "a group of disparate functions," as Oliver also liked to call it. Based on their discussions and dialogue, that concept initially became "total supply chain management"; later, it was shortened to just "supply chain management," the term we know today. It was all crystalized, initially, at least, in that *Financial Times* interview in 1982.

This means that we celebrated the thirtieth anniversary of the formalized modern understanding of supply chain management in 2012. So, what is the logistics tie-in? Well, prior to his dialogue with Mr. Van t'Hoff and his interview with Arnold Kransdorff, Oliver, according to Damon Schechter, played a critical role in the development of logistics in the 1970s and 1980s.[1] Oliver drove the concept that interconnected links in a chain was a better illustration and strategic focus than a stand-alone view of logistics. It is fascinating that logistics was initially perceived as an outbound/downstream function of the supply chain, since Keith Oliver, as a logistics professional, was the first to coin the term *supply chain management* and establish definitional boundaries for SCM. Today, however, logistics spans the full length of the supply chain, including important transportation, inventory management, packaging, and materials-handling issues that are strategically imperative to the full functioning of the global supply chain.

Going back in history, the term *logistics* dates from the late nineteenth century and has its roots in the French word *logistique*. More generally, logistics is broadly considered to have originated with the military's need to supply itself with arms, ammunition, and other necessities as the troops moved from a base position to a more forward position. And, going back (way back) to the ancient Greek, Roman, and Byzantine Empires, military officers who were responsible for supply distribution–related activities were given the title *Logistikas*. It's no wonder, then, that even today, many of the logistics professionals in academic circles and in industry have a military background, where their skills and knowledge were first honed.

FIGURE 4.1 A Focus on Global Logistics

Global logistics is the part of global supply chain management that plans, implements, and controls the efficient and effective forward and reverse flow and storage of goods, services, and related information between the worldwide point of origin and the worldwide point of consumption in order to meet global customers' requirements (see Figure 4.1).[2] It involves the worldwide management of order processing, inventory, transportation, and the combination of warehousing, materials handling, and packaging, all integrated throughout a network of facilities. This means that issues such as global distribution center network orchestration, integrated inventory management, packaging and materials handling, reverse logistics (including backhaul logistics), and various forms of transportation (ocean, air, land, and intermodal) are key strategic and operational elements of global logistics.

Strategically, within the integrated global supply chain of multinational corporations, it is predicted that logistics as a function will become 13 percent more globalized in the next five years (2013 to 2018) and 30 percent more globalized in the next ten years (by 2023). Figure 4.2 illustrates these increases. In 2013, logistics scored 61 out of 100 points in terms of being globalized (where 100 is fully globalized and zero is purely domestic). A score of 61 places logistics ahead of operations and market channels, but behind purchasing, in terms of the degree of globalness permeating that function of the supply chain. Logistics is also found to be the second most important of the four functions (logistics, purchasing, operations, and market channels), scoring a 94 out of a possible 100 points on the degree of importance in contributing to overall global supply chain management for the multinational corporation. (Market channels is at the top with 96, followed by logistics with 94, operations with 92, and purchasing with 89.) Logistics is expected to fall slightly in importance, from 94 to 93, over the next five years vis-à-vis the other core supply chain functions. Figure 4.3 illustrates the changes in logistics in the 2013 to 2018 time period.

As we elaborated on earlier, global logistics includes the activities related to transportation, inventory management, packaging, and materials handling. While these are the operating functions that are generally included in logistics, they are all brought together at the distribution center (DC) or warehouse. The DC or warehouse is the place where the product is transported from or to, the inventory is stored or staged, and packaging and materials handling are often completed. The DC may be as simple as a fenced area, or it may be a highly automated facility with more than a million square feet (93,000 square meters) under one roof. This brings us to a story! On a trip to Ireland, one of the authors looked down on the village of Kilkenny and saw the ruins of a church surrounded by what looked like aluminum barrels. With a closer look, the sign on the fence confirmed

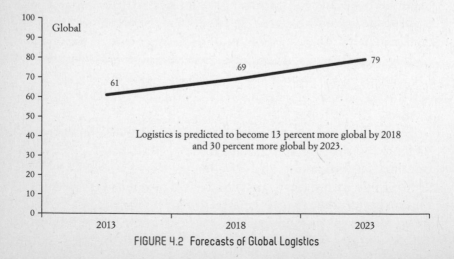

FIGURE 4.2 Forecasts of Global Logistics

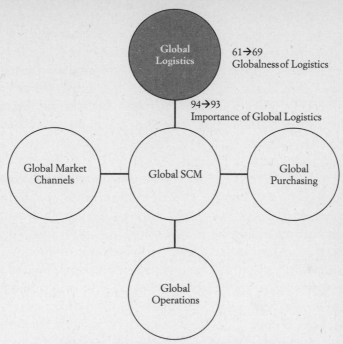

FIGURE 4.3 Globalization of Logistics, 2013 to 2018

that it was a Guinness distribution center for full and empty kegs. So, DCs come in all shapes, forms, and foundations.

Beginning with the distribution center as the center of integration for most logistics activities, the following sections describe the characteristics, activities, and recommendations for global distribution centers, inventory management, packaging and materials handling, transportation, and reverse logistics. The chapter concludes with general guidelines for global logistics.

GLOBAL DISTRIBUTION CENTERS

A global distribution center (or warehouse) is a facility that positions and allows customization of products for delivery to worldwide wholesalers or retailers, or directly to consumers anywhere in the world. On a global scale, distribution centers are used by manufacturers, importers, exporters, wholesalers, retailers, transportation companies, and customs agencies to store products and provide a location where customization can be facilitated. When warehousing shifted from passive storage of products to strategic assortments and processing, the term *distribution center* became more widely used to capture this strategic and dynamic aspect of not only storing but adding value to products that are being warehoused or staged. A DC is at the center of the global supply chain, specifically the order processing part of the order fulfillment process. DCs are the foundation of a global supply network, as they allow either a single location or satellite warehouses to store quantities and assortments of products and allow for value-added customization.

Global DCs should be located strategically in the global marketplace, considering the aggregate total transportation cost of moving products from plants or suppliers through the distribution center and then delivering them to customers. Once a site or sites have been identified, other factors to consider are labor and community acceptance; a reliable and productive workforce; environmental issues such as water, air, or traffic restrictions; and infrastructure capabilities such as electricity, telecommunications, and sewer.

Distribution centers exist for both economic and service reasons. The four most common types are the consolidation DC, the break-bulk DC, the cross-dock DC, and the order assembly DC. Using the European cities of Amsterdam, Copenhagen, Frankfurt, and Paris as examples, let us briefly illustrate the activities that each type may carry out. A consolidation DC located in Frankfurt, for example, may be used to receive products from the plants in Amsterdam, Copenhagen, and Paris, which are then combined into the exact quantity needed for a large shipment to a retailer in Eastern Europe.

A break-bulk DC in Amsterdam, on the other hand, may receive a single large shipment from a plant in Frankfurt and then arrange for shipments to retailers in Belgium, France, and the Netherlands. The rationale for a break-bulk DC is that it allows for one long-haul movement and three short-haul moves rather than three individual long-haul moves. The single long-haul move is for a larger quantity, which also means that the cost per unit is less than it would be for the three individual long-haul moves.

In a cross-dock DC, a facility in Paris, for example, receives product shipments from three plants—one plant in each of the other three cities—and then creates specific assortments for retailers around Paris. The rationale for the cross-dock DC is that truckloads of a single plant's products can be brought into the cross-dock facility and then be moved "across the dock" to other trucks that can move a full truckload of combined manufacturers' products to each retail site. This allows both the inbound movement to the cross-dock facility and the outbound movement to the retailer to be in truckload quantities.

An order assembly DC, called a first-tier supplier, such as one in Frankfurt, supports the plant in Frankfurt by orchestrating the assembly of parts from the second-tier suppliers around Europe.

The service rationale for warehousing is to position a mix or combination of products near customers to allow for customization or to provide for value-added services. As an example, there may be a DC in Paris that stores healthcare products and delivers them to hospitals around Paris. The facility exists to collect products from multiple manufacturers in a location near the hospitals so that supplies are available quickly. DCs in Paris and Frankfurt could become value-added facilities by offering packaging with the specific language and regulatory requirements for a specific country.

Once the type and location of each DC have been determined, the next consideration is the operational activities that will take place within the DC. As a general rule of thumb, the breakdown of a DC's costs is allocated as 15 percent receiving (products, raw materials, and work in process), 20 percent storage, 50 percent order picking, and 15 percent shipping (see Figure 4.4). These activities interact

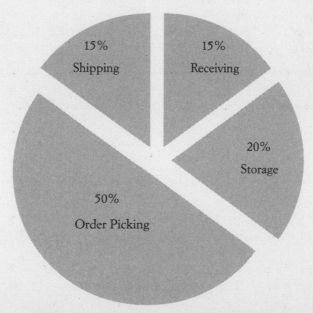

FIGURE 4.4 Typical Breakdown of Key Global DC Activities

with one another, and performance in one area often affects performance in another. Our experience and preferences suggest that five key performance indicators (KPIs) should be used when evaluating DC operations in the areas of receiving, storage, order picking, and shipping. These are cost, productivity, utilization, quality, and cycle time (see Table 4.1).[3]

Receiving is central to DC operations. Properly receiving the raw materials, work in process, or products is critical to the subsequent handling of those items. Products may be received for the purpose of temporary storage or for the purpose of moving them across the dock for loading into an outbound vehicle. Preferred KPIs relating to DC receiving include the following: cost of receiving per receiving line available at maximum capacity (cost), volume received per person-hour of available work time (productivity), percentage utilization of the receiving dock door (utilization), percentage of accurate receipts (quality), and time taken to process the receipt of items (cycle time[4]).

Storage is what we often think of when we mentally envision a DC. Storing items creates value in that it makes them available when and where they are needed in the global supply chain. However,

TABLE 4.1 Key Performance Indicators for Global Distribution Centers

KPI	Receiving	Storage	Order Picking	Shipping
Cost	Cost of receiving per receiving line	Storage cost per product item	Cost of picking per order line	Cost of shipping per order
Productivity	Volume received per person-hour	Inventory per square meter (or square foot)	Order lines picked per hour	Order process for shipping per person-hour
Utilization	Receiving dock door utilization, percent	Percent location and cube occupied	Picking employees and equipment utilization, percent	Utilization of shipping docks, percent
Quality	Accurate receipts, percent	Percent location without inventory discrepancies	Perfect picking lines, percent	Perfect shipping, percent
Cycle Time	Time taken to process a receipt	Product inventory days on hand	Order picking cycle time per order	Shipping time per order

storage also incurs cost in that storing an item in a DC does consume resources (for example, money, space, and tracking), and thus the amount stored and the length of time it is stored should be minimized. While a just-in-time (JIT) inventory philosophy has reduced the demand for storage, there are still critical economic and service requirements for distribution centers. Preferred KPIs for storage include storage cost per product item (cost), inventory per square foot (productivity), percentage of the location and cube occupied (utilization), percentage of the location without inventory discrepancies (quality), and product inventory days on hand in storage (cycle time).

Order picking or selection is where DCs can add significant value to the global supply chain. Effective and efficient order picking enhances the performance of the rest of the supply chain. It is much like an end customer trying to buy a basket of products from a grocery store. If the customer gets all ten of the items he sets out to buy, he is satisfied. If he is able to find only nine of the ten items, he is probably not going to be satisfied with the grocery run. In the case of a DC, the order pickers (whether manual or automated) must be able to access the correct product and quantity in a minimum amount of time and at a minimum cost. The order picking process includes the activities of picking the products from the shelves and moving them to the staging area at the truck docks. If order pickers are able to find all the products or parts for the next entity in the global supply chain, they are creating positive performance and collaboration in the chain. The critical KPIs for order picking include the cost of picking per order line (cost), order lines picked per hour or per day (productivity), percentage utilization of picking employees and equipment (utilization), percentage of perfect picking lines (quality), and order picking cycle time per order (cycle time).

Shipping is often not seen as a DC activity, but it is very much integral to the DC's operations. Shipping refers to the actions of taking the staged product on the shipping dock and loading it onto vehicles. It is often viewed as the last step in handling products and/or raw materials on their way to the customer or in the handling of stock transfers. Critical KPIs for shipping in conjunction with a DC's operations include cost of shipping per order (cost), order process for shipping per person-hour or person-day (productivity), percentage utilization of shipping docks (utilization), percentage of perfect shipping process (quality), and shipping time from the DC to the next step in the global supply chain (cycle time).

GLOBAL INVENTORY MANAGEMENT _____

Global inventory management can be viewed as the decision making regarding the raw materials, work-in-process, and finished goods inventory for a multinational corporation. The decisions include how much inventory to hold, in what form to hold it, and where to locate it in the supply chain. Examining the largest 20,910 multinational corporations (MNCs) with headquarters in 105 countries, we find that these MNCs, on average, carry 32.30 percent of their inventory in raw materials, 17.94 percent of their inventory in work in process, and 49.76 percent of their inventory in finished goods (see Figure 4.5 and Table 4.2). The global inventory strategy must effectively trade off the service and economic benefits of making products in large quantities and positioning them near customers against the risk of having too much stock or the wrong items.

However, as the data in Table 4.2 indicate, these inventory statistics differ depending on the industry examined. The table summarizes major indicators to gauge the value and cost of inventory among the largest multinational corporations in 2011 (the latest data available at the time this book was written). The data and calculated ratios include Inventory—Raw Materials, Inventory—Work in Process, Inventory—Finished Goods, Inventory—Total, Inventory Turnover, Inventory to Assets, Research and Development (R&D), Return on Assets (ROA), and Sample Size (n) of Companies. The data analyzed were gathered from Compustat Global, using annual data representing fiscal year 2011.

While the relative mix of inventory by industry (raw materials, work in process, and finished goods) is important, the most interesting information can be gleaned using the inventory turnover, inventories to assets, and return on assets values. These ratios can be calculated using different methods, but three of the most common are given in Figures 4.6 to 4.8.

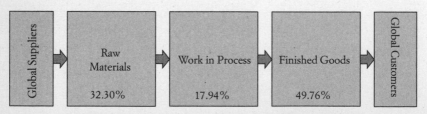

FIGURE 4.5 Inventory Positions of Multinational Corporations, 2012

TABLE 4.2 Global Inventory Statistics Across Industries (20,910 Companies in 105 Countries)

	Agriculture, Forestry, and Fisheries	Mineral Industries	Construction Industries	Manufacturing	Transportation, Communications, and Utilities	Wholesale Trade	Retail Trade	Finance, Insurance, and Real Estate	Service Industries	Public Administration	Overall Analysis
SIC Codes	0–999	1,000–1,499	1,500–1,799	2,000–3,999	4,000–4,971	5,000–5,100	5,101–5,999	6,000–6,799	7,000–8,999	9,000–9799	0–9,799
NAICS Codes	111–115	211–213	233–235	311–339, 511	221, 481–493, 513	421–422	441–454	521–533	512, 514, 541–814	921–928	111–928
Inventory—Raw Materials	11,213	1,239	9,005	11,431	5,817	595	788	0.06	387	N/A	7,674
Inventory—Work in Process	6,671	3,013	11,925	5,731	1,047	702	351	0.09	1,200	N/A	4,263
Global channels	32,808	4,419	6,183	14,887	5,905	11,665	21,711	0.23	1,728	N/A	11,822
Inventory—Total	46,990	8,546	30,344	31,139	12,667	16,513	22,200	82	3,207	N/A	23,759
Inventory—Turnover	2,681	92,630	656,165	18,462	5,8449	3,240	3,531	105,368	268,027	N/A	80,714
Inventory to Total Assets	18.43	3.35	21.00	18.41	3.40	22.35	19.91	5.50	5.28	N/A	14.41
Research and Development	465	206	3,907	7,246	7,762	510	441	0.63	2130	N/A	6,161
Return on Assets	10.90	−26.48	9.98	5.99	14.51	7.52	15.15	20.47	7.35	N/A	6.20
Sample Size (n) of Companies	196	1,486	712	11,837	1,878	649	1,275	22	2,855	N/A	20,910

$$\text{Inventory turnover}$$

$$= \frac{\text{sales (net)}}{\left(\dfrac{\text{total inventory } (t) + \text{total inventory in } (t-1)}{2} \right)}$$

FIGURE 4.6 Calculation of Inventory Turnover

$$\text{Inventory to assets}$$

$$= \frac{\text{total inventory}}{\text{total net property, plant, and equipment} + \text{total current assets}}$$

FIGURE 4.7 Calculation of Inventory to Assets

$$\text{Return on assets}$$

$$= \frac{\text{operating income before depreciation} - \text{depreciation and amortization}}{\text{total net property, plant, and equipment} + \text{total current assets}}$$

FIGURE 4.8 Calculation of Return on Assets

Inventory statistics also differ for different multinational corporations. Based on the 20,910 multinational corporations that we studied, the average MNC carries 14.41 percent of its total assets in some form of inventory. For example, Toyota (www.toyota.com) from Japan, one of the largest automobile firms in the world, has 8.71 percent of its total assets in inventory, with a mix of 25.87, 13.62, and 60.50 percent in raw materials, work in process, and finished vehicles, respectively.

Another example is Sinopec (www.sinopec.com), a petroleum firm and the largest firm in China. Sinopec has 21.46 percent of its total assets in inventory, with a mix of 36.58, 42.50, and 20.92 percent in raw materials and component parts, work in process, and finished goods, respectively. Note that Sinopec maintains a much higher percentage of its inventories in work in process and a much lower percentage in finished goods than Toyota does. This suggests that petroleum firms want more flexibility in deciding exactly how to formulate the finished product.

Siemens (www.siemens.com), the German integrated technology company with a primary focus on energy, water, and healthcare, has 24.28 percent of its total assets in inventory. Of that inventory, the Siemens mix is 17.50, 67.20, and 15.30 percent in raw materials and component parts, work in process, and finished goods, respectively.

GLOBAL PACKAGING AND MATERIALS HANDLING

Packaging comes in all shapes, sizes, forms, and uses. It can be divided into three different types: primary, secondary, and transit. Primary packaging holds the product itself. These are the packages brought home from the store, usually a retailer, by the end consumer. Secondary packaging (sometimes called case lot packaging) is designed to contain several primary packages. Bulk buying or warehouse store customers may take secondary packages home (for example, from Sam's Club), but this is not the typical mode for retailers. Retailers can also use secondary packaging as an aid when stocking shelves in the store. Transit packaging comes into use when a number of primary and secondary packages are assembled on a pallet or unit load for transportation. Unit load packaging, through palletizing, shrink-wrapping, or containerization, is the outer packaging envelope that allows for easier handling or product transfer between international suppliers, manufacturers, distribution centers, retailers, and any other intermediaries in the global supply chain.

Packaging has become a sophisticated science that serves a very important role in global supply chains. For example, issues such as labeling, packaging accessibility, messaging, packaging design, safety and security, sustainability, reusability, application of radio frequency identification, temperature requirements, regulatory requirements, and quality of package designs are some of the topics studied in packaging research at Michigan State University's world-leading School of Packaging (www.packaging.msu.edu).

Regardless of where the product is in the global supply chain, packaging is intended to achieve a set of multilayered functions. These can be grouped into perform, protect, and inform (see Figure 4.9).[5] *Perform* refers to (1) the ability of the product in the package to handle being transported between nodes in the global supply chain, (2) the ability of the product to be stored for typical lengths of time for a particular product category, and (3) the package providing the

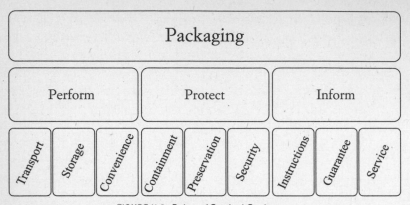

FIGURE 4.9 Roles of Product Packaging

convenience expected by both the supply chain partners and the end customers. *Protect* refers to the package's (1) being able to contain the products properly, (2) being able to preserve the products to maintain their freshness or newness, and (3) providing the necessary security and safety to ensure that the products reach their end destination in their intended shape. *Inform* refers to the package's (1) including logical and sufficient instructions for the use of the products inside the package, including specific requirements to satisfy local regulations, (2) providing a statement of a compelling product guarantee, and (3) providing information about service for the product, if and when it is needed.

According to *World Packaging News* (worldpackagingnews.com), there were a number of key global packaging trends in 2012. Several that have already been turned into slogans include "eyeballs everywhere," "private labels prevail," "information overload," and "green goes mainstream." Starting with the eyeballs everywhere notion, we can expect more mandated packaging regulations and universal global packaging standards. Packaging is under attack on a global scale by a number of detractors for a number of reasons (such as sustainability and the need for recycling).

Interestingly, almost every retailer now has its own private-label brand, whereas private labels were previously used on a limited scale. Regardless of what your private-label packaging looks like, consumers want value brands, and this will be at the expense of the premium and consumer product brands. The shift toward private labels increases supply chain complexity by dramatically increasing the number of stock-keeping units moved through the global supply chain.

Packaging and marketing often go hand in hand. Marketing typically wants every element of product packaging to be meaningful to the consumer. Specifically, do not overload the primary marketing space with meaningless phrases and symbols unless their message is integral to the firm's mission and brand. There is only so much space for a message on a package, and that message needs to be recognizable and the right one for the audience.

Finally, packaging accounts for about 35 percent of the waste stream, and consumers are becoming increasingly concerned about its aggregate impact. They are demanding less packaging or packaging that serves a secondary purpose or can be recycled or reused. So, "green goes mainstream" is not just a packaging slogan, but a concept driven heavily by some customer segments. Gone are the days of pretty packages sitting on the shelf in the retail store. There is too much competition worldwide (partially because of the much more effective and efficient global supply chain infrastructure these days), so firms are looking for unique ways to engage their consumers. Package marketing is a major challenge for the future for global business professionals.

The final considerations are the materials-handling technologies for receiving, storing, and selecting products in distribution centers. There are different ways of handling products, of course, ranging from mechanized materials handling to semiautomated materials handling to automated materials handling to information-directed materials handling. Mechanized materials-handling systems use a variety of types of equipment, including lift trucks, rider trucks, towlines, flow racks, tractor-trailers, conveyors, carousels, and radio frequency technologies for tracking products in the warehouses. Semiautomated materials-handling systems often complement mechanized systems by automating specific activities, such as product selection or lane selection for loading products into a transportation vehicle. Typical equipment used in semiautomated systems includes automated guided vehicle systems, computerized sorting, robotics, and live racks. Live racks trigger the automated release of a case based on a digital command. Automated materials-handling systems still remain relatively costly and have a low degree of flexibility. They are characteristically used for high-rise storage, retrieval, and master carton order selection systems. Information-directed materials-handling systems use mechanized handling controlled by information technology, such as using Wi-Fi systems and light-directed operations.

Several guidelines for materials handling should be taken into account when designing global supply chains. First, equipment for materials handling should be as standardized as possible throughout the global supply chain. Standardization across countries is much more possible today than it was in the past. Second, the materials-handling system should be designed to provide maximum continuous materials flow. Materials usually pass through a complex and lengthy system in global supply chains, and having a continuous materials flow is important. Third, investments should be made in materials-handling equipment rather than in stationary equipment. Stationary equipment limits the operational possibilities in global supply chains. Fourth, materials-handling equipment, rather than personnel, should be utilized to the maximum extent possible. There are different job restrictions on workers in different parts of the world, and equipment also helps minimize lifting injuries and accidents. Fifth, in terms of the selection of equipment for materials handling, the ratio of dead weight (or how much is lifted) to payload (or maximum capacity) should be minimized. This means that firms should minimize the weight of the carton, pallet, or container relative to the weight of the product. Safety and flexibility in material handling are keys to success in global supply chains.

TRANSPORTATION

Transportation typically represents the largest percentage of any logistics budget and an even greater percentage for MNCs because of the distances involved. Global supply chains are directly or indirectly responsible for transporting raw materials from their suppliers to the production facilities, work-in-process and finished goods inventories between plants and distribution centers, and finished goods from distribution centers to customers. The primary drivers of transportation rates and the resulting aggregate cost are distance, transport mode (ocean, air, or land), size of load, load characteristics, and oil prices. As would be expected, longer distances require more fuel and more time from vehicle operators, so transport rates increase with distance. Transport mode influences rates because of the different technologies involved. Ocean is the least expensive because of the size of the vehicles used and the low friction of water. Land is the next least expensive, with rail being less expensive than motor carriers. Air is the most expensive, since there is a substantial charge for defying gravity. Transportation rates are heavily influenced by economies of scale, so larger shipments are typically relatively less expensive than smaller shipments. The characteristics of the shipment also influence transportation rates through such factors as product density, value, perishability, potential for damage, and other such factors. Finally, oil prices have a major impact on transportation rates, since anywhere from 10 to 40 percent of most carrier costs, depending on the mode, are related to fuel. The following sections provide an overview of the characteristics of each mode.

Ocean Transportation

Ocean transportation has long been and will continue to be the primary mode of transportation for lots and lots of raw materials, work in process, and finished goods. Since 1975, world seaborne trade has increased by more than 400 percent to some 8.7 billion tons annually.[6] In fact, around 80 percent of international trade volume is moved by ocean, and the percentage is even higher for most developing countries. This shipment mode also represents more than 70 percent of the value being transported in all global supply chains. Asia is a key to this trade; the Asian continent is the source or destination for roughly half of all ocean cargo. In addition, the ocean transportation business is regulated and structured. It generally follows industry-specific guidance for shippers and container stuffers, as suggested by the World Shipping Council (worldshipping.org).

In the most recent year for which data are available (2011), the volume of seaborne trade grew by 4 percent and the tonnage of the world fleet grew by 10 percent (or an even more astounding 37 percent in the last four years). This expansion was primarily the result of rapid growth in dry cargo volumes (5.6 percent), container loads (8.6 percent), and major bulk trades (5.4 percent). While the aggregate fleet capacity is increasing, this can be somewhat misleading. First, much of the capacity results from an increase in ship size (container ships going from 8–10,000 TEU to 13–15,000; a TEU is a "20-foot equivalent unit," or a container that is 20 feet in length). While this increase in size adds capacity, it correspondingly reduces flexibility, as the owners of these ships want to operate them only on lanes where they fill that much capacity. Second, while there are more ships, many of them are being held out of service because there is not enough demand and they are not fuel-efficient enough given current oil prices.

That said, the numbers illustrate the magnitude of ocean transportation's importance. For example, container ships have the capacity to carry several large warehouses' worth of goods on a single journey. A 15,000-TEU ship carries a value equivalent to that carried by about twenty 100-car trains. A large container ship's engine weighs up to 2,300 tons and has about 1,000 times more power than a regular family car. Large container ships can also be operated by relatively few people, typically small teams of about a dozen people using sophisticated computer systems. Most ships' computer systems today are highly advanced, enabling the precise routing, transport, loading, and unloading of thousands of containers for every voyage. In an average year, a large container ship travels three-quarters of the distance to the moon. That means that during its lifetime, it travels the distance to the moon and back around 25 times.

As just one example, a container of refrigerators can be moved from a factory in Malaysia to Los Angeles—a journey of roughly 9,000 miles or 14,484 kilometers—in just 16 days by container ship. However, while the actual transit time may be only 16 to 20 days, the total time in transit may be double that because of the time required for loading containers, consolidating loads, security, and clearing customs in both ports. The cost of transporting a bicycle from Thailand to the United Kingdom in a container, as another example, is about $10. The typical cost for shipping a DVD player from Asia to Europe is roughly $1.50, that for shipping a kilogram (2.2 pounds) of coffee just 15 cents, and that for shipping a can of beer only a penny. Depending on which product is carried, the type of ship may also vary, of course. Generally there are five vessel groupings: oil tankers, bulk carriers, general cargo ships, container ships, and a series of other specialized ships.[7] Container cargo represents about 52 percent of ocean transportation, with tanker (22 percent), general cargo (20 percent), and dry bulk shipping (6 percent) making up the remainder.

A number of emerging trends affect ocean transportation.[8] First, a new global design in ocean transportation is being created because the advanced economies of the European Union and the United States, along with several others, are having a diminished influence. This diminished global supply chain and shift of economic influence from the North and the West to the South and the East has altered the seaborne industry's operating context, and it can be expected to evolve further as cargoes, markets, and trade patterns also change in response to the new global design.

Second, energy security, oil prices, and transport costs are all interconnected in the global marketplace and global supply chains. The growth in global trade over the past few decades has been powered by available and affordable oil. Ocean transportation is, of course, heavily reliant on oil for propulsion, and, as evidenced by the recent surges in oil prices, the era of easy and cheap oil is most likely coming to an end; this will affect energy security, oil prices, and ocean transportation costs. That said, after some oil price increases, we are also seeing prices come down and predictions of more stable prices. All of this makes estimating oil prices tough, but we do know that inexpensive oil is not likely to be part of the outlook. Most important, higher fuel costs have a disproportionate effect on transportation companies, since fuel is a necessary cost input and resource. The impact of higher fuel prices, particularly for ocean and air transportation, is forcing more firms to consider reshoring for both raw materials and finished goods.

Third, the need for cutting carbon emissions from international shipping and adapting to climate change are becoming a practical reality in firms' strategy considerations. Naturally, ocean transportation carriers are forced to be a part of the solution. Carbon emissions from international shipping result from the burning of heavy oil in ships' bunkers. Addressing the issue of bunker fuel through, for example, technology or other operational means that provide incentives or deterrents can help cut emissions and become part of the solution to the carbon emissions problem.

Fourth, environmental sustainability and corporate social responsibility are being stressed more and more in ocean transportation, just as they are throughout the business world. Basically, greater public awareness is driving the demand that industries adopt the principles of corporate social responsibility (CSR), including environmental sustainability. Whether this is realistic or not, the pressure is on ocean transportation carriers to improve their efficiency, effectiveness, and quality of service, all the while considering the cost of the externalities generated by their activities, including environmental and social costs.

Fifth, despite international efforts to address the problem of maritime piracy, there are some 500 reported actual or attempted acts of piracy and armed robbery against ships annually. The scale of the attacks and the size of the ships being targeted are raising serious concerns in the international community, especially among maritime professionals. This also threatens to undermine one of the world's busiest shipping routes (Asia–Europe) and choke points (the Suez Canal).

Sixth, over the past several years, developing countries have led a global transformation in international trade, global supply chains, and business input/output. This means that the historical shipping routes on the world's waters will change as different countries, especially developing and emerging markets, become more engaged in the global marketplace. For example, the OECD projects that by 2050, world freight flows will be two to four times what they are now, mainly driven by growth outside of the OECD countries, where the prediction of trade flow is two to six times higher than today.

Air Transportation

Since 2001, world air cargo tonnage has grown 3.7 percent annually, with a big jump of 18.5 percent from 2009 to 2010, but with stagnation and even contraction in the last two years (down 1 percent from 2010 to 2011 and roughly a 2 percent contraction between 2011 and 2012).[9] Despite these figures, Boeing's 2012–2013 World Air Cargo Forecast predicts that air cargo traffic will more than double over the next 20 years, representing an average 5.2 percent annual growth rate. As a comparison, world air cargo traffic grew, on average, by 6.9 percent annually in the 1980s, by 6.1 percent per year in the 1990s, and by 3.7 percent annually in the 2000s. At this time, total cargo volume handled by airports is about 94 million tons.

One bright spot in air transportation in the last couple of years is global air express traffic, which grew 24.8 percent in 2010 and 10.2 percent in 2011. In fact, global air express traffic grew at about triple the rate of total worldwide air cargo traffic in the 1990s (about 22 percent annually) and then at about 6.8 percent annually in the 2000s. This pattern of growth is similar to the growth seen in the air express traffic in the United States in the 1970s and 1980s. Clearly, there is a role for companies like DHL, FedEx, and UPS in the air express category, but also for other postal system competitors that either offer their own service or partner with one of the traditional air express companies.

In terms of passenger traffic, as a comparison to air cargo traffic, worldwide air passenger numbers increased by 5.3 percent in 2011 to 5.44 billion passengers.[10] This included increases in five of the six major regions in the world, Latin America–Caribbean (8.5 percent), the Middle East (7.7 percent), Asia-Pacific (7.0 percent), Europe (7.0 percent), and North America (1.8 percent), and a decrease in Africa (–3.5 percent). At this time, we have passenger numbers that are about the same for the Asia-Pacific, Europe, and North America regions (about 1.6 billion for each). Africa, the Middle East, and the Latin America–Caribbean regions fall between 152 and 408 million passengers annually. At the airport level, Atlanta (United States), Beijing (China), London (United Kingdom), Chicago (United States), and Tokyo (Japan) are the five busiest passenger airports, with Atlanta having 92 million passengers passing through in 2011.

We have seen increases in cargo volume in four of the six global regions, Latin America–Caribbean (7.6 percent), the Middle East (1.2 percent), Europe (1.4 percent), and Africa (2.6 percent), with a decrease in Asia-Pacific (–0.5 percent) and North America (–1.3 percent). The same regions that lead in passengers lead in air cargo as well, with Asia-Pacific in the clear lead with about 34 million tons, followed by North America with 28 million tons and Europe with 18 million tons. Each of the other three regions is below 6 million tons annually. At the airport level, Hong Kong (China), Memphis (United States), Shanghai (China), Anchorage (United States), and Incheon (South Korea) are the top five busiest cargo airports, with Hong Kong and Memphis being virtually tied at roughly 4 million tons. Memphis, of course, is easy to explain: FedEx's main airport hub is there.

Memphis and all other airports are assessed in the Air Cargo Excellence Survey, which was established in 2005. It is carried out and published annually by *Air Cargo World*.[11] The survey is based on a rating system that measures airlines and airports on specific criteria and subsequently ranks them to identify above- or below-average performance. There are two surveys, one for airlines and one for airports, based on their performance during the previous 12 months. The average rating for each measurement is calculated within each group, and that average is indexed to a value of 100. Ratings for airlines and airports are presented as an indexed score, relative to the average, to allow for easy comparisons. Scores greater than 100 represent above-average performance, scores less than 100 represent below-average performance, and scores of 100 represent exactly average performance.

Airlines are rated by freight forwarders based on customer service (claims are handled with expediency), problems solved in a prompt and courteous manner (reflecting a professional and knowledgeable sales force), performance (fulfills promises and contractual agreements, is dependable, and achieves scheduled transit times), value (competitive rates, rates commensurate with required level of service, and value-added programs), and information technology (tracking and tracing of shipments and electronic commerce capabilities). Based on the 2012 ratings, Lufthansa was the top-scoring airline, followed by Singapore Airlines, Korean Air, Cathay Pacific, and FedEx. More on the methodology and complete results can be found on *Air Cargo World*'s website.[12]

Airports are rated by airlines on performance (fulfills promises and contractual agreements); dependable, prompt, and courteous customer service; allied services (ground handling, trucking, and so on); value (competitive rates, rates commensurate with the service level required, and value-added programs); facilities (apron, warehousing, perishables center, access to highways and other modes); and regulatory operations (customs, security, and foreign trade zone). Based on the 2012 ratings, Dubai (DXB), Anchorage (ANC), Santiago (SCL), Hong Kong (HKG), and Frankfurt (FRA) rank as the top five best airports. Again, more on the methodology and the complete results can be found on *Air Cargo World*'s website.[13]

Land and Intermodal Transportation

Most of the time, land transportation refers to the movement of people, animals, or goods using trucks and rail. Pipelines are technically a form of land transportation as well. Land transportation goes back as far as we can think, of course, with early land transportation using horses, oxen, and even people to carry cargo on dirt roads. These early roads often followed game trails, which was an easy way to have some form of road infrastructure without having to build an actual road as we think of it today. Early stone-paved roads were, by all accounts, built in Mesopotamia and the Indus Valley civilizations. The first real network of roads, however, was built as the Royal Road across the Persian Empire.

The Persian Royal Road network was an ancient highway system that was rebuilt by Persian king Darius the Great (Darius I) of the Achaemenid Empire in the fifth century BC.[14] Darius had ulterior motives for his reorganization and rebuilding of the Royal Road system. He wanted to facilitate rapid communication and transportation throughout his very large empire, which stretched from Susa to Sardis. While various other developers (for example, the Assyrian kings) had a hand in the Royal Road, Darius is credited with making the roads the way they are recognized today.

Today, networks like the Royal Road have become modernized and globalized into Interstates and European highways, among many such systems. Think of the Interstate Highway System in the United States. For example, I-10 stretches from the Pacific Ocean at State Route 1 (Pacific Coast Highway) in Santa Monica, California, to Interstate 95 in Jacksonville, Florida (I-10 is the southernmost transcontinental highway in the United States). Its European counterpart example is the so-called international E-road network. E18, for example, stretches from Craigavon in Northern Ireland, United Kingdom, to Saint Petersburg, Russia (passing through Scotland, Sweden, Norway, and Finland). Given the maps of these countries, E18 actually requires transportation on ferryboats for some connections. This means that the volume of trucks that we see in the United States could not possibly move as easily on such a highway. You can fit only so many trucks on a ferry, or even on the large cruise ships that go between Kapellskär, Sweden, and Turku, Finland. E18 has a total distance of 1,890 km or 1,170 miles. While water is an obstacle to large-scale transportation, the E-road system is very important as an infrastructure for European travel and land transportation. Beyond the interstate and E-road systems, other continents have similar highway networks (for example, the Pan-American Highway network in the Americas, the Trans-African Highway network, and the Asian Highway network).

In the United States, it takes nearly 9 million people to move about 11 billion tons of freight annually. Trucks represent more than 80 percent of the freight bill in the United States, as just one example of the importance of motor carriers throughout the world. In CNNMoney's analysis of the world's most admired trucking, transportation, and logistics companies, J. B. Hunt Transport Services, Inc. (jbhunt.com), was the top trucking company. J. B. Hunt started in 1961 and has its headquarters in the northwest Arkansas city of Lowell. Its annual revenue tops $3 billion.

J. B. Hunt and others have many relatively good-quality roads to transport goods on in the United States. The United States leads the world in road length (6,544,199 km or 4,066,377 miles). China, India, Brazil, Japan, and Canada follow, in that order. What is more interesting, however, is that these top six countries accounted for more than 25 percent of the world's road infrastructure in 2013. However, while these countries have the most miles of roadways, the quality differs dramatically, as developing countries like China, India, and Brazil have a significant percentage of relatively low-quality or congested roadways.

Railroads have a history similar to that of roads and highways, although it is not as lengthy because relevant technology and machinery were invented later. Broadly, rail transport refers to the conveyance of passengers or goods using railroad cars. The obvious difference between rail and trucks is that railcars are directionally guided by the tracks on which they run, and the cars on the tracks have far lower frictional resistance than highway vehicles. Power for the train locomotives comes from either electricity from a railway system or their own power source (for example, diesel generators powering electric drive engines).

The oldest railroads are believed to be from the sixth century BC. Periander, one of the seven Sages of Greece, is credited with the invention of the oldest man-hauled railway known to exist. Modern rail transportation became popular with the British introduction of the steam engine as a source of power in the eighteenth century. Many consider the steam engine to have been a key component of the Industrial Revolution (for example, in the northern part of the United States).

It was more than 150 years ago that Abraham Lincoln signed the Pacific Railway Act of 1862, creating the original Union Pacific, one of America's iconic railroad companies. In CNNMoney's analysis of the world's most admired trucking, transportation, and logistics companies, Union Pacific Corporation (up.com) was the top railway company. Union Pacific has its headquarters in Omaha, Nebraska, and operates tracks in 23 U.S. states west of the Mississippi River. Its annual revenue is about $17 billion.

Union Pacific and many others have a large number of railway tracks that they can use in transporting passengers and goods. The United States leads the world in millions of freight ton-kilometers (at about 2,500,000), followed relatively closely by China and Russia, and then a drop to Canada (with each country in Europe lower in ton-kilometers for goods transportation).[15] Coordinating a lot of the railway effort in these and most other countries is the International Union of Railways (www.uic.org), a worldwide cooperative association of railway companies with more than 200 members across five continents.

Pipelines typically transport some form of liquids or gases, but pneumatic tubes using compressed air can also transport solid capsules of goods. There are three main forms of pipelines: gathering pipelines (interconnected pipelines forming complex networks), transportation pipelines (long pipes with large diameters), and distribution pipelines (interconnected pipelines with small diameters used to take the products to the final consumer). One prominent example of a pipeline is Russia's Druzhba ("Friendship") oil pipeline. It is a key energy source and the world's longest pipeline.

Pipelines experienced tremendous growth prior to the economic downturn in 2008. In fact, the industry grew from the low 20s in billions of dollars in 2006 to almost $40 billion in 2008 before faltering with the economic downturn. Beginning with 2012, pipelines are back in vogue. Almost 32,000 miles of North American pipeline, for example, are in the works, with some parts already functional. These include the Sand Hills Pipeline (developed by DCP Midstream, linking west to east Texas), the Pecos River Pipeline (developed by Bridger Group and Advantage Pipeline, linking the Delaware Basin and the Gulf Coast), and the Sterling III Pipeline (developed by Oneok Partners, linking Texas and Oklahoma on the one hand and the Gulf Coast on the other).

Intermodal transportation refers to the transfer of products in containers involving multiple modes of transportation—typically truck, railroad, air, or ocean carrier. It is becoming more and more popular as a way to move goods the most effectively, efficiently, and flexibly. Total intermodal volume has roughly doubled since the mid-1990s. According to the Intermodal Association of North America, intermodal transportation is growing faster than any other mode of transportation because it combines the best abilities of different transportation modes to deliver service, savings, and solutions to shippers. Typical products shipped using intermodal transportation include electronics, mail, food, paper products, clothes, appliances, textiles, and auto parts (some 25 million containers are shipped annually in the United States alone).

By working together, trucking companies, intermodal marketing companies, ocean steamship lines, air carriers, and railroads can provide a cost-effective, seamless, reliable, efficient, safe, and environmentally friendly way to move freight from origin to destination.

For example, shipments can be moved from a container ship directly to a truck or a railroad and then delivered to their final destination. Another common variation, popularized by FedEx and UPS, is air and truck, where products move by air for the long distances and motor carriers perform the pickup and delivery. Throughout the process, intermodal facilitators (often third-party logistics providers, freight forwarders, and consolidators) arrange for each piece of the move from pickup to drop-off and the end consignees.

REVERSE LOGISTICS

Product returns cost manufacturers and retailers more than $100 billion per year in the United States, or an average of 3.8 percent in lost profits.[16] Overall, manufacturers spend about 9 to 14 percent of their sales revenue on returns. Even more staggering, each year, consumers in America return more than the GDP of two-thirds of the nations in the world. Just these sample numbers suggest that reverse logistics is an incredibly important part of the global supply chain. Think about it—suppose you ship your product from East Lansing, Michigan (home to Michigan State University), to Uppsala, Sweden (where the first author of this book was born). What if the customer in Sweden does not like the product and wants to ship it back? Well, some firms have very good solutions to this reverse logistics problem, and others do not.

Based on the definition from the Reverse Logistics Executive Council (rlec.org), reverse logistics is the process of planning, implementing, and controlling the efficient, cost-effective flow of raw materials, in-process inventory, finished goods, and related information from the point of consumption to the point of origin for the purpose of recapturing value or proper disposal. In parallel, based on the definition from the Reverse Logistics Association (reverse logisticstrends.com), reverse logistics refers to all activities associated with a product or service *after* the point of sale. (The term can also occasionally pertain to the effective use of a transportation unit for the backhaul leg of a transfer.) The ultimate goal is to optimize the aftermarket activity or make it more efficient, thus saving money and environmental resources. Figure 4.10 provides an illustration of reverse logistics, with each step's counterpart in the forward logistics chain illustrated.

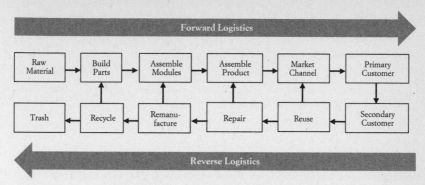

FIGURE 4.10 Forward and Reverse Logistics

The goal of the reverse logistics portion of the global supply chain is to move returned, overstocked, and/or obsolete products from the normal business value chain to an alternative place in order to maximize their value and reduce the risks that production companies, intermediaries, and customers take by engaging in the chain. Another goal of reverse logistics is to send items that have outlived their useful life to a reprocessing center. At the reprocessing center, many such items can be remarketed, refurbished, remanufactured, or decomposed into their basic materials for reuse as raw materials.

With the world becoming more globalized, products that are in the decline stage and/or slightly defective products no longer have a market in less developed nations to the same extent as they once did. This places increased burdens on firms to have effective and efficient reverse logistics systems built into their global supply chain networks. For example, in China, the rate of returns is about 4 percent for all industries, making up about 6 percent of the costs of total logistics. By some estimates, roughly half of all Chinese firms are now investing heavily in reverse logistics solutions, and half of those companies are outsourcing reverse logistics to third-party logistics providers (which creates a fantastic opportunity for third-party providers that are so inclined).

There are some important guidelines and conclusions about what firms can do to manage their product return policies to maximize profits. In a research study published in the *MIT Sloan Management Review*, Andrew Peterson and V. Kumar summarize the implications in terms of three core issues.[17] First, marketers can target and manage customers by taking information about both their purchase and their return behaviors into account. Second, lenient product return policies yield more profits than strict product return policies. Third, managing product returns in an optimal way increases profits even during tougher economic times.

GUIDELINES FOR LOGISTICS IN GLOBAL SUPPLY CHAINS

Logistics is one of the four critical functions that must be integrated at the strategic and tactical levels in global supply chains and as a part of the firm's global strategy. As in the earlier discussion of infrastructure, some logistics issues are major items that you can see, and some are intricate details of doing global business that are not readily obvious or understood. Everyone can figure out that the transportation of goods from point A to point B is important, but what about reverse logistics strategies or inventory management at each node of the global supply chain? Clearly, there are numerous issues to consider that relate to logistics in global supply chains. In assessing global logistics, we suggest these guidelines as a starting point:

- Strategic global supply chain management involves the continual evaluation and development of chains that incorporate the most efficient and effective network of transportation and inventory management systems. How global is your firm now, and how global are the logistics components of your supply chains? Are they global enough for today, five years from now, and ten years from now? Reasonable alignment of the globalness of the industry with the globalness of your logistics is critical. If you are underglobalized, you are not taking full advantage of the available and critical logistics options and the resulting market potential. If you are too globalized, there are other considerations that can impinge on your infrastructure and the resources available to you for conducting well-orchestrated global logistics (all of which is great for the industry, but could strain your budget and resources).
- How much inventory do you carry? Is it about the same amount as your largest competitor? Is it about the same amount as all your main competitors in the industry? The bottom line is, you need to know the average inventory (raw materials, work in process, and finished goods) of your

main competitors and your industry and have this knowledge for each major region of the world in which you operate. Why? Again, alignment is the key. If you have much more or much less inventory in a major category, you need to either *strategically* justify this inventory or bring the amount you have into line with the competitive averages in the respective world regions.

- You need to consider your inventory strategy (make to stock, configure to order, assemble to order, or make to order) when reviewing your inventory levels and mix profile. A make-to-stock strategy results in more finished goods inventory relative to raw materials or work-in-process inventory and more risk, but it is probably more responsive to customer demand. A make-to-order strategy results in less finished goods inventory relative to raw materials or work-in-process inventory and less risk, but it is probably not as responsive to customer demand in terms of availability.

- Packaging is a science in itself. Are you taking advantage of the state-of-the-art science in the area? Are you using the appropriate technology (for example, RFID tags, two-dimensional bar coding, and anticounterfeiting measures) on the containers, pallets, boxes, and individual packages? These and many other questions and issues pertaining to packaging must be asked regularly, since packaging science is making exponential improvements by innovating constantly.

- You should strategically and tactically consider taking advantage of potential intermodal transportation options. Intermodal is becoming a key solution for transportation of goods, and your options today are more plentiful and better than they have ever been before. Let's be clear: we are not suggesting that intermodal should be part of the solution for all companies and all situations. We are simply saying that the containers used, the vehicles used, the routes adopted, and so forth are all becoming much more universal and user-friendly. In that sense, intermodal should be evaluated as a strategic option for transportation more than it was before.

- Are products that you sold coming back to you? Some are. What are you doing with them, and how are you handling them? If you operate global supply chains—at least on the outbound/downstream side of the chain—you will have customers returning products to you. A clear strategy, an effective and efficient reverse logistics system, and a way to put the products back into the system at the right places are must-haves for all companies engaging in global supply chains.

CHAPTER 5

Purchasing in Global Supply Chains

Purchasing provides the input into global supply chains.

GLOBAL PURCHASING STRATEGY

Purchasing as a strategic function has a clearly defined role in global supply chains. It takes place in the inbound or upstream portion of the global supply chain, it involves buying something (such as raw materials, component parts, work in process, products, or services), and it should be strategically and tactically integrated with the elements of the production cycle for multinational corporations (MNCs). However, this is where the clarity stops! We will use the term *global purchasing* (and sometimes just *purchasing*) to elaborate on the concept within strategic global supply chain management (SCM) and within global supply chains as processes.

While purchasing as an activity has been around since the beginning of civilization, the idea of purchasing as a strategic field has been common only since the early 1970s, when the field of marketing—often using the term *organizational buying behavior*—called for giving more attention to business-to-business buying patterns and behaviors that were integrated with a firm's corporate strategy.[1] These days, marketing uses phrases such as "business buyer behavior" in the same context, with the idea that purchasing centers on the organizations involved in it. These terms refer to the purchasing behavior of producers, government units, institutions, and resellers.[2]

Prior to the early 1970s, purchasing was viewed as an administrative function rather than as having a strategic role in the firm. Indeed, this tripartite (tactical, administrative, and operational) focus still persists in many companies, especially among small and medium-sized enterprises (SMEs) that focus their strategic attention on a select set of core competencies. SMEs and even many larger corporations seldom view purchasing as one of their core, unique capabilities. We clearly disagree with this notion; purchasing—especially global purchasing—is and should be strategic. The use of corporate buying centers is one strategic decision that many firms routinely make. The buying center consists of the group of people within the organization that makes business purchasing decisions. It typically consists of users of what is bought, influencers of what should be bought, corporate buyers responsible for the administrative buying process, deciders, and, in some cases, gatekeepers.[3]

It is interesting to note that the field of purchasing has gone through a rather remarkable evolution in definitions and terminology, in many cases, to stress the strategic aspect of purchasing and to operate more within a buying center mentality than before. Terms such as *purchasing*, *procurement*, *sourcing*, *strategic sourcing*, and *supply management* have connections to what many would consider the field of purchasing. Broadly, *purchasing* refers to the functions associated with buying the raw materials, component parts, work in process, products (goods), and services required by the organization to perform its value-added activities and ultimately satisfy its end customers. At one time, *procurement* was a term used for purchasing involving one or more government organizations. *Requisitioning*, or *acquisition*, was another term that was sometimes used in this context. In that sense, procurement consists of governments and other public policy and regulatory bodies conducting purchasing activities.

The concept of *sourcing*, or purchasing practices aimed at finding, evaluating, and engaging suppliers of raw materials, component parts, or products and services, then elevated the nature of purchasing to some degree. *Sourcing* is an all-encompassing term that connects issues such as outsourcing and offshoring, and many others, to purchasing activities in general. The inclusion of these activities—and there are many of them—stretches the boundaries of purchasing into a clearer global arena as well. At an even more strategic level, *strategic sourcing* refers to the process of determining long-term supply requirements, finding suppliers and sources to fulfill those needs, negotiating the purchase agreements, and managing the suppliers' performance relative to the specifications and the (expected) long-term relationship between the supplier and buyer organizations.

Perhaps the most strategic term of all, at least to this point, is *supply management*. Supply management refers to the identification, acquisition, access, positioning, and management of resources and related capabilities that the organization needs or potentially needs if it is to attain its strategic objectives.[4] This definition is rooted in the complexities and intricate details offered by the official definition of the Institute for Supply Management (ISM, www.ism.ws). ISM has been in the forefront of the purchasing profession since its founding in 1915.

Global purchasing is the part of global supply chain management that refers to the functions associated with the worldwide buying of the goods, services, and/or information required by the multinational corporation (see Figure 5.1).[5] As we described earlier, a number of terms can be used within the general context of "global purchasing"; consequently, we will use the terms *purchasing*, *procurement*, *sourcing*, *strategic sourcing*, and *supply management* interchangeably (there are, of course, some technical and detailed differences among these terms that we have already highlighted). Global purchasing involves the following: worldwide management of a multinational corporation's

FIGURE 5.1 A Focus on Global Purchasing

evolution from international to global purchasing (assuming that this is the progression the MNC is undertaking), various types of purchasing strategies, outsourcing and offshoring, global customer and channel management, order fulfillment and delivery, global supplier selection, and global supplier networks.

Strategically, within the integrated global supply chain of multinational corporations, it is predicted that purchasing as a function will become 13 percent more globalized in the next five years (2013 to 2018) and 29 percent more globalized in the next ten years (by 2023). Figure 5.2 illustrates these increases. In 2013, purchasing scored 62 out of 100 points in terms of being globalized (where 100 is fully globalized and zero is purely domestic). A score of 62 places purchasing at the top of the functions within global supply chains in terms of being globalized—ahead of logistics, operations, and market channels. However, purchasing is found to contribute least to global supply chain management, albeit only marginally below the other three functions (logistics, operations, and market channels). The discipline scores an 89 out of a possible 100 points on the degree of importance in contributing to overall global supply chain management for the MNC. (Market channels is at the top with 96, followed by logistics with 94, operations with 92, and purchasing with 89). Purchasing is expected to maintain this degree of importance (89 on a 100-point scale) for the next five years. Figure 5.3 illustrates the changes in purchasing in the 2013 to 2018 time period.

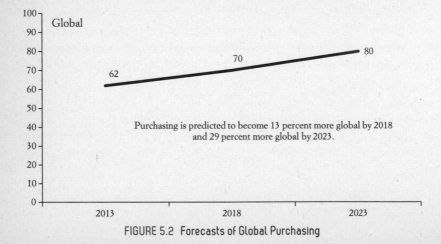

FIGURE 5.2 Forecasts of Global Purchasing

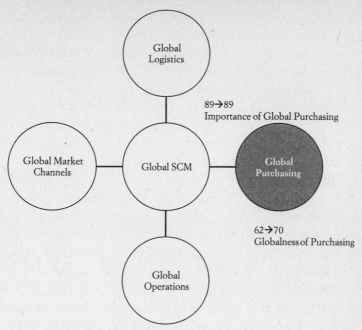

FIGURE 5.3 Globalization of Purchasing, 2013 to 2018

FROM DOMESTIC TO INTERNATIONAL TO GLOBAL PURCHASING

In 2005, Robert Trent and Robert Monczka wrote an article in the *MIT Sloan Management Review* in which they discussed how to achieve excellence in global purchasing. They made a strong case that global purchasing is an increasingly popular business strategy, but one that is difficult to execute. They argued that organizations that have developed outstanding global purchasing strategies have seven characteristics:[6] (1) executive commitment to global purchasing, (2) rigorous and well-defined processes, (3) availability of needed resources, (4) integration through information technology, (5) supportive organizational design, (6) structured approaches to communication, and (7) methodologies for measuring savings.

Each of these characteristics—or clusters of characteristics, as Trent and Monczka prefer to call them—is detailed in their article and is relatively straightforward to understand (and beyond the scope of this book). However, an important point that Trent and Monczka make is that very few, if any, organizations actually possess all seven characteristics. Instead, the seven characteristics should serve as benchmarks to use in developing strategic global purchasing in organizations. In addition, to help organizations better understand the resource commitments, time allocation, and purchasing practices that may be needed to extend the organization globally, Trent and Monczka introduced a continuum of five levels of purchasing and shared data. They based these levels upon the expectations for the next five years, ending in about 2010.

Using their five levels, we updated their data to 2013 and also provide forecasts (based on real data analysis) for the next five and ten years, respectively (2018 and 2023). We believe this form of benchmarking for current (2013), near future (2018), and somewhat distant future (2023) situations provides a great set of criteria for companies to use in developing their own global purchasing practices.

Let's start by highlighting the five levels of purchasing. Level I is simply companies engaging in domestic purchasing activities only. Often, these companies also stay close to their home base in their domestic market when purchasing raw materials, component parts, and the like for their operations (for example, a Michigan firm purchasing raw materials, such as cherries, from another Michigan firm). Other times, they use their home country's market to purchase needed inputs for their production process, but they do not venture outside their home country. The next four levels of purchasing include engaging in different degrees of international and global purchasing activities.

Levels II and III are both considered "international purchasing," but of various degrees and forms. Companies that are at Level II engage in international purchasing activities only as needed. This means that their approach to international purchasing is often reactive and uncoordinated among the buying locations within the firm and/or across the various units that make up the firm, such as strategic business units and functional units. Companies at Level III engage in international purchasing activities as part of the firm's overall supply chain management strategy. As such, at the Level III stage, companies begin to recognize that a well-formulated and well-executed worldwide international purchasing strategy can be very effective in elevating the firm's competitive edge in the marketplace.

Levels IV and V both involve "global purchasing" to various degrees. Level IV refers to global purchasing activities that are integrated across worldwide locations. This involves integration and coordination of purchasing strategies across the firm's buying locations worldwide. With Level IV, we are now dealing with a sophisticated form of worldwide purchasing. Level V involves engaging in global purchasing activities that are integrated across worldwide locations and functional groups. Broadly, this means that the firm integrates and coordinates the purchasing of common items, purchasing processes, and supplier selection efforts globally, for example. Trent and Monczka argue that only those companies that have a global design for their supply chain management can progress to Level V. In short, that also means that without global logistics, global operations, and global market channels that work well, global purchasing at Level V will not be achievable. We agree. It is critically important to integrate and coordinate efforts in logistics, operations, purchasing, and market channels to maximize global supply chain management.

Let us now move to some data for domestic, international, and global purchasing for 2013 and also forecast data for 2018 and 2023. This is where the situation surrounding multinational corporations gets interesting. It is intriguing simply to look at data for 2013, 2018, and 2023 to see where companies think they are heading in the next decade. But we thought we would take this up a notch by comparing data collected from purchasing professionals in multinational corporations and also so-called C-suite executives from these multinational corporations. A professional working in the trenches in a field such as purchasing may have a different view of his or her home field from that of the top-level managers in the firm. The C-suite executives are the companies' top-level executives, those whose abbreviated title begins with C. In other words, this pertains to executives with titles such as CEO (chief executive officer), COO (chief operating officer), and CFO (chief financial officer).

For the sample of purchasing professionals (such as purchasing managers, corporate buyers, senior buyers, and contract managers), we find that the results are relatively steady over the next decade. Figure 5.4 illustrates the expected changes. Clearly, there is movement at some levels, such as Level I, with its focus on engaging solely in domestic purchasing activities. In Level I, we forecast a downward trend from 33 percent of the companies engaging in only domestic purchasing in 2013 to 26 percent in 2023. Level II is predicted to be very steady, with roughly 22 percent of the companies engaging

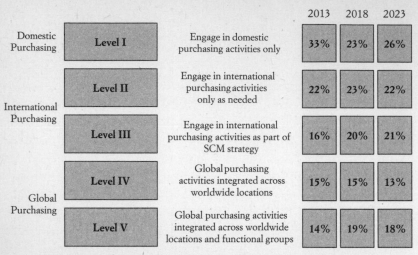

FIGURE 5.4 Purchasing Activities: The View from Purchasing Professionals

in international purchasing activities only as needed. The same goes for Level IV (global purchasing activities integrated across worldwide locations), where we will see about 15 percent of the companies allocating their purchasing efforts over the next decade. The significant changes, based on the input from purchasing professionals, will mainly be in the Level III and Level V categories. This means that companies will actively engage more in international purchasing activities as a part of their overall supply chain strategy (Level III), and they will also engage in more concerted efforts to integrate global purchasing activities across worldwide locations and functional groups (Level V). At the former level, we will see movement from 16 to 21 percent in the next 10 years, while the forecasted upward trend for Level V will take us from 14 percent to 18 to 19 percent in the next decade.

Now the comparison starts in earnest. For the sample of C-suite executives (such as CEOs, COOs, and CFOs), the results are dramatically different and much more global. Figure 5.5 illustrates the expected changes. Let's keep in mind that we are talking about the same multinational corporations here; basically, the idea is that the results should be the same if the C-suite executives and purchasing professionals are aligned with each other and have a common strategic view of purchasing as a part of their global supply chains. What we find is that the C-suite executives' understanding of the way their companies are purchasing today includes only a small number (9

			2013	2018	2023
Domestic Purchasing	Level I	Engage in domestic purchasing activities only	9%	5%	5%
International Purchasing	Level II	Engage in international purchasing activities only as needed	23%	15%	12%
	Level III	Engage in international purchasing activities as part of SCM strategy	19%	15%	12%
Global Purchasing	Level IV	Global purchasing activities integrated across worldwide locations	19%	13%	10%
	Level V	Global purchasing activities integrated across worldwide locations and functional groups	30%	52%	61%

FIGURE 5.5 Purchasing Activities: The View from C-Suite Professionals

percent) engaging only in domestic purchasing. They see roughly the same amount at Levels II, III, and IV, and the largest percentage (about 30 percent) being at Level V. The most remarkable results from the C-suite executives' feedback is that, based on all data collected, our predictions show that they expect a movement to some 61 percent being engaged in global purchasing activities that are integrated across worldwide locations and functions by 2023. This is a significant increase from their views of their activities today, which show 30 percent in this Level V category. (This is already significantly higher than the views of their purchasing professionals, who see this as 14 percent.)

A few more comparisons between C-suite executives and purchasing professionals may be in order. After all, C-suite executives often set the tone for what the firm does in terms of strategy. While we argue that supply chain executives should have a seat at the table when corporate strategy is being discussed, decided on, and implemented, this is, of course, not always the case. But, thankfully, more and more companies today are involving SCM executives on corporate boards and corporate leadership teams compared with the 1990s and early 2000s. Ideally, we would see at least one person on the board representing each of the four core areas of supply chain management: logistics, purchasing, operations, and market channels (we often see the latter two functions being represented, but seldom the first two, and that needs to change if global strategy is to be effectively developed and implemented).

What we see now is a relative disconnect between the C-suite and purchasing professionals. This is remarkably well illustrated by the fact that they do not even agree on what is going on today. For example, C-suite executives think that Level V global purchasing takes place roughly twice as often as the purchasing professionals do (30 percent versus 14 percent). This difference involves both definitional boundaries and practical understandings of reality. That is, C-suite executives may simply define certain purchasing activities as more global than their counterparts in purchasing do. This definitional explanation resolves some of the differences. Unfortunately, the differences also include the fact that one or both groups of firm employees may underestimate the level of global purchasing if they are not directly aware of each purchasing activity. In either case, alignment and coordination across hierarchies in multinational corporations obviously have to improve to make purchasing more strategic, better aligned with firm objectives, and beneficial to other supply chain functions.

TYPES OF PURCHASING STRATEGY

Beyond the domestic, international, and global purchasing strategies we discussed in the previous section, purchasing includes a number of basic choices that companies make in deciding how to engage with markets. Figure 5.6 illustrates the basic options that are available. We draw on Masaaki Kotabe and Kristiaan Helsen's work in this section.[7] Their labeling and some of their definitional boundaries are a bit different from ours, but the overarching schema we present here is very much aligned with theirs. The basic choices in purchasing strategy relate to the use of imports, product assembly, or complete production within a country to serve the global marketplace. Another important decision relates to the use of internal or external suppliers for component parts or finished products to be used in the firm's production operations.

The purchasing decision-making tree we present in this section begins with the choice of internal purchasing versus external purchasing—in other words, "how to purchase." We find that roughly 35 percent of the purchasing in multinational corporations today is internal, with 65 percent being classified as external. The next decision, in both internal and external purchasing, is to figure out "where

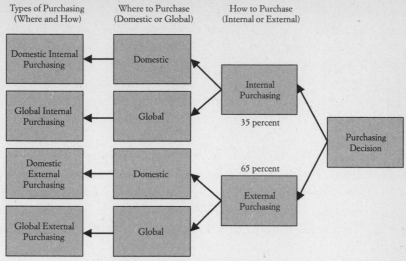

Types of Purchasing   Where to Purchase   How to Purchase
(Where and How)   (Domestic or Global)   (Internal or External)

FIGURE 5.6 Types of Purchasing Strategy

to purchase" (domestically or globally). This takes us ultimately to the "types of purchasing" (where and how) and the four choices for purchasing strategy: domestic internal purchasing, global internal purchasing, domestic external purchasing, and global external purchasing.

The two internal choices are involved in 35 percent of the purchases made by today's multinational corporations. Based on our estimation, we have no reason to expect the 35/65 split between internal and external purchasing to change in the foreseeable future. As an example, domestic internal purchasing could occur when a multinational corporation buys components from one of its own affiliates that produces them domestically in one of the firm's factories. This could also be referred to as domestic in-house sourcing. Global internal purchasing could occur when a multinational corporation buys components from one of its own subsidiaries that produces them in one of the firm's global factories. This could also be referred to as offshore subsidiary sourcing.

The other two choices are chiefly external in scope and are involved in 65 percent of the purchases made by multinational corporations. Domestic external purchasing could occur when a multinational corporation buys components from one of its suppliers that produces them in one of its factories in the firm's home country. This could also be referred to simply as purchasing from vendors. Global external purchasing could occur when a multinational corporation buys components from one of its suppliers that produces them in one of its global factories. That could also be referred to as outsourcing or sometimes offshore outsourcing. We expect continued growth in external purchases well into the future.

OUTSOURCING, OFFSHORING, AND THEIR DERIVATIVES ____

The types of purchasing activities and strategies discussed previously come with a set of generic options for the "international arena." But we all know that outsourcing and offshoring, along with many derivatives and other similar yet quite different options, exist in the purchasing world today. At this stage of the book and, in particular, at this stage of the purchasing chapter, we feel it is important to go over the outsourcing-related terms and options that companies have, especially the following terms that are often confusing to understand, develop strategy around, and implement: outsourcing, insourcing, offshoring, offshore outsourcing, nearshoring, crowdsourcing, multi-sourcing, homesourcing, and co-sourcing.

Outsourcing occurs when a multinational corporation buys products or services from one of its suppliers that produces them somewhere else, whether domestically or globally. In that sense, we are also referring to external purchasing when we talk about purchasing strategy.

Insourcing occurs when a multinational corporation decides to stop outsourcing products or services and instead starts to produce them internally; insourcing is the opposite of outsourcing. Therefore, we are dealing with internal purchasing in the context of purchasing strategy.

Offshoring occurs when a multinational corporation buys products or services from one of its suppliers that produces them somewhere globally (outside the MNC's home country). Offshoring takes us to a form of global external purchasing in terms of purchasing strategy.

Offshore outsourcing refers to a multinational corporation buying products or services from one of its suppliers in a country other than the one in which the product is manufactured or the service is developed. This again is a form of global external purchasing in terms of purchasing strategy.

Nearshoring happens when a multinational corporation transfers business or information technology processes to suppliers in a nearby country, often one that shares a border with the firm's own country. While nearshoring is not a purchasing activity per se, it involves facilitating global external purchasing.

Crowdsourcing refers to a multinational corporation outsourcing tasks to a distributed group of people; this process can occur both online and offline. The difference between crowdsourcing and typical outsourcing is that the task is outsourced to an undefined entity rather than to a specific firm or person. Crowdsourcing is not a supply chain phenomenon per se, but it applies to all four forms of purchasing strategy that we discussed in the previous section, especially with regard to supplier involvement in innovation processes.

Multisourcing occurs when a multinational corporation buys parts of its business and information technology services from the optimal set of internal and external providers in the pursuit of business goals; the term is typically applied to information technology services, but it can be used for any business area.

Homesourcing (sometimes called *homeshoring*) refers to a multinational corporation transferring service industry employment from the firm's physical offices to home-based employees with appropriate communication technology, who can be located anywhere in the world. Again, this is not a form of purchasing strategy per se, but it applies to a wide variety of purchasing scenarios.

Co-sourcing occurs when a multinational corporation uses both its own employees from inside the firm and an external supplier to perform certain tasks, often in concert with each other. This applies to all four forms of purchasing strategy that we discussed in the previous section. However, co-sourcing implies that the relationship between the firm and its supplier is rather strategic in nature—often, this involves the top suppliers in a particular product or component category.

GLOBAL CUSTOMERS AND CHANNELS

Global business customers are somewhat distinct in that they purchase raw materials, component parts, and products on a centralized or coordinated basis for decentralized use in the firm's production and operations. We draw on George Yip and Tomas Hult's work in this section.[8] They provide some descriptions and illustrations of firms over the years that have engaged with different types of customers, and we encourage the reader to check out those scenarios. In this section, we illustrate the five different types of customers outlined by Yip and Hult by using fictitious scenarios involving real companies.

Internationalization of purchasing refers broadly to the types of purchasing done—for instance, buying from domestic suppliers in domestic markets, buying from foreign suppliers in domestic markets, and buying from foreign suppliers in foreign markets. Globalization of purchasing is tied to the level of headquarters involvement (that is, no headquarters involvement, headquarters recommends standards and/or products, headquarters mandates standards and/or products, and headquarters does the purchasing). In essence, we build on the earlier sections on purchasing activities and purchasing strategy by involving a layer of centralization at the headquarters for the purchasing decision making.

The "free local customer" buys from domestic suppliers in domestic markets with no involvement by the headquarters of the multinational corporation. This customer type is exemplified by low internationalization of purchasing and low globalization of purchasing. An example of a free local customer could be a Detroit-based General Motors plant purchasing laundry and uniform services from StarSource Management Services in Detroit.

The "foreign customer" buys from foreign suppliers in foreign markets with no involvement by the headquarters of the multinational corporation. This customer type is exemplified by high internationalization of purchasing and low globalization of purchasing. An example of a foreign customer could be a General Motors plant purchasing components for its cars from one of its foreign suppliers, Müller—Die lila Logistik from Besigheim, Germany, for use in GM's German operations.

The "international customer" buys from foreign suppliers in domestic markets, with the multinational corporation's headquarters recommending standards and/or products. This customer type is exemplified by medium-level internationalization of purchasing and medium-level globalization of purchasing. An example of an international customer could be General Motors of Detroit purchasing components for its cars from one of its suppliers, Gestamp U.S. Hardtech, which is located in Mason, Michigan, but is owned by the Spanish firm Gestamp, for use in GM's operations in Detroit.

The "controlled local customer" buys from domestic suppliers in domestic markets with the multinational corporation's headquarters mandating standards and/or products. This customer type is exemplified by low internationalization of purchasing and medium globalization of purchasing. An example of a controlled local customer could be General Motors in Detroit purchasing components for cars from one of its domestic suppliers, Lear Corporation from Detroit.

The "global customer" buys from foreign suppliers in domestic or foreign markets, with the multinational corporation's headquarters mandating standards and/or products. This customer type is exemplified by medium to high internationalization of purchasing and medium to high globalization of purchasing. An example of a global customer could be General Motors of Detroit purchasing components for its cars from one of its foreign suppliers, Yasunaga Corporation from Japan, with the GM headquarters' corporate buying unit being in charge of the purchasing. In this case, General Motors is providing both guidance and control.

ORDER FULFILLMENT AND DELIVERY

If we have global customers, as indicated in the previous section, it is reasonable to assume that we should have purchasing strategies to go along with those customers. In particular, using the framework of center-led or centralized purchasing (often headquarters-based), we can anchor purchasing both in domestic versus global order fulfillment and in domestic versus global delivery as well. Such two-by-two thinking is nicely aligned with and strategically oriented alongside the purchasing activities and purchasing strategy sections presented earlier in this chapter. The result is a synergy in thinking about how to orchestrate purchasing in the firm.

Order fulfillment and delivery is a tricky business that takes place in the last mile of the global supply chain, often referred to as the market channels portion of the chain, where we deal with end customers. (In a purchasing sense, it is simply referred to as order fulfillment when dealing with business-to-business customers such as purchasing between companies.) These two issues are seldom discussed together, but we find that we can effectively draw on last-mile knowledge to capture the essence of the strategic choices and decisions that need to be made in both cases (that is, strategies for centralized global purchasing and strategies for extending the global supply chain). In particular, Kenneth Boyer, Markham Frolich, and Tomas Hult suggest four different strategies that we will apply to both two-by-two matrices: fully extended, centralized extended, semiextended, and decoupled.[9]

This means that, initially, the strategies for centralized global purchasing (fully extended, centralized extended, semiextended, and decoupled) can effectively be represented by a two-by-two matrix (see Figure 5.7). Let's use the scenario of the auto manufacturer Ford Motor Company, which is based in Michigan but has extensive global operations, and look at its options for order fulfillment and delivery within the framework of centralized global purchasing. In 1903, Henry Ford started the Ford Motor Company with $28,000 in cash, and his automobiles changed the way the world moved. According to its corporate philosophy, Ford Motor Company is focused on creating a strong business that builds great products that contribute to a better world (ford.com).

If we start with the lower left quadrant and the scenario of a fully extended global supply chain—where purchasing takes place in the home country and delivery is also to a home country location—we are talking, of course, about domestic order fulfillment and domestic delivery. An example of this scenario could be Ford purchasing car

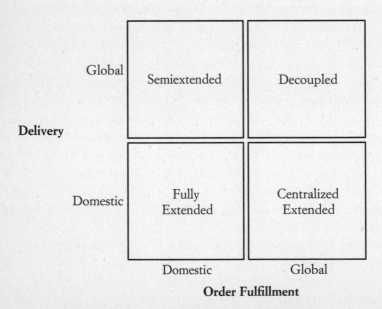

FIGURE 5.7 Strategies for Centralized Global Purchasing

seats from Magna, based in Excelsior Springs, Missouri, for delivery to its River Rouge Plant in Dearborn, Michigan.

Moving over to the lower right quadrant and the scenario of a centralized extended global supply chain, where purchasing takes place in a foreign country and delivery is to a home country location, we are looking at global order fulfillment and domestic delivery. An example of this scenario could be Ford purchasing axles from Dana-Talesol, based in Montevideo, Uruguay, for delivery to its plant in Flat Rock, Michigan.

The top left quadrant illustrates the semiextended strategy (purchasing in the home country and delivery to a foreign country location), so domestic order fulfillment and global delivery is the scenario. An example of this situational model could be Ford purchasing car seats from Magna, based in Excelsior Springs, Missouri, for delivery to its plant in Saint Petersburg, Russia.

The top right quadrant illustrates the decoupled strategy (purchasing in a foreign country and delivery to a foreign country location), where the scenario is global order fulfillment and global delivery. An example of this scenario could be Ford purchasing axles from Dana-Talesol, based in Montevideo, Uruguay, for delivery to its plant in Saint Petersburg, Russia.

The strategies for extending the global supply chain can also be effectively represented by a two-by-two matrix (see Figure 5.8). Let's use a scenario of grocery companies from Canada, England, and the United States, and look at their options for order fulfillment and delivery within the framework of extending the global supply chain. In 1916, Piggly Wiggly was the first self-service grocery store, and it has since evolved into a supermarket chain operating in the midwestern and southern regions of the United States. Peapod was one of America's first pure online grocery delivery services; the firm is based in Skokie, Illinois, and has been in business since 1989.

If we start with the lower left quadrant and the scenario of a fully extended global supply chain, here we are dealing with purchased products that are delivered from the global supplier's store directly to the firm. Examples of customer companies using this scenario include the grocery firms Tesco and Sainsbury in England and Albertsons in the United States.

Moving to the right, to the lower right quadrant and the scenario of a centralized extended global supply chain, we are addressing purchased products that are delivered from the global supplier's

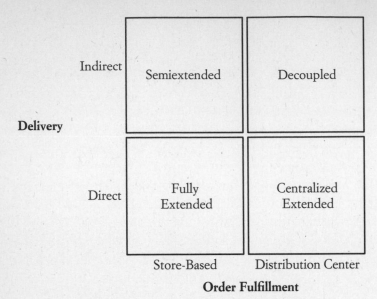

FIGURE 5.8 Strategies for Extending the Global Supply Chain

distribution center directly to the firm. Examples of customer companies using this scenario include the grocery firms Grocery Gateway in Canada and Ocado in England.

The top left quadrant illustrates the semiextended strategy, focusing on purchased products that are picked up from the global supplier's store by the firm. An example of a customer firm using this scenario includes the grocery firm Lowes Foods in the United States.

The top right quadrant illustrates the decoupled strategy with a focus on purchased products that are picked up from the global supplier's distribution center by the firm. At the end-customer level, an example of a firm using this scenario includes the U.S. grocery firm FreshDirect.

GLOBAL SUPPLIER SELECTION

Global supplier selection (even more than domestic supplier selection) should use a structured approach to ensure that the end result is the selection of an ideal global supplier. This means that the selection process for a global supplier needs to be as comprehensive as possible, given time and resource constraints. It also means that the global supplier selection process needs to be as objective as possible, given the available resources internal and external to the firm. A step-by-step process for global supplier selection ensures an orderly, strategic, and ultimately appropriate selection of the perfect global supplier for a particular purchase scenario. So we build a seven-step process for global supplier evaluation, suggest a set of main dimensions for this evaluation, and illustrate our thinking by including a sample "scorecard" for global supplier selection criteria.

As with any strategic initiative, a global supplier selection plan should be rigorous, be process-oriented, and result in an effective outcome that is defendable, both internally in the multinational corporation and also externally to current and potential global suppliers. We find that the following seven-step plan works well when selecting a global supplier for a new purchasing scenario or selecting a new or existing global supplier for an existing purchasing category.

1. Identify the main dimensions for global supplier evaluation.
2. Assign weights to the main dimensions for evaluation.
3. Identify subdimensions for global supplier evaluation.
4. Assign weights to the subdimensions for evaluation.
5. Define the scoring system for the main dimensions and subdimensions.
6. Evaluate each global supplier (initially screened as acceptable).
7. Make the decision as to which global supplier to select.

Step 1 entails identifying potential dimensions for global supplier evaluation and then selecting the main dimensions to be used in the assessment. The pyramid in Figure 5.9 illustrates starting points for thinking about and evaluating the potential dimensions to be used. These dimensions follow the logic of this book, focusing on industry globalization drivers and supply chain infrastructure (discussed in Chapters 2 and 3) along with competitive priorities (discussed in more detail in Chapter 6, when we deal with global operations). As a result, we find the seven main dimensions illustrated in the pyramid to be unique and appropriate starting points for global supplier evaluation and selection.

To illustrate the use of these seven main dimensions in global supplier selection, we have provided a draft of a scorecard that includes the seven main dimensions, subdimensions for each main dimension, weights allocated to the main dimensions and subdimensions,

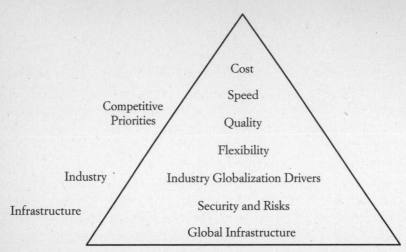

FIGURE 5.9 Sample of Main Dimensions for Global Supplier Evaluation

a fictitious illustrative score for each subdimension, the calculated weighted score based on the subweights and scores, an overall dimensional score, and finally an overall score for the global supplier we evaluated (see Table 5.1). In this case, we scored this fictitious global supplier as a 68.0 on a 100-point scale, where 100 is the maximum and 0 is the minimum. We like using weights that add up to 100 points at all times for ease of understanding and to facilitate comparisons across global suppliers, time periods, and purchasing categories, but there is nothing magical or necessary about the 100-point scaling format.

In this global supplier selection and evaluation scorecard, we include the seven main dimensions: cost, speed, quality, and flexibility from the competitive priorities framework (see Chapter 6), plus the industry drivers and two core aspects of supply chain infrastructure (security and risks and general infrastructure). For each main dimension, we also include logical and important subdimensions. For example, as the scorecard illustrates, we selected total cost analysis and financial stability for the cost dimension. Total cost is included because we find it incredibly valuable to evaluate the total cost, including the cost of each node, actor, and link in the global supply chain. With this information, we can make decisions based on the total cost of all the nodes, actors, and links collectively. This is in contrast to the result of summing the costs associated with each of those nodes, actors, and links (we will cover total cost analysis in

TABLE 5.1 Global Supplier Selection Scorecard

Dimensions	Weight	Subweight	Score (0–3)	Weighted Score	Dimensional Score
Cost	20				17.3
Total cost analysis		40%	2	5.3	
Financial stability		60%	3	12.0	
Speed	10				6.6
Timely delivery		70%	2	4.6	
Convenience		30%	2	2.0	
Quality	20				16.7
Quality management system		50%	2	6.7	
Experience		50%	3	10.0	
Flexibility	5				2.5
Life-cycle service		50%	1	0.8	
Agility to meet specs		50%	2	1.7	
Industry Drivers	20				9.9
Market drivers		30%	1	2.0	
Cost drivers		40%	1	2.6	
Government drivers		10%	2	1.3	
Competitive drivers		20%	3	4.0	
Security and Risks	10				6.6
Security issues		50%	2	3.3	
Risk issues		50%	2	3.3	
Infrastructure	15				8.4
Transportation		70%	2	6.9	
Communication		10%	0	0.0	
Utilities		10%	1	0.5	
Technology		10%	2	1.0	
				TOTAL	68.0

much more detail in Chapter 6). The financial stability of the global suppliers evaluated is critically important in terms of, among other things, long-term delivery of purchased goods.

For the speed dimension, we selected timely delivery and convenience as two subdimensions. Timely delivery, or cycle time, is always important for global supplier selection. It may be the most important factor for commodity-based goods and far lower in importance for other types of goods, but it should always be on the radar screen for what should be included for evaluation, with at least at some minimum weight. In this case, we opted to allocate 70 percent of the speed score to timely delivery and 30 percent of the weight for that main dimension to convenience. We include convenience because many companies operate close to or totally within just-in-time frameworks. That means that speed is evaluated not only in terms of fast cycle time, but also in terms of speed to get goods to the firm at the right time.

For quality, we selected the quality management system and experience as the two subdimensions. Obviously, additional subdimensions for quality purposes should be considered and are likely to be added, depending on what type of purchase is being considered, whether the global supplier is new or has previously been used by the firm, and so on. In this case, we refer to the quality management system as the global supplier's processes and its management of those processes to ensure that quality is achieved in the component parts and products delivered to the buyer. Ultimately, your firm becomes the quality assurance to the customer, and you need to be assured that the global supplier plays its role in this quality achievement. Experience, of course, goes a long way toward building a relationship in which you can trust the supplier to deliver and achieve quality. But the overall scorecard is also structured to address trust issues, including quality initiatives for new global suppliers as well.

For flexibility, we selected life-cycle service and agility to meet specifications as the two subdimensions. Basically, we are looking for subdimensions here that address the global supplier's flexibility in terms of working with your firm to meet whatever demands you face from the customers within your industry. This brings us to life-cycle service issues as well as meeting the specifications that you set, no matter what they are and no matter how often they may change. We did allocate fewer overall points (5 points, or 5 percent of the 100 points total for the scorecard) to this dimension, but it is important at the margin (and sometimes much more than that) in meeting end-customer demands over time.

For the industry globalization drivers, security and risks, and general infrastructure items, we built on what we discussed in Chapters 2 and 3. Therefore, we suggest that market drivers, cost drivers, government drivers, and competitive drivers should be evaluated for each global supplier in the context of the industry in which they operate (which may be your industry or a nearby industry). As a result, in addition to the competitive priority factor of cost, we include cost drivers as a part of the industry drivers. This means that costs that are directly related to the global supplier are evaluated in the competitive priorities portion of the scorecard, and cost as it pertains to the industry in a specific country or world region is evaluated in the industry globalization driver portion. Similarly, issues related to security, risk, transportation, communication, utilities, and technology are all relevant in the context of the country and/or world region environment when finding or verifying a global supplier.

As for scoring, select a scoring system that you are comfortable with. You probably already have a scoring system that you use for purchasing in the domestic setting. Can it be applied and/or adapted for global suppliers? What needs to be done, and how many changes need to be made to allow you to use your existing supplier evaluation scorecard in the global setting? These questions serve as the starting point for the global supplier selection and evaluation scorecard, since they are probably the scoring anchors that will make those in the C-suite and purchasing professionals the most comfortable. Our preferred scoring method is to use a system that is easy to use and hard not to use, while being rigorous enough to serve the process well. With that in mind, we prefer a 0 to 3 scoring system with labels to go along with each incremental score:

Major nonconformity (score = 0). You would give a score of 0 to a global supplier when you think it very likely that there would be a total breakdown of an activity pertaining to the global purchasing system.

Minor nonconformity (score = 1). You would give a score of 1 to a global supplier when you think it is likely that there would be a failure of its quality system or a reduction in its ability to ensure high-quality processes and/or products.

Conformity (score = 2). You would give a score of 2 to a global supplier when you believe that no major or minor nonconformities were noted during the evaluation (based on all available documents and/or past experiences).

Adequacy (score = 3). You would give a score of 3 to a global supplier when you think the supplier's performance record and/or objective documentation meets the purchasing needs based on the scope of the planned operations.

GLOBAL SUPPLIER NETWORKS

The term *global supplier networks* has commonly been used to refer to any form of association and/or network of global suppliers dealing with firm-based or non-firm-specific alliances. The general idea of global supplier networks takes purchasing to a higher strategic level than transactional relationships. We classify these strategic initiatives as an international purchasing office, a global supplier association, and a global supplier network. The bottom line is that in today's global economy, a multinational corporation can rarely be successful without a supplier base that is competitive on a worldwide basis. The three kinds of global supplier networks play a significant role in creating and maintaining a competitive global supplier base for the firm. Are you engaged in one? If yes, great (assuming it works!). If not, then why not?

An international purchasing office (IPO) is where the main purchasing executive is located in many multinational corporations. The purchasing executive is generally important, as indicated by the following numbers. In medium and large companies, the highest-level purchasing executive reports to the highest-level executive or one level below in 65 percent of the companies. In small companies, the highest-level purchasing executive reports to the highest-level executive or one level below in 90 percent of the companies. Our ideal scenario is one in which global supply chain management, with a particular focus on logistics and purchasing, has a seat at the corporate strategy table at all times. From a global supplier (internal) network perspective, a typical international purchasing office in a multinational corporation has the responsibility for (1) identifying supplier opportunities in the global marketplace, (2) selecting global suppliers for partnerships, and (3) coordinating input from buyers, deciders, gatekeepers, influencers, and users that are involved in specific global sourcing situations. In other words, this is where centralized purchasing resides and where integration and coordination across strategic business units and functional departmental units are front and center.

Another form of global supplier network occurs when a multinational corporation forms a so-called global supplier association. In this arrangement, As such, a global supplier association refers to a multinational corporation brings together its key global suppliers as a formal group (a global supplier association) on a regular basis (for example, "annual global supplier conferences") in order to achieve strategic and tactical alignment. Toyota was the first firm to form a supplier association in 1939; today, Toyota's supplier association has more than 200 members. Supplier associations are linked to a variety of benefits that facilitate global supplier development. This includes reducing costs, sharing best practices, training and development, and strengthening the trust and mutual benefit of the relationship among members.

Global supplier networks, as defined here, are supplier networks that are independent of any one firm (which is not the case with global supplier associations). In essence, these global supplier networks provide a link between many global suppliers and many global buyers, sometimes with a broad product assortment and sometimes very industry- and/or very product-specific. For example, Ariba was started in 1996 by Bobby Lent, Boris Putanec, Paul Touw, Rob Desantis, Ed Kinsey, Paul Hegarty, and Keith Krach based on the idea of using the Internet to help companies facilitate and improve the purchasing process. The Ariba Network has more than 700,000 buyers and sellers doing business in more than 140 countries without being tied to any one firm.

CRITICAL SUCCESS FACTORS FOR PURCHASING IN GLOBAL SUPPLY CHAINS

Based on research conducted by the world-leading supply chain management faculty at Michigan State University—through the Global Procurement and Supply Chain Benchmarking Initiative (a global, multiindustry benchmarking effort involving more than 200 companies worldwide)—the following eight factors have been identified as being critical to success for purchasing in global supply chains.

1. *Organizational support structure.* Does your firm have an organizational support structure for global purchasing in place, such as cross-functional/cross-locational teams, internal buy-in and cross-functional support, a globalization manager, staff to oversee the process, and international and global purchasing offices?

2. *Executive commitment.* Does your firm have executive commitment to global purchasing, including support for the development of a rigorous and well-defined process, providing budget and staff availability, developing performance measures that are reported to executives, promoting gains achieved throughout the organization, and participating on an executive steering committee to guide the process?

3. *Organizational resource availability.* Does your firm have resources available for global purchasing in four core areas: personnel with the required knowledge, skills, and abilities; systems with the required information and data; time for personnel to develop global strategies; and overall budget support?

4. *Information systems and technology.* Does your firm have information systems and technology in place to support global purchasing, including common coding for commodities and suppliers, information on historical usage and pricing, visibility concerning performance scorecards, and worldwide data availability?

5. *Well-defined global sourcing process.* Does your firm have a rigorous and well-defined approach to and process for global purchasing (a key differentiator between effective and highly effective efforts)?

6. *Availability of global suppliers.* Does your firm have access to global suppliers in support of global purchasing? In this case, a global supplier is not one that has locations in every part of the world. Rather, a global supplier is one that can supply the buying firm's worldwide requirements competitively.

7. *Performance measurement systems.* Does your firm measure performance in support of global purchasing, including recognizing, measuring, and rewarding the contributions of teams and individuals as well as measuring and reporting the performance gains achieved through global purchasing agreements?

8. *Communication and coordination mechanisms.* Does your firm have appropriate communication and coordination mechanisms in place to support global purchasing, including regular review meetings, postmortem review meetings, center-led strategy development efforts, web pages and chat rooms, co-location of personnel, and other e-mail, phone, and videoconferencing capabilities?

If a firm invests in these eight areas, the overall global purchasing effort is more likely to be successful. With these critical success factors in mind, we can now also provide strategic guidelines for purchasing in global supply chains.

GUIDELINES FOR PURCHASING IN GLOBAL SUPPLY CHAINS

Purchasing is one of the four critical functions that should be integrated at the strategic and tactical levels in global supply chains and as part of the global firm's corporate strategy. As in the earlier discussion of logistics, some purchasing issues are major items that you can see, and others are intricate details of doing global business that are not readily obvious or understood. Clearly, there are numerous issues related to purchasing in global supply chains that need to be considered. In assessing global purchasing, we suggest these guidelines as a starting point, in parallel to the success factors outlined previously:

- Develop mechanisms for creating understanding and alignment between the firm's purchasing professionals and the C-suite executives. This is an incredibly important task for any firm, but for a multinational corporation that does not have a supply chain executive on its corporate leadership team, creating and nurturing this alignment between purchasing professionals and C-suite executives is among the most significant internal aspects of purchasing's role in corporate strategy. It also enhances the degree of globalness that can ultimately be achieved through the goals that are set.
- In the case of purchasing, plan for and execute strategic initiatives to become at least as global as the average industry globalization drivers allow for and as the expectations for

global purchasing measures in the next ten years are. If you simply maintain your current level of globalness in purchasing, you will be losing a competitive edge in the next decade. This increased globalness in purchasing can be very effectively structured by adopting a strategy rooted in the issues discussed in the section, "From Domestic to International to Global Purchasing."

- Overall, 35 percent of the purchasing activities for multinational corporations involve internal purchasing of some kind (from domestic or global sources), while 65 percent of the purchasing activities involve external purchasing (domestic or global). Where does your firm fall in terms of this breakdown? If you are off significantly from the 35/65 split, why is this, and what does it mean for your competitive edge? Consider moving toward a better alignment with the 35/65 benchmark or make sure that you can justify the deviation strategically and explain why it is beneficial to your firm.

- Most likely, your firm is both a global customer and a global supplier. In the global supply chains in which you operate, do you have different expectations as a customer and as a supplier? Why or why not? This is not to say that you should, but you need to make sure that you are strategic, aligned, and consistent across the inbound and outbound purchasing actions that you engage in. This entails global channels, order fulfillment, and delivery options. It can also include constantly evaluating and considering options to join global supplier networks—both from the customer and from the supplier sides.

- What type of scorecard do you use for global supplier selection? Is it a universal scorecard that is applicable to all strategic business units, functional units, and any other purchasing scenarios in the firm, so that it covers all raw materials, component parts, and finished goods that you purchase? If not, why not? Can a standardized scorecard for global supplier selection be implemented? If so, you should attempt to do so. However, it is likely that global supplier evaluation and selection differ somewhat, depending on the purchase category. If so, strive for commonality across purchasing categories in some aspects of the scorecard (and preferably also with common items assessed by major competitors in the industry).

CHAPTER 6

Operations in Global Supply Chains

Operations integrates global supply chains.

GLOBAL OPERATIONS STRATEGY

The initial heading in this chapter, global operations strategy, is something of a conundrum in that operations is typically viewed as a group of activities, behaviors, or generally things that we do. Strategy, on the other hand, is a plan, a scheme, or even a policy-oriented undertaking. The former is normally focused on the short term, and the latter is characteristically long-term in orientation. So, what do we get when we combine "operations" and "strategy"? Then, of course, we add "global" to the phrase and do it in the context of supply chain management. Tracing "operations" may help you understand the logic that we are adopting in this book.

Operations research (or operational research in British usage) is a functional professional discipline that involves the application of advanced analytical methods to making decisions in a variety of contexts, such as supply chains. It is heavily rooted in the field of mathematics and connects to management science and decision sciences as two interdisciplinary fields that span business, engineering, statistics, and mathematics, to mention a few areas. The idea is to develop and arrive at optimal or at least near-optimal solutions to problems that are complex and involve decision making. Practically speaking, this means that operations research within a global supply chain context is concerned with determining the maximum or minimum of some real-world supply chain objective in the global marketplace. As an example, Massachusetts Institute of Technology's (MIT's) supply chain management (SCM) program, which started in 1998, is heavily grounded in principles of operations research (MIT's SCM program is currently number one in graduate education).

Operations management is also a functional professional field. It is concerned with management of the direct physical and/or technical functions of a firm, particularly those that relate to designing, developing, producing, and manufacturing products and/or services. This also includes redesigning business operations involved in the production of products and/or services. One way to understand the role of operations management is to compare it with engineering. Engineering blends art with applied science, and so does operations management. In some respects, operations management can be viewed as blending strategic and tactical issues from the field of management with art and science. Michigan State University's (MSU's) supply chain management program, which started more than half a century ago, incorporates a heavy operations management foundation along with an equal dosage of logistics and purchasing (MSU's SCM program is number one in undergraduate education).

We can all agree that operations as a form of practice has been around for centuries. One early example of operations comes from James Watt, a Scottish inventor and mechanical engineer. In 1763, he improved on the Newcomen steam engine, which had been in use for some 50 years, by causing the steam to condense in a chamber separated from the piston. This meant that very little heat was absorbed into the cylinder, and therefore more heat could be used by the steam engine to perform actual work. Basically, James Watt used operations principles to improve on an existing steam engine. Watt formed a successful partnership with Matthew Boulton that resulted in these types of "modern" steam engines being installed in commercial production facilities to serve as an integral component of that era's supply chains.

For our purposes, global operations management is the part of global supply chain management that refers to the systematic design, direction, and control of domestic and global processes that transform various inputs into services and products for internal and external global customers (see Figure 6.1).[1] A global operations strategy is the means by which operations implements the multinational firm's corporate strategy and facilitates the firm's being market driven. It involves the worldwide management of make-or-buy

FIGURE 6.1 A Focus on Global Operations

decisions in global supply chains, global production and manufacturing, competitive priorities in such supply chains, total cost analyses in global supply chains, process-based quality standards, guidelines within the supply chain operations reference model, and decisions on the usage of operational (logistics) providers within the realm of global operations across the supply chain.

Strategically, within the integrated global supply chain of multinational corporations, it is predicted that operations as a function will become 12 percent more globalized in the next five years (2013 to 2018) and 26 percent more globalized in the next ten years (by 2023). Figure 6.2 illustrates these increases. In 2013, operations scored 60 out of 100 points in terms of being globalized (where 100 is fully globalized and zero is purely domestic). A score of 60 places operations in a tie for last with market channels, behind purchasing at the top and logistics after that, in terms of the degree of globalness permeating that function of the supply chain. Operations is found to be the third most important of the four functions (logistics, purchasing, operations, and market channels), scoring a 92 out of a possible 100 points on the degree of importance in contributing to overall global supply chain management for the multinational corporation (MNC). Market channels is at the top with 96, followed by logistics with

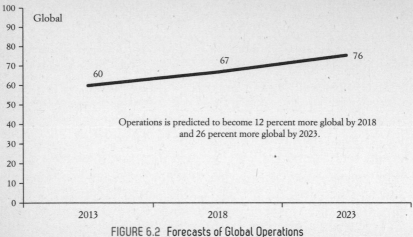

FIGURE 6.2 Forecasts of Global Operations

94, then operations with 92, and purchasing with 89. Operations is expected to increase slightly in importance, from 92 to 93, over the next five years. Figure 6.3 illustrates the changes in operations in the 2013 to 2018 time period.

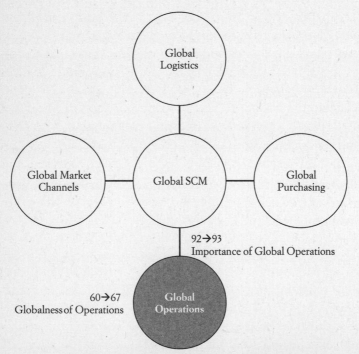

FIGURE 6.3 Globalization of Operations, 2013 to 2018

MAKE-OR-BUY DECISIONS IN GLOBAL SUPPLY CHAINS ___

The make-or-buy decision for a global firm is the strategic decision concerning whether to produce an item in-house ("make") or purchase it from an outside supplier ("buy"). Make-or-buy decisions are made at both the strategic and operational levels, with the strategic level being focused on the long term and the operational level being more focused on the short term. In some ways, the make-or-buy decision is also the starting point for operations' influence on global supply chains. That is, someone in the chain—within one firm—has to take the lead in deciding whether the global firm should make the product in-house or buy it from an external supplier. If the decision is to make it in-house, there are certain implications for that firm's global supply chains (for example, where to purchase raw materials and component parts). If the decision is to buy the product, that decision also has certain implications (for example, quality control and competitive priorities management).

A number of things are involved in determining which decision is the correct one for a particular global firm and in a particular situation. At a broad level, issues of product success, specialized knowledge, and strategic fit can lead to the make (produce) decision. For example, if the item or part is critical to the success of the product, including perceptions among primary stakeholders, such a scenario skews the decision in favor of make. Another reason for a make decision is that the item or part requires specialized design or production skills, and/or that equipment and reliable alternatives are very scarce. Strategic fit is also important. If the item or part strategically fits within the firm's current and/or planned core competencies, then it should be a make decision for the global firm.

However, these are strategic decisions at a general level. In reality, the make-or-buy decision is often based largely on two critical factors: cost and production capacity. Cost issues include such things as acquiring raw materials, component parts, and any other inputs into the process, along with the costs of finishing the product. The production capacity is really presented as an opportunity cost. That is, does the firm have the capacity to produce the product at a cost that is at least no higher than the cost of buying it from an external supplier? And, if the product is made in-house, what opportunity cost would be incurred as a result (for example, what product or item was the firm unable to produce because of limited production capacity)? Unfortunately, many, and perhaps most, global companies think that cost and production capacity are the only factors playing into the make-or-buy decision. This is simply not true!

Cost and production capacity are just the two main drivers behind make-or-buy choices made by global companies when they engage in global supply chains. The decision of whether to buy or make a product is a much more complex and research-intensive process than the typical global firm may expect, though. For example, how many times have we heard, "Let's move our production to China because we can get the same quality for a dime-on-the-dollar cost, and that will free up production capacity that we can use to focus on other products"? Of course, dime-on-the-dollar cost is not relevant because we have to take into account the costs of quality control measures that have to be instituted, raw materials that have to be purchased far away from home, foreign entry requirements, multiple-party contracts, management responsibilities for the outsourced production operations, and so on. Ultimately, we are unlikely to end up with a dime-on-the-dollar cost, but where do we end up and how do we get there? In other words, what are the core elements that we should be evaluating when we are determining whether the correct decision is to make or to buy?

To facilitate the make-or-buy decision, we have captured the dynamics of this choice in two figures that center on either operationally favoring a make decision or operationally favoring a buy decision. As we can see, the core elements in both cases are cost and production capacity. However, the other elements differ for each of the decisions and influence the choice differently. This means that we need to evaluate each decision separately, not jointly. In fact, through this process, we may end up thinking that both a make and a buy decision would be acceptable and strategically logical for our firm. Keep in mind that this simply means that we have a choice; if both choices seem positive for your firm, choose the one that is the best strategic fit with the least opportunity cost structure.

The elements that favor a make decision—beyond the core elements of cost and production capacity—include quality control, proprietary technology, having control, excess capacity, limited suppliers, assurance of continual supply, and industry drivers (see Figure 6.4). So, the starting point is lower (or at least no greater) cost than

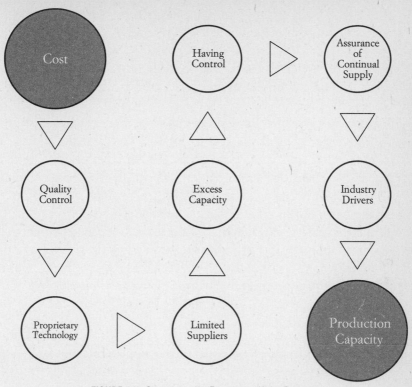

FIGURE 6.4 Operationally Favoring a Make Decision

what we can expect when we outsource the production to an external party in another country (or another external party in general). The limitation is that we must have excess production capacity or capacity that is best used by our firm for making the product in-house.

After the cost and production capacity decisions have been explored and made (really, after the cost and production hurdles have been overcome), the next set of decisions follows logically from the path in Figure 6.4. For example, if quality control is important to the global firm, cannot be relied on fully if the part is outsourced, and is at the center of the strategic core that customers expect from the firm, then the quality control issue favors a make decision. If there is proprietary technology involved in making the product that cannot or should not be shared with outsourcing parties, then the decision has to be make.

The idea that limited suppliers may influence the make-or-buy choice in the direction of the make selection is important as well.

Specifically, it could be that some suppliers do not want to work with certain companies in certain parts of the world. It could also be that a supplier cannot, because of various restrictions on production or location or because of international barriers, follow the production of your firm's products to wherever you see fit to locate your production lines.

Naturally, if the firm has excess capacity that otherwise would not be productively used, the decision should favor a make choice to allow that excess capacity to be used for the benefit of the firm in the global marketplace. Some companies also simply want to have control over certain elements of their production processes. This affects the make-or-buy decision in favor of the make choice.

A make decision is also favored if there is any chance that supply cannot be guaranteed if the firm moves its production overseas. And, finally, the industry globalization drivers may dictate that a make decision should be the choice for various trust and commitment reasons involving your industry and the marketplace that you engage with in order to find success.

Now, some of these elements that favor make can probably influence a buy decision as well. Naturally, if one of the make elements is not in favor of the make decision (for example, if there is no excess capacity), this would suggest that the global firm should think more seriously about a buy decision. However, again, the buy decision also involves a number of other elements that are not necessarily factors in the make decision (see Figure 6.5). As with the make decision, after the cost and production capacity decisions have been considered and made, the next set of decisions for the buy choice follow logically from the path in Figure 6.5. For example, if the global firm has minimal restrictions on which firms or companies it can source raw materials and component parts from, then a buy decision is more likely, since outsourcing production also increases the likelihood that other and/or more suppliers in those parts of the world will be used.

Another good reason to choose a buy scenario is if the firm lacks the needed expertise to make a product or component part, and the supplier or outsourced production choice has that expertise. Supplier competencies can affect the decision in favor of a buy choice as well, especially if those competencies reside closer to the production facility that you buy from than the ones that will be available if you make the product. Small volumes would also be a reason favoring a buy

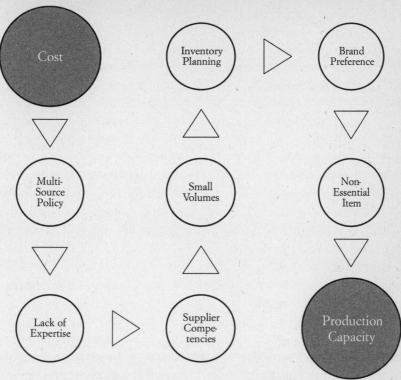

FIGURE 6.5 Operationally Favoring a Buy Decision

decision; cost efficiencies can seldom be achieved when only small volumes are produced.

Inventory planning is also of critical importance. Even if your firm can make the product equally well in terms of quality and expectations set, perhaps a better choice is to buy simply in order to strategically manage inventory (which is a cost center in the global supply chain). In certain cases, even brand preference is a reason to go with a buy decision; for example, many computer users favor Intel microchips in their computers, so many of the large computer manufacturers opt to buy chips from Intel instead of making them in-house for that reason (this was more true in the 1990s and 2000s than it is now, but it is still a factor). And, of course, if the item to be made is a so-called nonessential item that has little effect on the firm's core competencies and what the customers expect in terms of uniqueness, this is a factor in favor of a buy decision.

GLOBAL PRODUCTION AND MANUFACTURING _____

The growth of global production in parent companies with foreign affiliates has been tremendous in the last two decades, outdoing the home country production by more than tenfold. What this means is that since 1990, multinational corporations have opted to set up shop and production facilities outside their domestic home country ten times for every one time they have opted to create such production facilities at home. We predict that this trend will continue and perhaps even increase in the next decade. Are you ready to make the decision to open up a new production facility outside your home base, and if so, where? How will you go about it? Perhaps thinking about it in terms of the six roles we see for foreign factories will help you in making the appropriate and correct decision. Based on work by Kasra Ferdows, the strategic roles for foreign factories are offshore factory, source factory, server factory, contributor factory, outpost factory, and lead factory.[2]

An offshore factory is one that is developed and set up mainly for producing component parts or finished goods at a lower cost than producing them at home or in any other market (when a total cost analysis involving all supply chain activities has been conducted). Ferdows suggests that at an offshore factory, investments in technology and managerial resources should ideally be kept to a minimum to achieve greater cost efficiencies. Basically, the best offshore factory should involve minimal everything—from engineering to development to engaging with suppliers to negotiating prices to any form of strategic decisions being made at that facility. In reality, contrary to Ferdows, we expect at least some strategic decisions to include input from the offshore factory personnel.

A source factory's primary purpose is also to drive down costs in the global supply chain. The main difference between a source factory and an offshore factory is the strategic role of the factory, which is more significant for a source factory than for an offshore factory. Managers of a source factory have more of a say in certain decisions, such as purchasing raw materials and component parts used in the production at the source factory. They also have strategic input into production planning, process changes, logistics issues, product customization, and implementation of newer designs when needed. Centrally, a source factory is at the top of the standards in the global supply chain, and these factories are used and treated just like any factory in the global firm's home country. This also means that source factories should be located where production costs are low, where infrastructure is well developed (see Chapter 3), and where it is relatively easy to find a knowledgeable and skilled workforce to make the products.

A server factory is linked into the global supply chain for a global firm to supply specific country or regional markets around the globe. This type of factory—often with the same standards as the top factories in the global firm's system—is set up to overcome intangible and tangible barriers in the global marketplace. For example, a server factory may be intended to overcome tariff barriers, reduce taxes, and reinvest money made in the region. Another obvious reason for a server factory is to reduce or eliminate costly global supply chain operations that would be needed if the factory were located much farther away from the end customers. Managers at a server factory typically have more authority to make minor customizations to please their customers, but they still do not have much more input than managers in an offshore factory relative to the home country factories of the same global firm.

A contributor factory also serves a specific country or world region. The main difference between a contributor factory and a server factory is that a contributor factory has responsibilities for product and process engineering and development. This type of factory also has much more of a choice in terms of which suppliers to use for raw materials and component parts. In fact, a contributor factory often competes with the global firm's home factories for testing new ideas and products. A contributor factory has its own infrastructure when it comes to development, engineering, and production. This means that a contributor factory is very much stand-alone in terms of what it can do and how it contributes to the global firm's supply chain efforts.

An outpost factory can be viewed as an intelligence-gathering unit. This means that an outpost factory is often placed near a competitor's headquarters or main operations, near the most demanding customers, or near key suppliers of unique and critically important parts. An outpost factory also has a function to fill in production; it often operates as a server and/or offshore factory as well. The outpost factory can be very much connected to the idea of selecting countries for operations based on the countries' strategic importance rather than on the production logic of a location.[3] Maintaining and potentially even enhancing the position of the global firm in strategic countries is sometimes viewed as a practical factor. For example, the fact that Nokia has its headquarters in Finland may result in another mobile phone manufacturer locating some operations in Finland, even though the country market is rather small (about 5.5 million people).

A lead factory is intended to create new processes, products, and technologies that can be used throughout the global firm in all parts of the world. This is where cutting-edge production should take place, or at least be tested for implementation in other parts of the firm's production network. Given the lead factory's prominent role in setting a high bar for how the global firm wants to provide products to customers, we also expect that it will be located in an area where highly skilled employees can be found (or where they want to locate). A lead factory scenario also implies that managers and employees at the site have a direct connection to and say in which suppliers to use, what designs to implement, and other issues that are of critical importance to the core competencies of the global firm.

COMPETITIVE PRIORITIES IN GLOBAL SUPPLY CHAINS

The phrase "competitive priorities," as we will use it, originated in the field of operations management. The idea was that trade-offs in operations strategy were an important element of the firm's overall strategy and, more important, a way for operations to contribute to the competitive edge of the global firm.[4] At the outset, we want to say that we disagree with the concept that a firm needs to select one priority. In essence, the logic behind this concept is that a firm should select one competitive priority and base its edge on implementing that priority well—better than the competition. This means that companies should seldom, if ever, try to compete on multiple competitive priorities. Doing so would mean taking on too much, with the risk of not performing well on any of the priorities. Certainly there are many examples across strategy fields in general that support the idea of selecting one or a few focus areas and then implementing them really well compared with the competition.

For example, Michael Porter describes three main or generic strategies that businesses use to initially achieve and then maintain competitive advantages in the global marketplace: cost leadership, differentiation, and focus strategy.[5] A cost leadership strategy simply refers to the idea that producing high volumes of standardized products will also allow a firm to take advantage of economies of scale and experience curve effects. The emphasis in the differentiation strategy is on being superior in terms of quality, delivery, or flexibility. The focus strategy centers on the firm's targeting a few market segments by tailoring its offerings to these segments in unique ways. In essence, the competitive priorities in operations management are very much connected to Porter's cost leadership and differentiation strategies but are generally implemented at the operations management level of the global supply chain.

In today's global marketplace, though, we have moved beyond the need for operations in global supply chains to strategically focus on only one competitive priority (for that matter, this is true for the corporate strategy level as well, as in the case of Porter's work). Instead, we fully expect—as customers—that global companies are global for a reason; they solve customers' problems wherever the customers are, regardless of where the global firm has its headquarters. This challenges operations within global supply chains to be "all things to all people." Our benchmarking and research over a couple of decades provide foundational platforms for what to focus on in establishing world-class supply chains as well as supply chains that are more narrowly focused on one of the competitive priorities.

World-class supply chains emphasize operational issues that are directed toward three distinct areas (see Figure 6.6). First, world-class supply chains are incredibly good at storing knowledge that can be used for future global supply chain operations. They have developed appropriate storage bins—intangible (people) or tangible (such as electronic networks)—that can be readily accessed to infuse knowledge into the global supply chain. Second, world-class supply chains are very good at applying knowledge to solve specific global supply chain operations issues. Not only do they have the stored organizational memory, but they are also effective at using their knowledge in an appropriate way and at the appropriate time. Third, world-class supply chains are able to take actions that are based on global supply chain knowledge much more readily, effectively, and efficiently than other supply chains.

While we believe that global supply chains within global companies no longer have to select just one competitive priority as their focus, some chains should be targeted in terms of their scope and

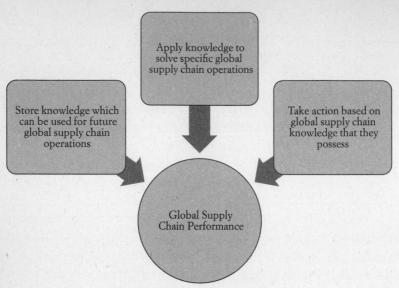

FIGURE 6.6 World–Class Supply Chains

what they try to achieve worldwide. Niche markets, targeted strategies, and a focused approach will work at some times and in some
industries or geographic locations. If the goal is to have a "first-mover
advantage," as we call it in global markets, then the competitive priority of speed has to take precedence, at least for some time, in the
introduction of a product into a new marketplace.

If the focus is on quality first and everything else second (for
example, for the approximately 100 restaurants in the world classified as three-star Michelin-ranked restaurants), then quality has to
come first, has to be the focus, and cannot be anything but the best.
By the same token, chains focusing on cost and flexibility stress attributes associated with each of those focus areas. What is important to
note, however, is that whether the focus is on speed, quality, cost, or
flexibility, each of those types of chain also exemplifies the three main
characteristics of world-class supply chains that we described earlier.

In addition to the world-class attributes of organizational memory,
knowledge use, and ability to take action, speed-focused global supply chains also focus on (1) delivering products in the shortest cycle
time, (2) being very customer-oriented, and (3) developing innovative processes. The additional characteristics of quality-focused
chains include (1) emphasis on delivering high-quality products, (2)
dependence on having high knowledge quality, and (3) preferences

for developing innovative products. Cost-focused chains focus on (1) delivering cost-efficient products, (2) accessing knowledge quickly, and (3) preferring to imitate competitors' successful practices. And flexibility-focused chains have a preference for (1) focusing on delivering highly flexible products, (2) filtering knowledge effectively, and (3) avoiding risks in products and processes.

TOTAL COST ANALYSIS IN GLOBAL SUPPLY CHAINS

Total supply chain costs include all costs across all companies in the global supply chain. This includes all costs associated with, for example, all first-tier suppliers, all second-tier suppliers, all third-tier suppliers, the producer, the agents and/or facilitators in the chain, the wholesaler, and the retailer (and many other potential actors in the supply chain). Total cost analysis is one of the most important aspects of the global supply chain.

If you are to run an effective and efficient global supply chain, such costs should not be measured as the sum of the costs for each individual link and entity. Instead, a total cost analysis and its outcome are measured by determining the lowest total cost when all operations in the global supply chain are included. Focusing on single individual companies may lead to suboptimization and even "gaming," where one firm tries to shift costs to another firm. The global supply chain has a number of cost centers that need to be analyzed not individually, but collectively (see Figure 6.7). Decisions then need to be made by key actors or even by all actors in the chain together to maximize the overall cost-efficiency of the global supply chain.

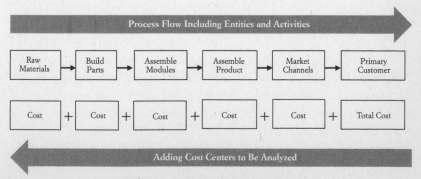

FIGURE 6.7 Total Costs in Supply Chains

Thus, a total cost perspective means that the focus is on reducing the total cost of the global supply chain. From that perspective, it is very possible that one firm may experience increased costs while other companies in the chain experience lowered costs. The idea is to lower the costs in the entire global supply chain, resulting in cost measures for the chain as a whole being improved. On the fairness principle, if some companies at some nodes in the chain agree to increase their costs in order to improve the total cost of the chain, then companies whose costs are lowered should share the benefits with those companies that had increased costs. Importantly, global companies participating in world-class supply chains are willing to share the benefits and risks associated with the effective and efficient operations and integration of the chain. This takes trust, commitment, and high-level management of the global supply chain.

A total cost analysis of the global supply chain can be done effectively using a five-step process. Robert Handfield and Ernest Nichols defined these five steps, which we have adapted: (1) identify total cost items to analyze, (2) map nodes, activities, and resources, (3) identify the scope of and costs in the model, (4) identify performance standards, and (5) document the model and use it.[6] The first step, identifying total cost items to analyze, is obviously a critical starting point for this exercise, as it involves all aspects of the global supply chain. Including all companies, products, and component parts across the chain in a total cost analysis is unrealistic. First, start with the "Pareto principle," also called the 80/20 rule: 20 percent of the products or parts are responsible for 80 percent of the total cost. Focus initially on those items and the companies involved. Second, zero in on "problem items"—products or parts that are strategically needed for each node. Third, focus on multiple items from or to the same supplier or customer and analyze them as a group.

The second step of the total cost analysis process is to map the nodes, activities, and resources in the global supply chain. Companies (nodes) in the global supply chain, the activities between them, and the resources used in each paired relationship depend on each other. A total cost analysis involves knowing and assessing each step of the order fulfillment process (for example, order processing, shipping, inspection, and inventory used). Knowing and assessing refers to the resources used for normal activity plus the resources used for secondary activity when or if the process fails.

The third step of the total cost analysis process is to identify the scope of and costs in the model. This is the stage of the total cost analysis at which decisions are made concerning the scope and the cost elements to be included. Again, not all items and all costs are relevant for a total cost analysis in global supply chains. The scope of the total cost analysis and its operations (nodes, activities, and resources) should not be too broad or too narrow. The costs included should be relevant, should occur in the forecasted future, and should be controllable.

The fourth step of the total cost analysis process, identifying performance standards that can span the full global supply chain, requires the establishment of a structured measurement system that is rigorous, is relatively easy to prepare, and can be operated without too much cost. Given that global supply chains are inherently heterogeneous in terms of the different nodes, activities, and resources used, the performance system should follow some standardized measurement and recording procedures. This takes trust, commitment, and ongoing relationship building among participants in the global supply chain.

The fifth step of the total cost analysis is to document the model and use it. The objective of such an analysis is to allow for the comparison of options at each critical stage of the global supply chain. A well-performing total cost analysis also incorporates real options theory in that the net present value of exercising an "option" in the chain can be evaluated against other options. And, finally, total costs take into account all product, service, and informational costs for each step of the supply chain in a holistic way, not in an additive way.

PROCESS-BASED QUALITY STANDARDS _____

In this section, we will tackle and highlight two quality systems: Six Sigma and ISO 9000. However, first, it is important to discuss some general issues related to quality as it pertains to operations in the context of global supply chains. Almost every field of business and engineering (and, frankly, almost any field at all) has quality as a staple construct that is considered daily by all working professionals. Obviously, this does not mean that organizations or global supply chains deliver on quality just because they are thinking about it in their daily work lives, but it does mean that quality is one of those issues that we cannot escape and that we should plan for strategically throughout the global supply chain. Thus, a good starting point is to look at a basic framework for quality within an operations context.

At the general level, quality should be divided into intangible and tangible quality issues, or, as Lee Krajewski, Larry Ritzman, and Manoj Malhotra suggest, intangible costs of quality and tangible costs of quality.[7] We will assume for now that the reader has an idea of the tangible issues related to quality. More important, we will also assume that these tangible quality issues are measured, assessed, and known for the firm's operations issues. We know that this may not be a fair assumption in all cases, but we are more interested in putting the intangible issues related to quality into focus.

Based on Krajewski, Ritzman, and Malhotra's work, we have constructed a basic model in Figure 6.8. The logic of the model is that the intangible plus tangible costs of quality have an additive effect on the firm's sales in the global marketplace. Intangible costs of quality include prevention costs, appraisal costs, internal failure costs, and external failure costs.[8] Prevention costs are investments in processes for preventing defects before they happen. Appraisal costs are investments in procedures for assessing the performance levels of a firm's processes. Internal failure costs are expenses incurred as a result of

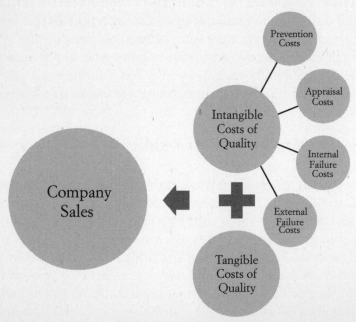

FIGURE 6.8 Costs of Quality

defects that are discovered during the production process. External failure costs are expenses incurred as a result of defects that are discovered after the customer receives the product. With these basic quality and cost issues in mind, let's move to Six Sigma first and then to ISO 9000 as examples of quality initiatives that have received a lot of positive feedback and have had a significant influence on global supply chains and across many global companies.

Six Sigma was developed at Motorola in 1986 by Bill Smith, with the help of Mikel Harry, then launched by Bob Galvin at Motorola in 1987 under the name "The Six Sigma Quality Program." Six Sigma became well known when Jack Welch made it a critically important aspect of his business strategy at General Electric in 1995; Welch implemented the concept and backed it with a strong salary incentive system (with 40 percent coming from Six Sigma results). The idea of Six Sigma is that if a process, such as a global supply chain, has six standard deviations between the process mean and the nearest specification limit, then practically no items will fail to meet specifications (the yield is 99.99966 percent).

The Six Sigma process includes five defined steps: define, measure, analyze, improve, and control. Putting these steps in the context of global supply chains, we can provide an effective framework for global supply chain quality initiatives. In the first step, the idea is to define the features of the global supply chain's output that are critical to customer satisfaction and identify gaps between these features and the supply chain's capabilities. The second step entails measuring the nature of the gap between the output desired and the global supply chain's capabilities. The third step is to analyze the gaps in the global supply chain and establish procedures to ensure that the desired outcome is routinely achieved. The fourth step highlights the idea that improvement is a key feature of the Six Sigma process. Here, we focus on improving the global supply chain processes by modifying and/or redesigning existing processes and methods to meet the desired performance outcomes. The fifth step in the Six Sigma process is to control and monitor the global supply chain to make sure that the desired levels of performance are achieved.

The International Organization for Standardization (ISO) developed ISO 9000 in 1987 as a quality management system. The top 10 nations with companies that have ISO 9001 certification (ISO 9001 includes the requirements for ISO 9000) are China, Italy, Japan, Spain, Russia, Germany, the United Kingdom, India, the United

States, and Korea. The overall family of ISO 9000 documentation includes ISO 9001:2008, which sets out the requirements for a quality management system; ISO 9000:2005, which covers the basic concepts and language; ISO 9004:2009, which focuses on how to make a quality management system more efficient and effective; and ISO 19011:2011, which sets out guidance on internal and external audits of quality management systems. There are eight principles that are key components of the ISO 9000 system: customer focus, leadership, involvement of people, a process approach, a system approach to management, continual improvement, a factual approach to decision making, and mutually beneficial supplier relationships.

At the basic level, starting with the first principle, customer focus, we know that organizations depend on their customers and therefore should understand current and future customer needs, meet customer requirements, and strive to exceed customer expectations. Second, leaders need to establish a unity of purpose and direction for the organization. They should create and maintain an internal environment in which people can become fully involved in achieving the organization's objectives. Third, people at all levels are the essence of an organization, and their full involvement enables their abilities to be used for the organization's benefit. Fourth, a desired result is achieved more efficiently when activities and related resources are managed as a process. Fifth, identifying, understanding, and managing interrelated processes as a system contributes to the organization's effectiveness and efficiency in achieving its objectives. Sixth, continual improvement of the organization's overall performance should be a permanent objective of the organization. Seventh, effective decisions are based on the analysis of data and information. And eighth, an organization and its suppliers are interdependent, and a mutually beneficial relationship enhances the ability of both to create value.

SUPPLY CHAIN OPERATIONS REFERENCE MODEL

The Supply Chain Council (SCC, supply-chain.org) is a global non-profit organization whose framework, improvement methodology, and benchmarking tools help member organizations improve their supply chain performance. The SCC developed and maintains a widely accepted framework for evaluating and comparing supply chain activities and their performance, the Supply Chain Operations Reference (SCOR) model. The SCOR model links performance metrics, processes, best practices, and people into a unified structure. This framework supports communication among supply chain partners and enhances the effectiveness of supply chain management, technology, and related supply chain improvement activities.

SCOR focuses on solving five critical global supply chain challenges. First, the SCOR model is intended to deliver a high degree of customer service throughout the supply chain, based on the assumption that effective supply chains deliver the right product in the right quantity and in the right condition with the right documentation to the right place at the right time at the right price. Second, the SCOR model sets out to control costs for the various nodes, activities, and resources in the supply chain. Third, the SCOR model provides for rigorous planning and risk management throughout the supply chain that involves all supply chain partners. Fourth, the SCOR model provides a framework for engaging in supplier and partner relationship management through encouraging trust and commitment. Fifth, the SCOR model offers a mechanism by which talent for the supply chain can be acquired, trained, and developed.

Overall, analysis in the SCOR model involves three levels. Level 1 refers to processes that describe the scope and configuration of a supply chain. Level 2 refers to processes that differentiate the strategies of the Level 1 processes. Level 3 refers to processes that are used to describe the steps performed to execute Level 2 processes. Most global companies that use SCOR focus a lot of attention on the first-level management processes and give them critical attention (perhaps more than they give the issues in Level 2 and Level 3). Plan, source, make, deliver, and return are the five process steps that are highlighted in Level 1 (see Figure 6.9). Each of these processes is rigorously detailed by the Supply Chain Council. We are not trying to "sell" or advocate for the SCOR model; rather, we include it as a

FIGURE 6.9 The First-Level Management Processes of SCOR Are Critical

good alternative for global supply chain operations. In that context, we will highlight each process and trust that interested parties will contact the SCC for more information.

Based on the SCC descriptions, the five processes can be defined as follows. The plan processes describe the planning activities associated with operating a supply chain (for example, determining customer requirements, collecting information on resources, and balancing requirements). The source processes describe the scheduling and receipt of products, component parts, and services. The make processes describe the activities associated with the conversion of materials or the creation of the content for services. The deliver processes describe the activities associated with the creation, maintenance, and fulfillment of customer orders. The return processes describe the activities associated with the reverse flow of goods back from the customer.

The SCOR model, by design, incorporates a heavy dose of performance measurement. The performance attributes are critically important for better understanding global supply chains, making improvements, and taking any necessary corrective actions before it is too late. Reliability, responsiveness, agility, costs, and assets are all among the performance attributes assessed within the SCOR model. The reliability attribute addresses the ability to perform tasks as expected (for example, on time, in the right quantity, and at the right quality). The responsiveness attribute describes the speed at which tasks are performed (for example, cycle time). The agility attribute describes the ability to respond to external influences and the ability to change. The costs attribute describes the costs of operating the process (labor costs, material costs, and transportation costs). The assets attribute describes the ability to utilize assets efficiently (for example, inventory reduction and in-sourcing versus outsourcing).

1PL/2PL/3PL/4PL/5PL

A third-party logistics provider (3PL) is a firm that provides outsourced logistics services for part or all of its customers' supply chain management functions. C. H. Robinson (chrobinson.com), founded in 1905, is one of the world's largest (more than $10 billion in 2011) and most well-respected 3PL companies, with 230 offices in North America, Europe, Asia, South America, Australia, and the Middle

East and with more than 53,000 transportation providers worldwide in its network; the firm offers comprehensive reverse logistics services.

Overall, for the typical person, 3PLs are clearly the best known and perhaps the only known logistics providers. However, by some definitions, we have 1PL, 2PL, 3PL, 4PL, and 5PL options available. We could have discussed these PL options in the logistics chapter, given the use of the word *logistics* in the titles. But in reality, the PLs are as much an operations issue as they are a logistics-connected aspect of global supply chains, so we opted to include their definitions and general boundaries in the operations chapter.

A first-party logistics provider is a firm that needs to have a product shipped from point A to point B. A second-party logistics provider is an asset-based carrier that owns or rents its transportation. A third-party logistics provider takes care of one or more activities in part or all of the supply chain. A fourth-party logistics provider assembles resources to offer comprehensive supply chain solutions. Finally, a fifth-party logistics provider aggregates demand from other PLs to utilize resources and collaborate well.

GUIDELINES FOR OPERATIONS IN GLOBAL SUPPLY CHAINS

Operations is one of the four critical functions that should be integrated at the strategic and tactical levels in global supply chains and as part of the firm's corporate strategy. As in the earlier discussions of logistics and purchasing, some operations issues are major items that you can see, and some are intricate details of doing global business that are not readily obvious or understood. Clearly, there are numerous issues related to operations in global supply chains that need to be considered. In assessing global operations, we suggest these guidelines as a starting point:

- The make-or-buy decision regarding the products and component parts that a firm needs if it is to provide value in the global marketplace should be a starting point, and it should be continually assessed and evaluated. Keep in mind that while both the make and the buy decision are rooted in cost and production capacity, the critically important secondary knowledge items and decision points for the make and the buy decisions are not the same. Each decision—make or buy—needs to be evaluated jointly on the basis of cost and production capacity, but also separately on a number of other measures explored in this chapter.

- Global production and manufacturing have increased dramatically in the last couple of decades. Parent companies with foreign affiliates are "mushrooming" in the marketplace. But it's not as simple as deciding to "go to China" (as just one example) and expecting a dime-on-the-dollar cost. You need to evaluate the strategic options for each production choice overseas, including whether you should establish factories that are used for offshoring, sourcing, serving, contributing, outposting, or leading.

- It used to be that global companies and global supply chains had to select one competitive priority to focus on and become the best at in the marketplace (speed, quality, cost, or flexibility). Those days are over—customers expect the best, and the best is usually a good combination of speed, quality, cost, and/or flexibility. Obviously, we do not expect a company to be the best in each area at all times, but over time, we expect a global firm to know its customers and to be able to create a mix (much like the so-called marketing mix) of the appropriate speed, quality, cost, and flexibility elements.

- We are strong advocates of a total cost analysis approach to global supply chain operations. Total supply chain costs include all costs across companies in the global supply chain. This means that to run an effective and efficient global supply chain, such costs should not be measured as the sum of the costs of the individual links and entities. Instead, the outcome of a total cost analysis is measured by resulting in the lowest total cost when all operations in the global supply chain are included. Focusing on single individual companies may lead to suboptimization and even "gaming," where one firm tries to shift costs to another firm.

- All global supply chains need structure. Some of the quality structures and processes that we like are Six Sigma, ISO 9000, and the SCOR model. You should assess the merits of one or more of those initiatives for your firm's global supply chains. Industry standards such as these are hard to beat with in-house and homegrown alternatives. Yes, in-house alternatives may be a better fit, better customized, and better liked in the short term, but they also have a tendency to develop idiosyncrasies that do not reflect the reality of the global marketplace over the long term. This is not to say that in-house and homegrown systems are not effective, but that there is a risk in using those systems, given their ability to be influenced by leaders within the global firm over time.

CHAPTER 7

Market Channels in Global Supply Chains

Market channels connect global supply chains with customers.

GLOBAL MARKET CHANNELS STRATEGY

Developing and manufacturing products and services are not enough to satisfy customers and the other major stakeholders of a multinational corporation. We are speaking chiefly here of customers and the other primary stakeholders of modern firms: shareholders, suppliers, employees, regulators, and the community at large. The products must also be available in adequate quantities, in accessible locations, and at the time the customers want them. This is a true market channels strategy, and if we also have customers in the global marketplace, then we are talking about a global market channels strategy. In essence, market channels close the customer gap in the "last mile" of global supply chains.

This last mile of the global supply chain is important, is unique, and often involves a high degree of variance in terms of what customers want, how they want it, when they want it, and so forth. And, although market channel decisions do not have to be made prior to other global supply chain decisions, they are a powerful influence on the rest of the core functions of the chain (logistics, purchasing, and operations). Market channel decisions are highly visible because of the exposure in the marketplace and their contact with the global supply chain's end customers.

Customers who have bad experiences often seek out alternative solutions, and such solutions affect the logistics, purchasing, and operations in the supply chain. At the same time, when the connection with customers—via the market channels and the last mile of the supply chain—works well, customers experience increased convenience, customization that is to their liking, higher quality, and/or more enriching exchanges with the multinational corporation.[1] These characteristics of market channels mean that channel decisions are critical because they determine the market presence of a product (or service) and customers' access to the product.

Without effective global market channels, even the best ideas, products, and services (the best of anything) will not be successful. A parallel is found in education. For more than half a century, the supply chain management (SCM) program at Michigan State University's Eli Broad College of Business has been top-ranked at the undergraduate, master's, doctoral, and executive training levels (MIT currently holds the top slot at the master's level). One unique aspect of MSU's SCM programs is that they integrate roughly an equal quantity of logistics, purchasing, and operations (and some market channels topics for students who select those as electives).

Its breadth, depth, and integration make MSU's program unique in the global marketplace. But what if MSU did not incorporate all these functions into its SCM program? Or what if MSU did not use its best professors to deliver the courses? What if MSU's SCM scholars did not stay on top of the SCM knowledge in the marketplace in order to integrate that knowledge into their SCM courses? Then the supply chain education would not be the best, no matter how great the structure of the program is. The same goes for market channels and products; the best products that are never delivered to the customer are, in essence, products that might as well not exist. There is utility in the global market channels, and that utility is what drives customer value and, ultimately, satisfaction.

Market channels create four utilities, and each needs to be taken into account when delivering on the last mile of the global supply chain: time, place, possession, and form. The time utility is straightforward: having products and/or services available to customers when they want them. The place utility refers to making products available in locations (such as retail stores or online) where customers wish to buy them. The possession utility is a bit more complex, but broadly, we are talking about customers having access to the product to either use it now or store it for some future use, when needed. The form utility is also complex and important. It refers to global market channel members assembling, preparing, and/or refining the product to suit the customers' needs and wants.

Global market channels involves the part of global supply chain management that includes all activities related to sales, service, and the development of relationships, preferably long-term relationships, with customers (see Figure 7.1).[2] A critical component of market channels is the last mile of the supply chain.[3] A number of terms can be used within the general context of global market channels; consequently, the terms *market channels*, *marketing channels*, *channels of distribution*, and *distribution channels* broadly mean the same thing for the purpose of this book, although there are technical and detailed differences among them. Global channel entities typically include some combination of producer, agent, broker, wholesaler, retailer, and consumer. Market channels include the worldwide management of customer value–creating global processes; international market entry modes; international wholesaling, retailing, and franchising; exporting and importing; going global online; place and the other three Ps (product, price, and promotion) within the marketing mix; and finally, finding and evaluating channel partners. We will introduce a series of globalEDGE diagnostic tools for global market channel partners as a part of this chapter.

LOGISTICS

Global logistics is responsible for transportation, inventory management, packaging, and materials handling

Global Suppliers

PURCHASING

Global purchasing is responsible for the boundary-spanning role with suppliers

MARKET CHANNELS

Global market channels is responsible for the boundary-spanning role with customers

Global Customers

OPERATIONS

Global operations is responsible for the managing of production, competitive priorities, vertical integration, and quality

FIGURE 7.1 A Focus on Global Market Channels

Strategically, within an MNC's integrated global supply chain, it is predicted that market channels as a function will become 12 percent more globalized in the next five years (2013 to 2018) and 26 percent more globalized in the next ten years (by 2023). Figure 7.2 illustrates these increases. In 2013, market channels scored 60 out of 100 points in terms of being globalized (where 100 is fully globalized and zero is purely domestic). A score of 60 places market channels in a tie for last with operations, behind purchasing at the top and logistics after that, in terms of the degree of globalness permeating that function of the supply chain. However, the market channels function is found to be the most important of the four functions (logistics, purchasing, operations, and market channels), scoring a 96 out of a possible 100 points on the degree of importance in contributing to overall global supply chain management for the multinational corporation, followed by logistics with 94, operations with 92, and purchasing with 89. The market channels are expected to decrease in importance from 96 to 94 over the next five years. Figure 7.3 illustrates the changes in market channels in the 2013 to 2018 time period.

CUSTOMER VALUE–CREATING GLOBAL PROCESSES

Within global supply chain management, our primary focus is on global market channels (or market channels management [MCM]) when interacting with and providing value to global customers.

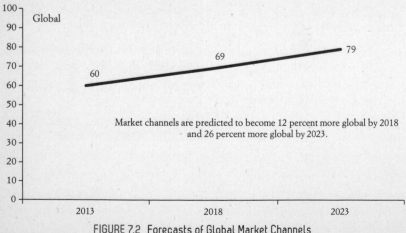

FIGURE 7.2 Forecasts of Global Market Channels

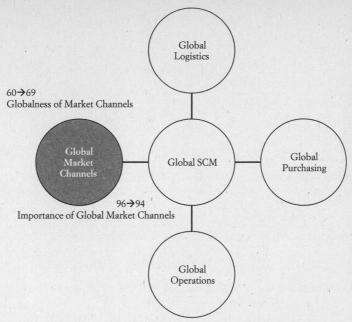

FIGURE 7.3 Globalization of Market Channels, 2013 to 2018

However, two other processes that work in concert with global market channels are viewed as customer value–creating processes (or
core business processes).[4] These are called product development
management (PDM) and customer relationship management (CRM).
MCM, PDM, and CRM are core processes in the last mile of the
global supply chain.

Customer value creation, which is at the center of a global firm's
connection to its customers, both globally and domestically, necessi-
tates the accomplishment of three related and reinforcing processes.[5]
First, the development of new customer innovations, the development of new solutions, and/or the reinvigoration of existing customer
solutions is central to achieving customer satisfaction that is commensurate with customers' expectations (PDM). Second, continually
enhancing the acquisition of inputs and their related transformation
into outputs through an integration of uniquely positioned out-
bound/downstream supply chain partners tends to drive a total cost
analysis toward value creation (MCM). Third, the creation and leveraging of connections to and relationships with external marketplace
actors are central to those actors perceiving that value is being created and customer satisfaction is being achieved (CRM). Figure 7.4

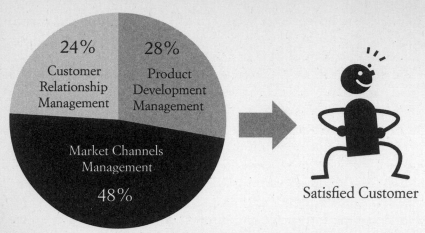

FIGURE 7.4   Customer Value–Creating Processes

illustrates the relative importance vis-à-vis one another that CRM, PDM, and MCM have in the last mile of the global supply chain.

These three macro processes, PDM, MCM, and CRM, include a number of subprocesses that operationally make each of them work in concert with the other two within each macro process and across such processes. In essence, a global firm has the chance to create synergies within each of the PDM, MCM, and CRM processes as well as between the subprocesses within each macro process (PDM, MCM, and CRM). Using the categorization and labeling of Srivastava, Shervani, and Fahey, a number of such subprocesses are possible and likely, and they should be carefully evaluated and addressed in making the customer value–creating processes a strategic resource for global companies.

The PDM subprocesses include determining new customer needs, designing new product solutions, identifying and managing internal functional and departmental relationships, developing and sustaining linkages with external organizations, and coordinating product design activities to speed business processes. Basically, one role of global supply chains is to bring the product development and innovation activities closer to the end customer to allow for better input, integration, and leveraging of knowledge to develop the best customer solution possible.

Based on our data on multinational corporations, we find that in terms of satisfying customers, 28 percent of the customer value–creating effort resides in PDM. A global firm should allocate 28 percent of its customer value–creating effort to product development management. Designers of global products and services should try to maximize the size of the common global core while providing for local tailoring around the core. The best global products are usually those that are designed as such from the start rather than being adapted from national products later. Global products reduce the duplication of development efforts and sourcing, production, and inventory costs in global supply chains, and in some cases supply chain processes can actually lower global product development costs and improve time to market (for example, supplier involvement in PDM).

The MCM subprocesses include selecting and qualifying desired market channel partners; establishing and managing outbound logistics; designing and managing internal logistics; designing work flow in product or solution assembly; running batch manufacturing; acquiring, installing, and maintaining process technology; processing order fulfillment, pricing, billing, rebates, and terms; managing multiple market channels; and managing customer services such as installation and maintenance. Broadly, the role of MCM is to manage the outbound/downstream portion of the global supply chain in concert with the global firm's PDM and CRM efforts.

Based on our data on multinational corporations, we find that in terms of satisfying customers, 48 percent of the customer value–creating effort resides in MCM. As in the PDM scenario, a global firm should allocate 48 percent of its customer value–creating efforts to market channels management. Finding the right balance between maximum efficiency (activities specialized for each country) and maximum effectiveness (activities duplicated in each country) is critically important. Satisfied customers in developed and emerging countries want the product at the right time, at the right place, and in the right way. This means redundancy in the global market channel. How much redundancy is needed has to be individually evaluated based on products, industry, and country dynamics.

The CRM subprocesses include identifying potential new customers, determining the needs of existing and potential new customers, learning about product usage and application, developing and executing advertising programs, developing and executing service programs, acquiring and leveraging information technology and systems for customer contact, managing customer site visit teams, enhancing customer trust and customer loyalty, and cross-selling and upselling product and service offerings. At a macro level, the role of CRM is to develop, maintain, and possibly enhance the

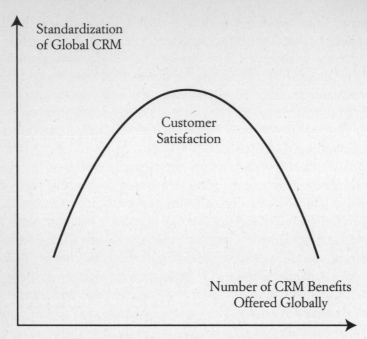

FIGURE 7.5 Global Customer Relationship Management

relationship with business-to-business partners and business-to-customer relationships.

Based on our data on multinational corporations, we find that in terms of satisfying customers, 24 percent of the customer value–creating effort resides in CRM. Again, a global firm should allocate 24 percent of its customer value–creating efforts to customer relationship management. CRM activities can be standardized globally and achieve great customer satisfaction up to a point. At some inflection point, however, CRM practices have to be customized based upon country differences so that they do not adversely affect customer satisfaction. This inflection-point phenomenon is illustrated in Figure 7.5. Global CRM should be implemented by focusing on similarities among customers first and then, and only if needed, satisfying the unique differences through customization.

INTERNATIONAL MARKET ENTRY MODES

Involvement and commitment are two separate yet often related issues in international market entry modes. The following question needs to be posed: how involved is your firm planning to be in the international market and, at whichever level of involvement your firm selects, what level of commitment to the global marketplace in which it engages will it adopt? Companies can enter international markets and engage in global supply chain activities at several levels of international involvement. The four basic levels are exporting and importing, multinational market channels, regional market channels, and global market channels.

At the initial level, which represents the lowest level of international involvement (none), we can start with purely domestic market channels. This is a market channel strategy that focuses on the market in the country of origin. The next level of involvement is exporting and importing. Here, there is no formal international market channel strategy aside from company sales overseas. Multinational market channels are next in companies' potential evolution. At this level, the international strategy has been developed and country markets are customized. The next level of involvement is the regional market channel: a strategy is developed for various regions of the world, and each region is targeted globally. Global strategy is the highest involvement for global companies operating worldwide supply chains; it is developed either for the world or for multiregional areas.

As with involvement, we can also discuss several different levels of commitment to a firm's engagement across the global marketplace. This means that, practically speaking, companies enter international markets and engage in global supply chain activities at several levels of international commitment. The four basic levels are exporting and importing, licensing and franchising, international joint ventures, and foreign direct investment.

The initial level for commitment is the same as the one we described for involvement. Again, we are simply pointing out that the initial level is domestic market channels, since not all companies should strive to be global companies. This level of commitment means that all market channel strategies are focused on the market in the country of origin. The next level is also the same for commitment as it is for involvement: in exporting and importing, there is no formal international market channel strategy other than company purchases and sales overseas. The third level of the commitment process is different from that for involvement, however. Now we are dealing with commitments related to licensing and franchising. Licensees sell a firm's products, and franchisors market a firm's brand

and products under contract. International joint ventures (IJVs) are next in the commitment order. An IJV is a partnership between a domestic and a foreign firm. The highest and most committed level of international presence involves foreign direct investment (FDI). Direct ownership is a situation in which a firm owns foreign subsidiaries or facilities.

For these modes of entry (exporting and importing, licensing and franchising, international joint ventures, and foreign direct ownership), as with many other strategic alternatives, there are conditions that favor their use, and they have certain strengths and weaknesses. Table 7.1 summarizes the favorable conditions, strengths, and weaknesses for each of the four entry modes in detail.

INTERNATIONAL WHOLESALING, RETAILING, AND FRANCHISING

Wholesaling, retailing, and franchising are three market channel options that can be used effectively to engage the global marketplace. These also place the global firm in the right situation and allow it to be successful through an arms-length connection to the customer or to be in direct contact with end customers around the globe. To illustrate the wholesaling, retailing, and franchising options, the best way is to use real-world examples to explain what each option can do for a firm.

Wholesaling involves transactions in which products are bought for resale, for making other products, or for general business operations.[6] The role of wholesalers is critical in supply chains since they often facilitate the cross-border flow of products within the outbound portion of the chain. A strong advocate for wholesalers, with some 40,000 members, is the National Association of Wholesaler-Distributors (www.naw.org). Three examples of wholesalers are Tech Data, Worldwide Brands, and International Wholesale Tile.

Tech Data, a U.S. company, has a unique position and business model for a wholesaler: "As one of the world's largest wholesale IT distributors, Tech Data is the conduit through which the power of technology flows to the world. In fiscal year 2011, we sold $24 billion of IT products to more than 125,000 technology resellers in over 100 countries. Every day, these resellers depend on us to help them cost-effectively support the technology needs of end users of all sizes,

TABLE 7.1 Modes of Entry: Favorable Conditions, Strengths, and Weaknesses

Mode of Entry	Favorable Conditions	Strengths	Weaknesses
Exporting and Importing	Limited or unclear sales potential in target countries Standardized product requiring little product modification Favorable import policies in target countries; unclear political stability	Minimizes involvement, commitment, and risk Increases speed and flexibility of engaging target countries Uses existing production facilities worldwide	Company and its products are viewed as outsiders and foreign market entrants Costs associated with, for example, trade barriers, tariffs, and transportation
Licensing and Franchising	Import and investment barriers exist in target countries, but moderate sales potential exists Large cultural distance between home and host countries Licensee has limited ability to become a future competitor	Moderate involvement and commitment, and low risk Moderate speed and flexibility of engaging target countries Can circumvent import barriers; sales potential	Licensee period is limited in contractual length, and licensee may become competitor Lack of control over the use of company and noncompany assets to promote products
International Joint Ventures	Import barriers exist in target countries, but government restrictions on foreign ownership exist Moderate to high sales potential of products Local JV partner can provide knowledge, skills, and network	Overcomes ownership restrictions and cultural distance Potential for learning and resource combination JV ownership >50% are typically viewed as domestic companies	JVs are new companies, legally independent from the original companies JVs are difficult to manage for the original companies, and there is a lack of control over strategic and tactical issues
Foreign Direct Ownership	Import barriers exist in target countries, but there is low political risk Small cultural distance between home and host countries High sales potential of products, but assets cannot be fairly priced	Viewed as being locally committed and involved Gain knowledge, over time, of the local market Can apply local skills to customize production	Higher risk being taken while being more committed and involved Requires more human and non-human resources, and interaction and integration with local employees

including small- and medium-sized businesses, large enterprises, educational institutions, government agencies, and consumers" (www. techdata.com).

Worldwide Brands, also a U.S. company, is another example of a wholesaler. "Since 1999 we have been finding and Certifying 100% genuine Dropshippers and Light Bulk Wholesalers that are willing to work with small home-based online sellers. We visit warehouses, meet the Manufacturers and find out who the real Dropshippers & small volume Wholesalers really are and then add them to our Directory. Our Directory represents MILLIONS of top-level wholesale products from THOUSANDS of 100% Certified Dropshippers and Bulk Wholesalers that you can use for your online store or auctions. These are the same Suppliers used by big Retail Stores" (www. worldwidebrands.com).

International Wholesale Tile, another U.S. wholesaler, "is a provider of premium quality porcelain, ceramic and natural stone tile products to retail floor covering stores, design centers and specialty tile shops. . . . We pride ourselves on being 'your quality supplier, not your competition,' and that's why we don't sell direct to the consumer. Our main facility, located in Palm City, Florida, houses an inventory that covers more than 14 million square feet. . . . We run several merchandising and marketing campaigns to raise visibility and awareness of our lines and drive traffic to our dealers' locations. IWT markets tile from Europe, South America and Asia. . . . Our focus remains true: sell the highest quality tile to independent dealers, stocking distributors and buying groups" (www.international wholesaletile.com).

Retailing refers to all transactions in which the buyer intends to consume the product through personal, family, or household use.[7] A retailer is "an organization that purchases products for the purpose of reselling them to ultimate consumers." A strong advocate for retailers, with members in some 45 countries, is the National Retail Federation (www.nrf.com).

From Sweden, the home country of the first author of this book, comes H&M as a great illustration of a retailer. "H&M's business concept is to offer fashion and quality at the best price. H&M maintains a strong position in more than 40 markets, and ever since opening the first store in 1947, H&M has pursued its quest for constant improvement. By demonstrating flexibility and listening to the customers, H&M is able to adapt quickly to rapidly changing environments and trends. A competitive combination of quality and fashion at the best price allows H&M to offer customers the best value for money in every market" (www.hm.com).

Another unique retailer is Ahold, from the Netherlands. "Ahold is an international retailing group based in the Netherlands, with strong local consumer brands in Europe and the United States. Our foundation is selling great food—and supermarkets are our core business. We also operate other formats and channels so that our customers can shop whenever and wherever is most convenient for them. We provide customers with the best possible value, assortment, and shopping experience. Our vision is to offer all of our stakeholders—our customers, employees, suppliers, shareholders, and the communities we serve—better choice, better value, better life, every day. We are committed to acting responsibly in all that we do" (www.ahold.com).

Like Ahold, Tesco, from the United Kingdom, is also a good illustration. "Tesco was founded in 1919 by Jack Cohen from a market stall in London's East End. Over the years, our business has grown and we now operate in 14 countries around the world, employ over 500,000 people and serve tens of millions of customers every week. We have always been committed to providing the best shopping experience. Today, we continue to focus on doing the right thing for our customers, colleagues and the communities we serve. . . . We are dedicated to bringing the best value, choice and service to our millions of customers each week" (www.tesco.com).

Franchising is the third alternative market channel. It is an arrangement in which a supplier (the franchisor) grants a dealer (the franchisee) the rights to sell its products in exchange for some type of consideration.[8] A strong advocate for franchising, with more than 1,100 franchisor members and more than 12,000 franchisee members worldwide, is the International Franchise Association (www.franchise.org).

Uniquely positioned in the global marketplace in 2013, the U.S. firm Subway has become the largest fast food chain in the world. "Back in 1965, Fred DeLuca set out to fulfill his dream of becoming a medical doctor. Searching for a way to help pay for his education, a family friend suggested he open a submarine sandwich shop. . . . With a loan of $1,000, the friend—Dr. Peter Buck—offered to become Fred's partner, and a business relationship was forged that would change the landscape of the fast food industry. . . . Fred soon learned the basics of running a business, as well as the importance of serving a well-made, high quality product, providing excellent customer service, keeping operating costs low and finding great locations. These early lessons continue to serve as the foundation for successful SUBWAY® restaurants around the world" (www.subway.com).

Let's go to Canada for another great example, Tim Hortons. "Tim Hortons opened its first restaurant in Hamilton, Ontario in 1964. Since then, the focus on top quality, always fresh product, value, exceptional service and community leadership has allowed the chain to grow into the largest quick service restaurant chain in Canada specializing in always fresh coffee, baked goods and homestyle lunches. Tim Hortons enjoys iconic brand status in Canada and a strong, emerging presence in select regional markets in the U.S." (www.timhortons.com).

Europcar from France is our final example of an international franchisor. "Europcar Groupe S.A., together with its subsidiaries, provides car rental services for business and leisure customers. It offers vehicles for short and medium term corporate and leisure rentals in Europe, Africa, the Middle East, Latin America, and the Asia-Pacific. As of April 24, 2012, the firm's fleet consisted of approximately 190,000 vehicles. It also engages in franchise operations and fuel sales activities. Europcar Groupe S.A., together with its strategic alliance with Enterprise Holdings, operates a car rental network with approximately 10,000 stations. The firm was founded in 1949 and is headquartered in Saint-Quentin-en-Yvelines, France" (www.europcar.com).

EXPORTING AND IMPORTING

Earlier, we dealt with involvement and commitment in going international in terms of the global market channels. What we found was that the first international level for both involvement and commitment was the exporting (outbound) and importing (inbound) option. The remaining options for involvement and commitment, although they overlapped in some areas, were a bit different. That places a lot of emphasis on exporting and importing as a mode of operations in global market channels, and we think that this area deserves a bit more coverage. This is, after all, the lowest level of involvement and the lowest level of commitment a firm can use when going international: selling to foreign markets (exporting) or purchasing raw materials, component parts, or finished goods for operations (importing).

The bottom line is that as the global supply chain becomes more complex over time, companies must adapt to this change and incorporate it into their supply chain strategies. This could mean using suppliers from developing nations, importing products from new sources, or exporting products to new markets. Companies that have traditionally operated within national or regional trading groups may feel ill equipped to extend their global supply chain. This may be as simple as feeling unable to select and manage a foreign supplier or not knowing how to sell products in a new country. But keep in mind that, by some accounts, 90 percent of the products and services that are needed locally are not produced locally; they are shipped in from somewhere else. Your firm is likely to have to get involved with global supply chains—probably through both exporting and importing—to maintain its competitiveness in the future.

The logic for both exporting (outbound international activity) and importing (inbound international activity) is very similar, as illustrated in Figures 7.6 and 7.7. Readiness to export and/or import is a large part of the story. Most companies that engage in international

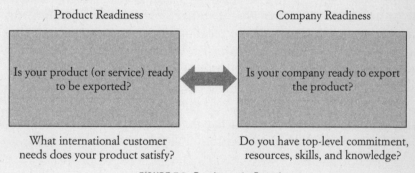

Product Readiness   Company Readiness

Is your product (or service) ready to be exported?   Is your company ready to export the product?

What international customer needs does your product satisfy?   Do you have top-level commitment, resources, skills, and knowledge?

FIGURE 7.6   Readiness to Export

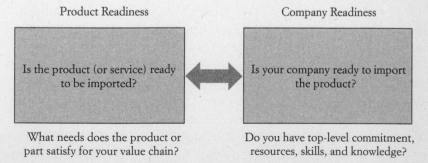

Product Readiness   Company Readiness

Is the product (or service) ready to be imported?   Is your company ready to import the product?

What needs does the product or part satisfy for your value chain?   Do you have top-level commitment, resources, skills, and knowledge?

FIGURE 7.7   Readiness to Import

trade enlist the help of export/import service providers, but there are many choices. Let's look at the main ones: freight forwarders, export management companies, export trading companies, export packaging companies, customs brokers, confirming houses, export agents and merchants, piggyback marketing, and economic processing zones.

Freight forwarders are mainly in business to orchestrate transportation for companies that are shipping internationally. Their primary task is to combine smaller shipments into a single large shipment to minimize the shipping cost. Freight forwarders also provide other services that are beneficial to the exporting firm, such as documentation, payment, and carrier selection.

Export management companies (EMCs) offer services to companies that have not previously exported products. EMCs offer a full menu of services to handle all aspects of exporting, similar to having an internal exporting department within your own firm. For example, EMCs deal with export documents and operate as the firm's agent and distributor; this may include selling the products directly or operating a sales unit to process sales orders.

Export trading companies export products for companies that contract with them. They identify and work with companies in foreign countries that will market and sell the products. They provide comprehensive exporting services, including export documentation, logistics, and transportation.

Export packaging companies, or export packers for short, provide services to companies that are unfamiliar with exporting. For example, some countries require packages to meet certain specifications, and the export packaging firm's knowledge of these requirements is invaluable to new exporters in particular. The export packer can also advise companies on appropriate design and materials for the packaging of their items. Export packers can assist companies in minimizing packaging to maximize the number of items to be shipped.

Customs brokers can help companies avoid the pitfalls involved in customs regulations. The customs requirements of many countries can be difficult for new or infrequent exporters to understand, and the knowledge and experience of the customs broker can be very important. For example, many countries have certain laws and documentation regulations concerning imported items that are not always obvious to the exporter. Customs brokers can offer a firm a complete package of services that are essential when a firm is exporting to a large number of countries.

Confirming houses, sometimes called buying agents, represent foreign companies that want to buy your products. Typically, they try to get the products they want at the lowest prices and are paid a commission by their foreign clients. A good place to find these potential exporting linkages is via government embassies.

Export agents, merchants, and remarketers buy products directly from the manufacturer, then package and label the products in accordance with their own wishes and specifications. They then sell the products internationally through their own contacts under their own names and assume all risks. The effort it takes for you to market the product internationally is very small, but you also lose any control over the marketing, promotion, and positioning of your product.

Piggyback marketing is an arrangement whereby one firm distributes another firm's products. For example, a firm may have a contract to provide an assortment of products to an overseas client, but it does not have all the products requested. In such cases, another firm can piggyback its products to fill the contract's requirements. Successful piggybacking usually requires complementary products and the same target market of customers.

There are now more than 600 export processing zones (EPZs) in the world, and they exist in more than 100 countries. The EPZs include foreign trade zones (FTZs), special economic zones, bonded warehouses, free ports, and customs zones. Many companies use EPZs to receive shipments of products that are then reshipped in smaller lots to customers throughout the surrounding areas. Founded in 1978 by the United Nations, the World Economic Processing Zones Association (wepza.org) is a private nonprofit organization dedicated to the improvement of the efficiency of all EPZs.

With all of these choices for exporting and importing assistance, the issues of financial resources, taking risks, and getting paid are money-related and thus are critically important for exporting and importing. So, let's look at three examples of export-import banks: those in the United States, China, and India. Keep in mind that many countries also have export credit agencies that operate in a similar way.

The Export-Import Bank of the United States (exim.gov) was established in 1934. It is the official export credit agency of the U.S. federal government, with the purpose of financing and insuring foreign purchases of American goods for customers who are unable or unwilling to accept credit risk. Broadly, the bank's mission is to create and sustain U.S. jobs by financing sales of U.S. exports to international buyers.

The Export-Import Bank of China (eximbank.gov.cn) was established in 1994. Its objective is to facilitate the export and import of Chinese mechanical and electronic products, including complete sets of equipment and new- and high-tech products; assist Chinese companies by providing comparative advantages in their offshore contract projects and outbound investment; and promote Sino-foreign relationships and international economic and trade cooperation.

The Export-Import Bank of India (eximbankindia.com) was established in 1982 with the objective of providing financial assistance to exporters and importers and functioning as the principal financial institution for coordinating the work of institutions engaged in financing the export and import of goods and services with a view to promoting India's international trade.

GOING GLOBAL ONLINE

The (ridiculous) saying goes something like this: you have a website; therefore you have a global business. The real story is that you do not have a true global business online until you attend to it as such. As professors, trainers, and authors, we have websites highlighting who we are, along with other useful (and perhaps not so useful) data and information about us that we and/or Michigan State University want to showcase. This does not make us a global business. Michigan State University is such a business, as it has operations in some 180 countries. However, we as individuals with websites are not. It takes a dedicated effort, a considered approach, and a strategic outlook on how best to engage and interact with customers to get the kind of sales a firm would be looking for in the marketplace.

In that vein, we can talk about three types of websites that have some implications, input, and potential for sales outcomes, either online or from the firm's brick-and-mortar stores: transactional sites, information delivery sites, and e-marketplaces.[9] A transactional site can be an electronic storefront for a retailer or a way for a manufacturer to sell directly to the customer. On these sites, customers are able to search for, order, pay for, and get after-sales service for products. An information delivery site typically generates sales by promoting a firm's brands, letting customers know that the firm exists, and providing general information about the firm—basically, it functions as an online brochure that is intended to create sales through the customer contacting the firm. E-marketplaces are "market makers" in that they bring buyers and sellers together to facilitate transactions (for example, eBay, Amazon, and Taobao).

Building on *A Basic Guide to Exporting*,[10] the five steps to going global online that are given there can serve as a great starting point for small and medium-sized enterprises (SMEs): selecting a domain name, registering with search engines, selecting a web host, localizing and internationalizing website content, and promoting the website. First, like any domain name, your URL for the global marketplace should be short, simple, descriptive, and memorable to customers in the intended global market. Locally branded domain names typically increase brand awareness, increase website recall, and influence sales and loyalty. Next, registering your website with all major search engines so that international customers can find information about your product is critically important. It is especially important that you register with search engines that are used by customers in the international market you are targeting. Third, when selecting a web host, ensure that the hosting firm's servers reside in a stable infrastructure, and that it is on the backbone of a web network that is maintained for optimal access reliability throughout all your potential markets. Fourth, consider localizing and internationalizing your web interface for your targeted customers; there is no need to change your main website, but consider adding site pages for the targeted audience. Language, cultural nuances, payment preferences, pricing in local currency, and metric measurements are issues to consider. Fifth, you will often be able to find locally oriented web networks— such as trade publications—that target customers in the markets you are considering. All your materials (products, packaging, and online brochures) should have your URL on them. Make sure your website has an opt-in mechanism so that customers can choose to interact with your site, your firm, and your products.

Let's say your firm uses one of the three types of websites—preferably a transactional site, since we want to sell products—and look at China as a viable market to sell into during the next several years. We all know China's market as a source for low-cost production, but what about China as a market to sell to? At the outset, we know that, for example, U.S. exports to China have gone up more than 500 percent in the last decade (from some $16 billion to some $104 billion)—an amazing number, especially when you compare it to the 116 percent increase in exports, on average, from the United States to all other countries. China is the United States's third largest export market, behind only Canada and Mexico. Crops, computers and electronics, chemicals, transportation equipment, and waste and scrap are the top five categories of exports to China (each with more than $11 billion in exports annually).

At the same time, the Chinese inbound market is still ripe for expansion. While the Chinese economy grew by a little more than 10 percent annually during the 2000 to 2010 decade, it is predicted to grow by roughly 8 percent annually during the 2010 to 2020 decade. This means that the Chinese economy could potentially double between 2010 and 2020, solidifying its global position as the second largest economy in the world, after the United States. This gets even more interesting in terms of the expected increase in the discretionary income of Chinese consumers. While only 6 percent of the Chinese population were middle-class consumers (by the standards of developed nations) in 2010, the expectation is that 51 percent of the Chinese population will be middle class by 2020. This takes us from some 17 million in 2010 to about 200 million Chinese households being middle class in 2020. That opens up sales opportunities because of the expected increase in incomes—if the trends truly turn out as projected.

Let's go back to discretionary income, which is really the most important issue. Advanced cities will see households move from about 5 percent middle class in 2010 to more than 70 percent in 2020. Developing cities see great projections as well: from 1 percent middle class in 2010 to some 70 percent in 2020. This trend is also projected for emerging cities; they are at virtually zero percent middle-class households in 2010 and are expected to have some 40 percent of households that are middle class in 2020. Even the lagging cities will see an increase in the middle class, from zero in 2010, like the emerging cities, to more than 20 percent by 2020. In each case, we will see a dramatic rise in discretionary income and the potential for spending on various products sold online.

China is expected to have about 700 million people online by 2015. The unique aspect of Chinese customers' online behavior is that only 20 percent of online shoppers in China go to official brand or manufacturers' websites, compared with about half of online shoppers in Japan, the United States, and Europe. Chinese consumers do not rely much on search engines to find products. They are prolific reviewers and readers of online reviews. Their trust in online information sources such as blogs, review sites, and social networking sites is far higher than their trust in offline sources such as TV ads or printed materials. However, social networking in China is very fragmented because of government policies. Also, there is a power in the Chinese online system that you will have to deal with: Taobao.com has virtually defined e-commerce in China. In 2010, it sold more than China's top five brick-and-mortar retailers combined. The site offers more than 800 million items and accounts for about 80 percent of China's online transaction value.

PLACE AND THE OTHER THREE Ps

For a long time, marketing has been centered on the tactical (or activities-based) issues related to the four Ps: product, place, price, and promotion. Place is where we find the concept of market channels, and for practical purposes, it is equivalent to market channels (we have referred to it as such throughout this book). But what marketing has to offer in the marketing mix is highly relevant for the connections among the four Ps and the effectiveness with which market channels can be developed and implemented globally.

For example, channel members ensure the flow of products from producers to customers via intermediaries (place). They participate in selecting the product assortments that match the needs of customers (product). They participate in the establishment of pricing policies and terms of sale for customers (price). They also coordinate advertising, personal selling, sales promotion, publicity, and packaging (promotion). This means that there are critical questions that need to be addressed, assessed, evaluated, and acted upon with respect to the four Ps. We use the work by Tomas Hult, William Pride, and O. C. Ferrell to provide a battery of questions that are useful for implementing each of the four Ps.[11]

Place

Many questions arise concerning place, such as what is the role of the channel intermediaries internationally, and where is value created beyond the domestic borders of the firm? These involve discussion of generic strategy issues for market channels. Is the movement of products from the home country to the foreign market or to a regional warehouse done in the most efficient way (a physical distributions issue)? What is the availability of different types of retail stores in the various country markets? That is a retail store issue. Where do customers typically shop in the targeted countries—downtown, in suburbs, or in malls? This question highlights a retailing strategy issue.

Product

Questions about the product emerge, such as whether there is a commonality in the customers' needs across countries and what the product will be used for and in what context. How is awareness of the product created in the various country markets, and how and where is the product typically bought? These are product adoption issues. How are truly new products managed in the country markets vis-à-vis existing products or modified products? This constitutes a product management issue. Is the brand accepted widely around the world, and does its home country help or hurt the consumer's perception of the brand? That is a critical branding issue.

Promotion

Questions arise here, too, such as whether some countries' customers prefer firm-specific advertising instead of product-specific advertising. Along this line is, how does this preference affect advertising? These are considered general advertising issues. How is public relations used to manage the stakeholders' interests internationally, and are the stakeholders' interests different worldwide? This involves public relations issues. What product types require personal selling internationally, and does international selling differ from the way those products are sold domestically? This question pertains to personal selling. Is coupon usage widespread in the targeted international markets, and what other forms of sales promotion should be used? Such a question is connected to sales promotion issues.

Price

Is price a critical component of the value equation for the product in the targeted country markets? That is a core pricing issue. Is the demand curve similar internationally to what it is domestically, and will a change in price drastically change demand? This has linkages to an analysis of demand. What are the fixed and variable costs when marketing the product internationally, and are they similar to the domestic ones in terms of the relationships among demand, cost, and profit for the global firm? Finally, how do the pricing strategy, environmental forces, business practices, and cultural values affect price as related to the determination of pricing that would work best globally?

GLOBALEDGE DIAGNOSTIC TOOLS AND MARKET POTENTIAL INDEX (MPI)

In Chapter 3, we introduced and discussed the main menu features of the globalEDGE website (globalEDGE.msu.edu), a product of the International Business Center in the Eli Broad College of Business at Michigan State University. To refresh your memory, globalEDGE has been the top-ranked website in the world for international business resources on Google since 2004. Businesspeople, public policy makers, academics, and college students have been using globalEDGE in some form since 1994, when it first started as "International Business Resources on the World Wide Web." The vast majority of the site has always been free; the only (small) fee-based portion of the site is the Diagnostic Tools section. In that section of the site, we have four diagnostic tools that focus on various portions of and solutions for the market channels function in the global supply chain. Each tool has been developed through sophisticated research and numerous Delphi studies with business and supply chain executives. The tools are CORE, PARTNER, DISTRIBUTOR, and FREIGHT.

CORE (Company Readiness to Export) assists firms in their self-assessment of their exporting proficiency, evaluates both the firm's and the intended product's readiness to be taken internationally, and systematically identifies the firm's strengths and weaknesses within the context of exporting (see Figure 7.8). The CORE tool also serves as a tutorial in exporting, and it has been the most successful and most widely used of the tools created by the International Business Center. PARTNER (International Partner Selection) assists in the analysis and evaluation of potential international partners. It covers a wide variety of types of partnerships: joint ventures,

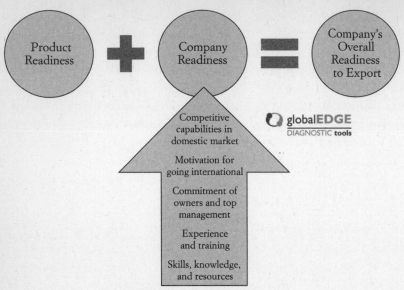

FIGURE 7.8 The CORE Diagnostic Tool

licensees, franchisees, contract manufacturers, and R&D partnerships. It is based on a multidimensional set of criteria that includes trust and relationship factors as well as operational criteria and contains individually identified strengths and weaknesses of each partner. DISTRIBUTOR (Foreign Distributor Selection) helps exporting firms evaluate and compare foreign distributor or agent candidates, given the type of product being sold and the market characteristics, and indicates areas that may require ongoing training and management throughout the life of the relationship. FREIGHT (Freight Forwarder Selection) assists companies in selecting the most appropriate international freight forwarder for their type and volume of business based on six sets of criteria; it evaluates each candidate, highlights the candidates' strengths and weaknesses, and compares the various candidates.

Another unique feature of globalEDGE is the Market Potential Index (MPI). Global marketing is becoming increasingly important, given that globalization of multinational corporations' subsidiaries is rampant and that trade across borders has far exceeded increases in home country production and the size of the home country economy. However, when a firm is planning to enter the global marketplace, having too many choices is a potential barrier to market entry. In that spirit, the focus of the MPI is on ranking the market potential of emerging economies. This indexing study is conducted annually by the International Business Center to help global companies and aspiring global companies compare emerging markets on eight dimensions, using a scale of 1 to 100. Each dimension is measured using a number of variables that are weighted to determine their relative contribution to the overall Market Potential Index. A recent MPI ranking is included in Table 7.2 for illustration purposes.

GUIDELINES FOR MARKET CHANNELS IN GLOBAL SUPPLY CHAINS

Market channels is one of the four critical functions that should be integrated at the strategic and tactical levels in global supply chains and as part of the global firm's corporate strategy. As in the earlier discussion of the other three functions (logistics, purchasing, and operations), some market channels issues are major items that you can see, and some are intricate details of doing global business that are not readily obvious or understood. Clearly, there are numerous issues to consider that relate to market channels in global supply chains. In assessing global market channels, we suggest these guidelines as a starting point:

- Analyze, evaluate, develop, and implement strategic initiatives commensurate with the relative importance of each customer value–creating process as a part of the firm's global market channels effort in global supply chains. A starting point is to allocate effort based on the data we presented in this chapter. That is, allocate 24 percent of the effort to customer relationship management, 28 percent to product development management, and 48 percent to market channels management.
- Involvement in international markets is not the same as commitment to international markets. Some overlap of involvement and commitment exists at the exporting and importing levels, but the higher levels of each are different and should be strategically evaluated as such. As we outlined, take into account favorable conditions, strengths, and weaknesses in making the level of commitment decision that fits your firm the best.

TABLE 7.2 Michigan State University's MPI, 2013

Overall Rank	Country	Market Size	Market Growth Rate	Market Intensity	Market Consumption Capacity	Commercial Infrastructure	Economic Freedom	Market Receptivity	Country Risk	Overall Score
1	Singapore	1	86	74	66	80	83	97	100	62
2	Hong Kong	1	44	100	58	100	90	100	92	61
3	China	100	100	1	70	39	8	4	54	56
4	South Korea	9	40	56	100	87	82	18	65	49
5	Israel	1	39	65	79	70	78	22	66	43
6	Czech Republic	1	11	45	95	88	88	16	71	43
7	Poland	3	33	55	82	72	81	8	63	41
8	Turkey	6	73	65	79	52	53	5	49	41
9	India	37	74	28	78	22	52	3	42	41
10	Chile	1	40	48	35	60	100	15	79	38
11	Hungary	1	1	58	88	77	78	20	37	37
12	Malaysia	3	60	29	58	63	52	21	61	37
13	Russia	19	45	36	68	73	17	4	43	36

Overall Rank	Country	Market Size	Market Growth Rate	Market Intensity	Market Consumption Capacity	Commercial Infrastructure	Economic Freedom	Market Receptivity	Country Risk	Overall Score
14	Peru	2	76	40	56	40	70	6	50	35
15	Mexico	9	31	53	49	47	63	21	53	35
16	Indonesia	10	68	28	77	32	54	3	39	34
17	Brazil	18	36	42	37	56	60	1	55	34
18	Argentina	4	68	49	67	60	45	4	11	33
19	Saudi Arabia	4	68	15	0	56	15	14	67	32
20	Thailand	3	19	31	66	47	49	17	48	30
21	Egypt	4	33	58	83	47	27	4	10	30
22	Colombia	3	44	42	31	45	62	4	52	29
23	Philippines	4	24	52	58	31	51	5	37	28
24	Pakistan	5	37	66	83	1	32	1	1	25
25	Venezuela	3	40	36	67	44	1	8	10	24
26	South Africa	5	29	40	1	25	66	5	50	22

- A firm's readiness to export does not automatically imply its readiness to import, and vice versa. Review our material on exporting and importing and figure out the landscape of your firm's operations. More important, we discussed nine different options for assistance in dealing with exporting and importing. Assuming that your firm does not have an international division or a dedicated team to tackle all exporting- and/or importing-related issues, contracting with service operations that can help is a great way to leverage knowledge across your firm and the service provider.
- globalEDGE has a set of market channels tools that can be particularly helpful in determining whether your firm is ready to export a product (CORE), finding the right international partner (PARTNER), selecting the best freight forwarder (FREIGHT), and selecting the most appropriate international distributor (DISTRIBUTOR). These tools are made available for a minimal fee; check them out.

CHAPTER 8

Managing Global Supply Chains

Coordination creates value for stakeholders in global supply chains.

VALUE OF MANAGING THE LOCATION OF GLOBAL ACTIVITIES

If you are interested only in tactically managing global supply chains, then you are not the main audience for this book. Global supply chain management is inherently both strategic and tactical (operational). While we find that the global strategy efforts of multinational corporations explain 70 percent of a firm's performance in the global marketplace, we also find that global supply chain efforts account for roughly 21 percent of that effort today and are predicted to account for 25 percent in five years (that is, global supply chains are becoming more important and more global). This is in the realm of strategy development, and strategy should include global supply chain management.

The impact of global strategy on performance has stayed consistent over the last decade and is forecast to stay the same over the next five years (we can estimate that it will stay about the same for the next ten years, but the data support at least the next five years). What is interesting and important is that the emphasis on the location of global activities—mainly via the focus on global supply chains—has increased significantly. Multinational corporations emphasized locating global activities 4 percentage points more in 2013 than in 2005 (a change from a 17 percent emphasis in 2005 to a 21 percent in 2013, with a prediction for even greater emphasis on the global supply chain in the next five years).

In 2005, the scores for the five global strategy levers for the world's multinational corporations were global market participation, 22 percent; products and services, 20 percent; locating global activities, 17 percent; global marketing, 22 percent; and making global competitive moves, 19 percent. In 2013, the scores for the five global strategy levers for the world's MNCs were global market participation, 20 percent; products and services, 20 percent; locating global activities, 21 percent; global marketing, 20 percent; and making global competitive moves, 19 percent. These results show a more balanced approach to global strategy development in 2013. They also indicate that locating global activities—and global supply chain strategy and activities play a core role within the location efforts—is the strategy area that is receiving the most clear-cut added focus. Our prediction, based on data, is that this global supply chain focus will increase even more in the next decade (locating global activities could be averaging a score of 26 in 2023 for the leading MNCs in the world).

To better understand individual companies' emphasis on certain global strategy levers (as identified by George Yip and Tomas Hult),[1] we gathered independent data and analyzed the relative efforts of 16 multinational corporations: ABB, AB InBev, American Express, ArcelorMittal, Cemex, Daimler, Dell, FedEx, Microsoft, Nestlé, Nokia, OMV Group, Siemens, Skandia, Swatch, and Unilever. Our analysis of these companies addresses the core emphasis that each places on the five global strategy levers (that is, market participation, products and services, locating activities, marketing, and competitive moves). However, we naturally focus more intense scrutiny on the global strategy lever called "locating global activities," since it inherently focuses primarily on the global supply chain efforts of these companies. Some basic information about the 16 firms is given in Table 8.1 for ease of readability. The first portion of the table provides descriptive information about the firms. The right-side columns provide the scores on the global strategy levers.

From these data, we can see that different firms emphasize different strategy levers for their success. For instance, ABB emphasizes global marketing first (24 percent) and the supply chain–focused lever of locating global activities second (22 percent). On the other hand, American Express most emphasizes global marketing participation (23 percent) followed by products and services (23 percent).

TABLE 8.1 Summaries of 16 Global Companies

Firm Name, Location, and Web Address	Overview/Description	GMP	P/S	LGA	GM	MGCM
ABB, Switzerland/Sweden www.abb.com	Asea Brown Boveri, or simply ABB, was the result of a 1988 merger of the Swedish corporation Allmänna Svenska Elektriska Aktiebolaget (ASEA) and the Swiss company Brown, Boveri, and Cie (BBC). ABB is a global leader in power and automation technologies. Now primarily based in Zurich, Switzerland, the company employs some 145,000 people and operates in more than 100 countries.	20%	14%	22%	**24%**	20%
American Express, USA www.americanexpress.com	American Express Company, or Amex, was founded in 1850 as an express mail business in Buffalo, New York. These days Amex is headquartered in Manhattan, New York, and is best known for its credit card, charge card, and traveler's checks businesses, which are accepted in more than 130 countries. Amex says that "we're a global services company that provides customers with access to products, insights and experiences that enrich lives and build business success."	**23%**	**23%**	16%	21%	17%
AB InBev, Belgium/Brazil www.ab-inbev.com	AB InBev is a Belgian-Brazilian beverage and brewing company headquartered in Leuven, Belgium, that is the world's largest brewer, with some 25 percent global market share. AB InBev has around 120,000 employees in more than 20 countries. With the integration of Anheuser-Busch in 2008, roughly 45 percent of the company's sales come from North America. It is one of the world's top five consumer products companies and is recognized as the top company in the beverage industry in *Fortune* magazine's list of "World's Most Admired" companies.	**25%**	23%	21%	15%	16%
ArcelorMittal, Liechtenstein www.arcelormittal.com	As indicated on its website, "ArcelorMittal is the world's leading steel and mining company. Guided by a philosophy to produce safe, sustainable steel, it is the leading supplier of quality steel products in all major markets including automotive, construction, household appliances and packaging. ArcelorMittal operates in 60 countries and employs about 245,000 people worldwide."	20%	**22%**	21%	20%	17%
Cemex, Mexico www.cemex.com	According to Cemex's website, "CEMEX is a global building materials company that provides high quality products and reliable service to customers and communities throughout the Americas, Europe, Africa, the Middle East, and Asia." The enterprise "produces, distributes, and sells cement, ready-mix concrete, aggregates, and related building materials in more than 50 countries, and maintains trade relationships in approximately 102 nations." Cemex is a top three producer of cement, is often named as one of the world's most admired companies, and has won several industry awards.	**30%**	13%	15%	18%	24%

(continued on next page)

GMP = Global Market Participation/ P/S = Products/Services; LGA = Locating Global Activities; GM = Global Marketing; MGCM = Making Global Competitive Moves

TABLE 8.1 Summaries of 16 Global Companies *(continued)*

Firm Name, Location, and Web Address	Overview/Description	GMP	P/S	LGA	GM	MGCM
Dell, USA www.dell.com	According to its website, "Dell has empowered countries, communities, customers and people everywhere to use technology to realize their dreams." The company states that "customers trust us to deliver technology solutions that help them do and achieve more, whether they're at home, work, school or anywhere in their world."	21%	18%	**23%**	20%	18%
FedEx, USA www.fedex.com	FedEx has become a conglomerate of "supply chain companies" from its beginnings in 1971 as an air/ground express company. The company states on its website that "FedEx Corporation provides customers and businesses worldwide with a broad portfolio of transportation, e-commerce and business services. With annual revenues of $43 billion, the company offers integrated business applications through operating companies competing collectively and managed collaboratively, under the respected FedEx brand." Consistently ranked among the world's most admired and trusted employers, FedEx has more than 300,000 team members, as the company calls its employees, operates in more than 220 countries, and includes among its companies the largest express transportation company in the world (FedEx Express).	21%	20%	14%	**23%**	22%
Daimler, Germany www.daimler.com	Daimler is one of the world's most successful automotive companies. With its divisions of Mercedes-Benz Cars, Daimler Trucks, Mercedes-Benz Vans, and Daimler Buses, the Daimler Group is one of the biggest producers of premium automobiles and the world's biggest manufacturer of commercial vehicles for the global marketplace. The company's founders, Gottlieb Daimler and Carl Benz, invented the modern automobile in the year 1886, with Karl Benz being given the most credit by the popular press.	20%	21%	13%	16%	**30%**
Microsoft, USA www.microsoft.com	Based on the company's website, "at Microsoft, we're motivated and inspired every day by how our customers use our software to find creative solutions to business problems, develop breakthrough ideas, and stay connected to what's most important to them." Microsoft was founded on April 4, 1975, by Bill Gates and Paul Allen and is headquartered in Redmond, Washington. At this time, Microsoft is divided into eight business divisions to serve its customers: Online Services Division, Server and Tools Business, Microsoft Business Solutions, Microsoft Office Division, Interactive Entertainment Business, Windows Phone Division, Windows Division, and Skype.	**22%**	20%	19%	**22%**	17%
Nestlé, Switzerland www.nestle.com	Nestlé has some big goals within its industry domain. Based on its website, "Nestlé's objectives are to be recognized as the world leader in nutrition, health and wellness, trusted by all its stakeholders, and to be the reference for financial performance in its industry."	**22%**	18%	21%	19%	20%
Nokia, Finland www.nokia.com	The Nokia story and history are fascinating. In the last 150 years, Nokia has evolved from a paper mill in Tammerkoski Rapids in Southwestern Finland into a global telecommunications leader connecting more than a billion people worldwide. In the century and a half since its founding, Nokia has made rubber boots and car tires, generated electricity, and manufactured TVs. On Nokia's website, the company is proud of this heritage: "changing with the times, disrupting the status quo—it's what we've always done … and we fully intend to keep doing it."	18%	20%	21%	**24%**	17%

Firm Name, Location, and Web Address	Overview/Description	GMP	P/S	LGA	GM	MGCM
OMV Group, Austria www.omv.com	OMV Aktiengesellschaft (formerly Österreichische Mineralölverwaltung) is Austria's largest listed industrial company and employs almost 30,000 people. What started in 1956 as a state-owned company has developed into arguably the most successful industrial corporation in the country and an international flagship. OMV's main business areas are exploration and production, gas and power, and refining and marketing.	19%	21%	17%	**24%**	19%
Siemens, Germany www.siemens.com	On its website, Siemens claims that "from a small back building workshop in Berlin to a global firm—there are few industrial corporations that can look back on such a long history of success in the way that we look back." Siemens is the largest European-based electronics and electrical engineering company and is headquartered in Munich, Germany. The company is organized in five main divisions: industry, energy, healthcare, infrastructure and cities, and Siemens Financial Services. Siemens employs about 360,000 people in nearly 190 countries.	21%	19%	**22%**	19%	19%
Skandia, Sweden www.oldmutual.com/skandia	Often viewed as a "knowledge management" company, Skandia is one of the world's leading providers of solutions for long-term savings and investments. The company offers products and services that cater to various financial needs and security areas. Skandia pioneered the so-called MultiManager approach, which has now been adopted by most life insurance providers worldwide. With a history that started in 1855, through mergers and acquisitions, the old Swedish-based company is now owned by Skandia Liv (with the remainder being majority owned by Old Mutual).	**21%**	**21%**	19%	19%	20%
Swatch, Switzerland www.swatch.com	The Swatch story can best be described by the company itself: "In 1983, the unexpected appearance of an affordable, Swiss made, plastic watch turned the watch world upside down. Suddenly, a watch was much more than a way to measure time. It was a new language, a way to speak from the heart without words. A Swatch watch was an expression of joy, a provocative statement, a warm smile delivered with a flick of the wrist." Almost everyone around the world knows a Swatch when he or she sees one. There is clearly something that makes Swatch uniquely different from other watches made today.	**23%**	22%	18%	19%	18%
Unilever, Netherlands www.unilever.com	Unilever is an Anglo-Dutch consumer goods company that focuses on foods, beverages, cleaning agents, and personal care products. Unilever is the third-largest consumer goods company in the world (after Procter & Gamble and Nestlé) and the world's largest maker of ice cream. Amazingly, Unilever owns more than 400 brands (e.g., Ben & Jerry's, Dove, Knorr, Lipton, VO5). The company was founded in 1930 by the merger of the British soap maker Lever Brothers and the Dutch margarine producer Margarine Unie. Now, "working to create a better future every day" is part of its story line and is something inherent in how the company drives its global strategy.	19%	20%	**21%**	**21%**	19%

GMP = Global Market Participation/ P/S = Products/Services; LGA = Locating Global Activities; GM = Global Marketing; MGCM = Making Global Competitive Moves

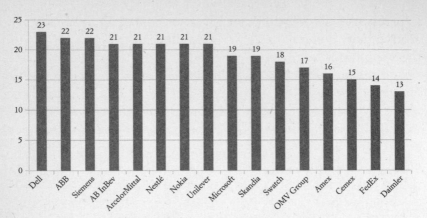

FIGURE 8.1 Emphasis on Locating Global Activities

Other comparisons can be made by careful examination of the data. Looking more specifically at the locating global activities lever, Figure 8.1 lists the 16 firms based on their relative efforts on the locating global activities lever.

The importance of locating global activities and developing global supply chains cannot be understated. The range of possibilities, sustainable efforts, and methods for addressing the needs of the global marketplace is wide. For example, despite some negative media coverage in various areas, Walmart is another fascinating driver of global supply chain development, efficiency, and even infrastructure development.[2] An argument can even be made that Walmart has helped increase the purchasing power of the "bottom of the pyramid" customers, who are often viewed as the world's poorest people.[3] Walmart has achieved a competitive edge by being better than other firms at coordinating the raw-material-to-end-customer global supply chain to maximize efficiencies in total costs (that is, to provide greater total value than many other firms). And it is particularly good at orchestrating global supply chains that produce low-cost versions of products that are wanted (and needed) by customers at the bottom of the pyramid.

IMPORTANCE OF COORDINATION IN GLOBAL SUPPLY CHAINS

Let's go back to the example we used in Chapter 1 about turning an aircraft. Again, consider how to turn an aircraft, and think in terms of coordination and leverage points. That is, aircraft are typically steered using an integrated system of ailerons on the wings and the rudder at the tail of the aircraft. In comparison to the aircraft, the ailerons and the rudder seem very small. However, leverage allows the coordinated effort of the ailerons and the rudder to turn the aircraft. In other words, putting the right combination of a little leverage on the right places through a coordinated effort leads to incredible maneuvering ability for the plane. Global supply chains are the same. Integration and coordination are critically important.

When we presented the general framework of what we include in global supply chain management in Chapter 1 (in the section "Integration of Global Supply Chain Functions"), we focused heavily on logistics, purchasing, operations, and market channels. Figure 1.6 also included keywords such as "strategic and operational," "industry globalization drivers," "worldwide infrastructure," and "managing coordination and integration." We have tackled strategic and operational issues throughout this book and specifically covered the other two topics in Chapter 2 (industry globalization drivers) and Chapter 3 (worldwide infrastructure). What remains to be addressed further is the coordination aspect of running effective, strategic global supply chains. In some way, coordination needs to take place at every cross section of the basic model we introduced in Chapter 1 (in the section "Global Location of Value-Added Activities"), as illustrated in Figure 8.2.

Our data collectively indicate that the coordination of global supply chain efforts is as important for operating a strategically effective and efficient chain as any of the functions in it (logistics, purchasing, operations, and market channels). We find that the importance of coordination for global supply chain management receives a score of 88 out of 100 in 2013 and is predicted to move to 93 on the 100-point scale by 2018. Likewise, the globalization efforts of coordination (how much coordination is done across the companies' global markets), which is at 60 on a 100-point scale (with 100 being fully globalized) in 2013, is predicted to go to 69 by 2018. As such, compared with the supply chain functions, coordination is expected to rival market channels for the most improvement in globalization while gaining in importance so that it is on a par with the supply chain functions by 2018. What are you doing about coordinating your efforts across the global markets you are in and across the

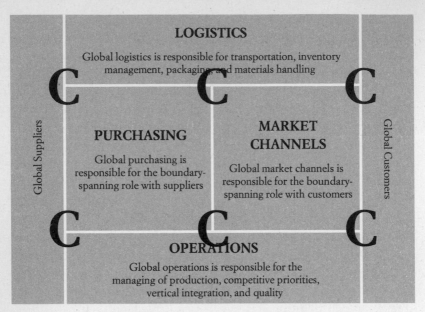

FIGURE 8.2 Coordination at Every Intersection

critical supply chain functions of logistics, purchasing, operations, and market channels?

COORDINATION MECHANISMS IN GLOBAL SUPPLY CHAINS

Global supply chain coordination—across the functions and activities of logistics, purchasing, operations, and market channels—refers to shared decision-making opportunities, operational integration and collaboration, and common information systems pertaining to key global supply chains (see Figure 8.3).

Shared decision making, such as joint consideration of replenishment, inventory holding costs, collaborative planning, costs of different processes, frequency of orders, batch size, and product development, creates a more integrated, coherent, efficient, and effective global supply chain. Shared decision making is not joint decision making; it is decision making involving joint considerations. Shared decision making helps in resolving potential conflicts among supply chain members and fosters a culture of coordination and integration.

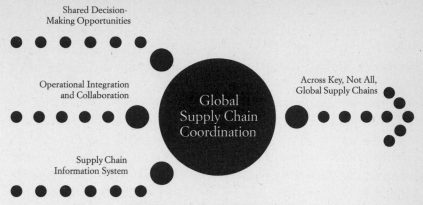

FIGURE 8.3 Coordination Mechanisms

To achieve operational integration and collaboration within a global supply chain, six operational objectives should be addressed: responsiveness, variance reduction, inventory reduction, shipment consolidation, quality, and life-cycle support.[4] Responsiveness refers to a global firm's ability to satisfy customers' requirements across global supply chain functions in a timely manner. Variance reduction refers to integrating a control system across global supply chain functions to eliminate global supply chain disruptions. Inventory reduction refers to integrating an inventory system controlling asset commitment and turn velocity across global supply chain functions. Shipment consolidation refers to using various programs to combine small shipments and provide timely, consolidated movement. This includes multiunit coordination across global supply chain functions. Quality refers to integrating a system so that it achieves zero defects throughout global supply chains. Finally, life-cycle support refers to integrating the activities of reverse logistics, recycling, aftermarket service, product recall, and product disposal across global supply chain functions.

To achieve operational integration and collaboration within a global supply chain, an information system should address four areas: transaction systems, management control, decision analysis, and strategic planning.[5] Transaction systems use formalized rules and procedures, the processing of large volumes of transactions, and an operational day-to-day focus to help coordinate activities in global supply chains. Management control helps coordinate the supply chain's activities by measuring and reporting on performance. Decision analysis helps to coordinate the activities in global supply chains by focusing on tools that assist in identifying, evaluating, and comparing strategic and operational alternatives. Strategic planning helps coordinate the activities through organization and synthesis of data and information to assist in evaluating global supply chain strategies.

There are a variety of supply chain information system options. Electronic data interchange (EDI) refers to the electronic interchange of data between two or more companies. Enterprise resource planning (ERP) is a wide-ranging business planning and control system that includes supply chain–related subsystems (for example, materials requirements planning, or MRP). Collaborative planning, forecasting, and replenishment (CPFR) was developed to fill the interorganizational connections that ERP cannot fill. Vendor management of inventory (VMI) allows for a holistic overview of the supply chain with a single point of control for all inventory management. A warehouse management system (WMS) often operates in concert with ERP systems; for example, an ERP system defines material requirements, and these are transmitted to a distribution center for a WMS.

INTERORGANIZATIONAL RELATIONSHIPS IN GLOBAL SUPPLY CHAINS

Interorganizational relationships have been studied and talked about in various contexts for decades. The two keys are trust and commitment. If we always had 100 percent trust within relationships and 100 percent commitment to them, most global supply chains would ultimately be incredibly efficient and effective. But we don't! So, let's take a look at the building blocks of global interorganizational relationships that are inherent in global supply chains. Developing global supply chain relationships is much like pouring a drink—blending three different liquids into one smooth and silky sensation. All three parts have to be coordinated, integrated, and blended well if the end result is to be right. The parts are actor bonds, activity links, and resource ties.[6]

The actors in the global supply chain are organizations, nodes in the chain, individuals, and other intermediaries. Each of these actors performs certain supply chain activities and has certain specialized knowledge that adds to the value created in the global supply chain.

These actors also control certain resources, some alone and others jointly with supply chain partners. Activities link resources to one another, and they are also used to change or exchange resources through the use of other resources. In a way, global supply chains can be thought of as a complex web of relationships rooted in actor bonds, activity links, and resource ties. These interorganizational relationships have certain dynamics that companies should be aware of, including issues related to functional interdependencies, the power structure, the knowledge structure, and intertemporal dependence.[7]

Global supply chain actors, activities, and resources together form a system in which heterogeneous demands are satisfied by heterogeneous resources. They are functionally related to one another across actors and supply chain functions (that is, logistics, purchasing, operations, and market channels). Based on the control of activities and resources in global supply chains, there are important power relationships among actors. The performance of the activities in global supply chains is to some extent organized based upon those power relationships. The design of the activities and the use of the resources are bound together by the knowledge and experience of present and earlier actors in the global supply chain. The knowledge of those actors, based on the cultural fabric embedded in the global supply chain, is related. The global supply chain is a product of its history in the form of organizational memories, investments in global relationships, knowledge, and routines. Changes in the global supply chain fabric must typically be accepted by at least a large part of the actors in the chain if they are to be workable.

If the blending of actors, activities, and resources is done well and fits within the dynamics of the forces and fabric of the global supply chain, not only is the end result likely to be a smooth, silky mixture, but it is also likely to have the synergy of extra garnish on the side (as captured in Figure 8.4). Effective and efficient global supply chains can give companies amazing strategic and operational leverage.

VALUE PROPOSITIONS IN GLOBAL SUPPLY CHAIN RELATIONSHIPS

By looking at the building blocks for global supply chains within the functional interdependencies, power structure, knowledge structure, and intertemporal dependencies, we would also assume that not all

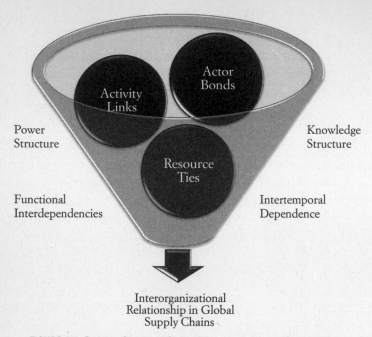

FIGURE 8.4 Building Blocks of Global Interorganizational Relationships

relationships in global supply chains are equally valuable, and that they should not be treated as if they were. To help you think strategically, we developed two illustrations centered on upstream/inbound and downstream/outbound supply chain activities. Figure 8.5 focuses on the upstream (sometimes called inbound) supply chain relationships, and Figure 8.6 focuses on the downstream (sometimes called outbound) supply chain relationships.

For the upstream/inbound portion of the global supply chain, we labeled the three logical scenarios of interacting entities as vendors,

FIGURE 8.5 Upstream/Inbound Relationships

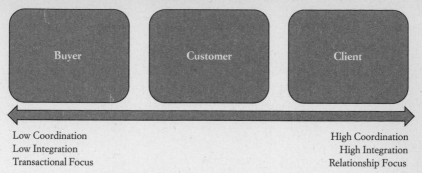

Low Coordination
Low Integration
Transactional Focus

High Coordination
High Integration
Relationship Focus

FIGURE 8.6 Downstream/Outbound Relationships

suppliers, and partners. Each scenario is based on the degree of coordination, integration, and transactional versus relationship emphasis that the firm should adopt in partnering with other entities in the global supply chain. For instance, a firm uses vendors to obtain raw materials and component parts through a transactional relationship that can change easily. A given firm may use suppliers to obtain raw materials and parts and maintain a relationship with those suppliers based on experience and performance. Another firm may engage with partners to obtain raw materials and parts, maintaining a relationship based on trust and commitment.

For the downstream/outbound portion of the global supply chain, we labeled the three logical scenarios of interacting entities as buyers, customers, and clients. As with the upstream/inbound examples, each downstream/outbound scenario is based on the degree of coordination, integration, and transactional versus relationship focus that the firm should adopt in partnering with other entities in the global supply chain. One firm may sell products and parts to buyers through a transactional relationship that can change easily. Another firm may sell products and parts to customers and maintain a relationship that's based on experience and performance. Yet another firm may sell products and parts to clients and maintain a relationship that's based on trust and commitment.

Having reviewed the three scenarios for the upstream/inbound and downstream/outbound portions of the global supply chain, let's look at the emphasis a multinational corporation should place on the relationships with each entity: the benefits to be expected, favorable points of distinction, and resonating focus in the relationship.[8] First, however, some basics on value are appropriate. Value between nodes and actors in global supply chains is a function of the cost (money and nonmoney resources) given up in return for the quality (products, services, information, trust, and commitment) received. Basically, greater value is achieved if the quality is greater while the cost remains the same or is reduced, or when the cost is reduced and the quality remains constant.

Based on our research and strategic thinking, a multinational corporation should allocate 20 percent of its efforts to the vendor category, 30 percent to the supplier category, and 50 percent to the partner category in the upstream/inbound portion of the global supply chain. Likewise, a multinational corporation should allocate 20 percent of its efforts to the buyer category, 30 percent to the customer category, and 50 percent to the client category in the downstream/outbound portion of the chain.

In the vendor (upstream) and buyer (downstream) portions of the supply chain, the benefits that can be expected include those typical of a transactional exchange (costs equal to quality for the goods bought, but not necessarily the best goods in the marketplace). In the supplier (upstream) and customer (downstream) stages, the expectation is that the firm will receive all the favorable points that the raw materials, component parts, and/or products have relative to the next best alternative in the global marketplace. This takes into account the ideas that the costs are equal to quality for the goods bought and that the goods are among the best goods in the marketplace. Finally, in the partner (upstream) and client (downstream) portions of the supply chain, the benefits that the firm can expect to receive include the one or two points of difference for the raw materials, component parts, and/or products whose improvements will deliver the greatest value to the customer for the foreseeable future (quality greater than cost).

STAKEHOLDERS AND GLOBAL SUPPLY CHAIN SUSTAINABILITY

Up to this point, we have dealt with a variety of supply chain players in both the upstream/inbound and downstream/outbound portions of the global supply chain, dealt with the core functions of the chain (logistics, purchasing, operations, and market channels), and stressed the importance of coordination and integration of these core functions. What we have not yet considered are different stakeholders and issues related to supply chain sustainability. Both of these areas—which are sometimes orchestrated and tackled jointly by multinational corporations—have significant implications for global strategy and global supply chain management.

We like to think of sustainability and stakeholder issues as being in the same "value chain." Figure 8.7 illustrates this value chain idea in that the sustainability of global supply chain performance has an effect on how the stakeholders react and respond; stakeholders subsequently have an effect on the performance of the multinational corporation. Importantly, what one category of stakeholders wants and needs (and expects) may not be what another category of stakeholders wants and needs (and expects). In addition, focusing too much on one category of stakeholders and passing over the needs and wants of another category of stakeholder often results in less than optimal overall performance for the firm.

This logic, of course, assumes that we know our stakeholders. There are six categories of primary stakeholders: shareholders, employees, customers, suppliers, regulators, and communities.[9] Shareholders and employees are the key firm-based individuals driving global supply chain strategy and operations. Suppliers and customers are the key upstream/inbound and downstream/outbound groups, respectively, in global supply chains. Regulators and local communities are a part of the infrastructure, either facilitating or hindering the development of global supply chains. They often guide sustainability and greening efforts. Our data indicate that, on average, multinational corporations emphasize customers the most (20 percent of the time), followed by employees (18 percent), shareholders (16 percent), suppliers (16 percent), regulators (15 percent), and communities (15 percent).

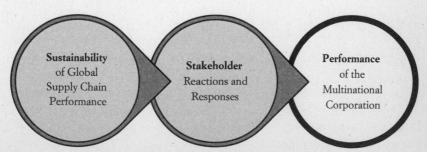

FIGURE 8.7 Sustainability, Stakeholders, and Performance

While still receiving the least focus of all stakeholders, local communities (now emphasized by 15 percent) is also the stakeholder category that has seen the greatest increase in focus between 2003 and 2013 (an increase of 3 percent). Overall, emphasis on the regulators and communities categories of stakeholders has increased in intensity during the last decade. One reason for this change is the increased focus on sustainability and the greening of global supply chains. Companies now place a greater emphasis on corporate social responsibility efforts throughout their organizational systems, including global supply chains. These results are not surprising, since about 70 percent of top business executives consider sustainability efforts to be essential to long-term profitability.

Stakeholders and sustainability efforts in global supply chains can take various forms and have various emphases, depending on the specific multinational corporation's needs and interests. The International Organization for Standardization (ISO) has developed two sets of guidelines that pertain to sustainability, social responsibility, and the greening of global supply chains: ISO 14000 and ISO 26000. ISO 14000 deals with environmental management; the ISO suggests that the benefits of using ISO 14000 include reduced cost of waste management, savings in consumption of energy and materials, lower distribution costs, and an improved corporate image among regulators, customers, and the public. ISO 26000 deals with social responsibility; the areas covered are organizational governance, human rights, employment practices, environmental issues, fair operating practices, consumer issues, and community involvement and development.

GUIDELINES FOR MANAGING GLOBAL SUPPLY CHAINS

There are numerous issues in global supply chain management that should be continually evaluated and decided upon. As always, some are major items that you can see, and some are intricate details of doing global business that are not readily obvious or understood. Given the web of relationships in global supply chains and the many actor bonds, activity links, and resource ties involved in such chains, managing the chain at both the strategic and the operational level is critically important for achieving excellence. Corporate strategy should not dictate what the global supply chain strategy should be, and global supply chains should not dictate what can be developed at the corporate strategy level. In that spirit, a number of guidelines for managing global supply chains can be further explored.

- Do not assume that industries are either global or not global. Nearly every industry has global supply chain potential in some areas, but not in others. Importantly, different industry globalization drivers can operate in different directions, with some favoring global supply chain management and others making it more difficult. Companies should respond selectively to industry globalization drivers and globalize those supply chain activities (purchasing, logistics, operations, and market channels) that are affected by favorable drivers.
- Companies need to select countries for global supply chain activities based on comparative advantage and alignment with the firm's competitive advantages. Different countries can play different strategic roles, such as inbound value-added (purchasing) and outbound value-added (market channels).
- Similarities and differences in potential supply chain partners are important factors to consider. In the inbound portion of the global supply chain, the idea is to evaluate whether similarities synergistically enhance the value-added elements in the chain and whether differences are positive and uniquely valuable. In the outbound portion of the global supply chain, the idea is to evaluate whether the similarities outweigh the differences and stress those relationships in which they do (and when the differences outweigh the similarities, consider pulling back and not engaging in those relationships).
- The best global supply chains are usually those that are designed as such from zero-based assumptions and constraints. However, realistically, supply chains become globalized when the benefits of doing so outweigh the costs. Such a cost/benefit analysis needs to be done for the inbound and outbound parts of the supply chain separately and for each of the "value relationships" (nodes and actors) in the chain, including vendors, suppliers, and partners on the inbound side and buyers, customers, and clients on the outbound side.
- The best pattern of global supply chains usually allows for some degree of redundancy in each link in the global supply

chain (node/actor to node/actor) to maximize value while minimizing supply chain risks.

- Each component of the global supply chain—purchasing, logistics, operations, and market channels—has its own unique opportunities and limitations in terms of global uniformity. Global supply chain managers (and businesspeople in general) typically have been trained to maximize the effectiveness and efficiency of their component of the chain. Creating a successful global supply chain requires a reorientation toward a holistic view of the chain, with managers considering potential sacrifices in their own part of the chain for the benefit of coordination, integration, and cooperation of the full global supply chain.

- Not globalizing a firm's supply chain—or parts of it—can be detrimental to the firm's performance in the long term, as the forecast is that companies will globalize more and more of their supply chain efforts.

- Global strategic supply chain management cannot succeed in the face of organizational barriers and resistance. Some parts of the supply chain will be more difficult to globalize, depending on the firm's culture and its historically established practices and behaviors. Often, it may be best to start by globalizing those parts of the supply chain that are the easiest to globalize, as a way of initiating cultural and behavioral changes before dealing with the more difficult parts. Market channels (especially selling to global customers) is typically a logical starting point for many companies, followed by sourcing globally for some commodity products used in operations and/or for commodity-oriented raw materials or component parts.

- Do not assume that global supply chain management is not for your firm or that "it can't happen here." Almost any industry or firm has the potential for globalization of supply chain activities. Global supply chains are not born; rather, they are created by companies based on need, cost/benefit analysis, opportunity, or diversification interests. Proactive globalization of supply chains is always preferred in order to reap some first-mover advantages, as opposed to taking a reactive approach to globalizing supply chains that is motivated by competitors' actions.

WRAP-UP OF THE INTRIGUING WORLD OF GLOBAL SUPPLY CHAIN MANAGEMENT _____

In the early parts of Chapter 1, we discussed how, no matter where in the world we are born and grow up, we are taught at a very young age to break down our daily lives into smaller pieces, often in a sequential way based on time. The rationale is that breaking down projects and undertakings into their component parts will make us focused and effective in succeeding at completing the task. Sometimes we refer to this as "division." The whole idea is that division creates a procedure whereby a problem is broken down into easier steps. The end result is expected to be a superior outcome if each step is completed fully, with high quality, and at high speed. In a way, we are all taught to be operational in living our lives, whether we're focused on our family life or our work life. But what about the bigger picture, where we can see critical leverage points?

The moral of that story is that, like people, global supply chains are "total cost systems" that work best if all aspects of the chain (such as linkages, resources, and connecting nodes) are strategically leveraged. For the global supply chain, the idea is to get the total chain to succeed, not to maximize the success of an individual entity in the chain. Don't misinterpret this: we want companies that are involved in global supply chains to maximize their value from being a part of the chain. However, strategically, such value-maximizing efforts should be at the 30,000-foot level, where most commercial airplanes fly, like the aircraft turning example we used in this chapter and in Chapter 1.

Therefore, the bottom line is that global supply chain management is not the additive utility of its core functions (logistics, purchasing, operations, and market channels), but instead is the integration and coordination of the strategic leverage points embedded in those supply chain functions along with the entities, activity links, and resources throughout the chain. Global supply chains have to be developed and implemented in such a way that they are both tactically operational and strategic. The corporate C-suite is as important as the service personnel suite, and all organizational layers in between those two must be leveraged appropriately at all mission-critical points in the chain. Just as multinational corporations are increasing their global supply chain efforts as part of their corporate strategies (as our data indicate in myriad ways), we encourage you and your firm to also develop strategic, operational, and cultural foundations to leverage your global supply chains in the most optimal ways possible.

We believe and hope that you will find the tools and ideas covered in this book beneficial. They do away with the illusion that supply chain management in the global marketplace is purely a task-oriented, sequential "chain" of operational activities that are combined into a whole once the chain has been completed. Our argument throughout has been that the supply chains that provide the best value are those that strategically leverage the upstream/inbound and downstream/outbound portions of the chain, from raw materials to finished products. Using critical leverage points, employing total cost analysis,[10] achieving alignment with industry globalization drivers, and embedding global supply chains in corporate strategies should be your focus in order to achieve effective and efficient chains and maximize performance.

Notes

Chapter 1

1. Donald J. Bowersox, David J. Closs, M. Bixby Cooper, and John C. Bowersox, *Supply Chain Logistics Management* (Boston: McGraw-Hill Companies, 2012).

2. Jagdish Sheth and Rajendra Sisodia, *The Rule of Three: Surviving and Thriving in Competitive Markets* (New York: Simon & Schuster, 2002).

3. G. Tomas M. Hult, "The BRIC Countries," *globalEDGE Business Review* 3 (no. 4): 1–2, 2009.

4. Klaus-Dieter Ruske and Peter Kauschke, *Transportation and Logistics 2030*, vol. 3. *Emerging Markets—New Hubs, New Spokes, and New Industry Leaders?* (Dusseldorf: PricewaterhouseCoopers, 2010), www.tl2030.com.

5. George S. Yip and G. Tomas M. Hult, *Total Global Strategy* (Upper Saddle River, NJ: Pearson, 2012).

6. Ibid.

7. Ibid.

8. G. Tomas M. Hult, "Toward a Theory of the Boundary-Spanning Marketing Organization and Insights from 31 Organization Theories," *Journal of the Academy of Marketing Science* 39 (no. 4): 509–536, 2011.

9. Yip and Hult, *Total Global Strategy.*

10. Bowersox et al., *Supply Chain Logistics Management.*

11. Ibid.

Chapter 2

1. George S. Yip and G. Tomas M. Hult, *Total Global Strategy* (Upper Saddle River, NJ: Pearson, 2012).

2. Kenneth Karel Boyer, Markham T. Frolich, and G. Tomas M. Hult, *Extending the Supply Chain: How Cutting-Edge Companies Bridge the Critical Last Mile into Customers' Homes* (New York: AMACOM, 2005).

3. United Nations Global Compact, *Supply Chain Sustainability: A Practical Guide to Continuous Improvement* (2012).

4. Yip and Hult, *Total Global Strategy.*

Chapter 3

1. Pierre David and Richard Stewart, *International Logistics: The Management of International Trade Operations* (Mason, OH: Cengage Learning, 2010).

2. Kenneth Karel Boyer, Markham T. Frolich, and G. Tomas M. Hult, *Extending the Supply Chain: How Cutting-Edge Companies Bridge the Critical Last Mile into Customers' Homes* (New York: AMACOM, 2005).

3. David J. Closs and Edmund F. McGarrell, "Enhancing Security Throughout the Supply Chain," IBM Center for the Business of Government, 2004, www.businessofgovernment.org.

4. Peter Kraljic, "Purchasing Must Become Supply Management," *Harvard Business Review* 61 (no. 5): 109–117, 1984.

5. James F. Foley, *The Global Entrepreneur: Taking Your Business International* (Dearborn, MI: Dearborn Financial Publishing, 2004).

6. Jean-Francois Arvis, Monica Alina Mustra, Lauri Ojala, Ben Shepherd, and Daniel Saslavsky, *Connecting to Compete: Trade Logistics in the Global Economy* (Washington, DC: World Bank, 2012).

Chapter 4

1. Damon Schechter, *Delivering the Goods: The Art of Managing Your Supply Chain* (New York: John Wiley & Sons, 2002).

2. Donald J. Bowersox, David J. Closs, M. Bixby Cooper, and John C. Bowersox, *Supply Chain Logistics Management* (Boston: McGraw-Hill Companies, 2012).

3. Vijay Sangam, "Warehouse Key Performance Indicators," *Supply Chain World*, 2010, http://vijaysangamworld.wordpress.com/.

4. G. Tomas M. Hult, David J. Ketchen, Jr., and Ernest L. Nichols, Jr., "Measuring Cycle Time in Organizational Processes," *Cycle Time Research* 6 (no. 1): 13–27, 2000.

5. D. A. Beeton, *Technology Roadmapping in the Packaging Sector* (Cambridge, U.K.: Institute for Manufacturing, University of Cambridge, 2004).

6. Review of Maritime Transport (2011, 2012), United Nations Conference on Trade and Development (UNCTAD), www.unctad.org.

7. Ibid.

8. Ibid.

9. World Air Cargo Forecast 2012-2013, http://www.boeing.com/commercial/cargo/wacf.pdf.

10. Airports Council International (2012), www.aci.aero.

11. *Air Cargo World* (2012), aircargoworld.com.

12. Air Cargo Excellence Survey (2012), *Air Cargo World*, http://www.aircargoworld.com/Air-Cargo-Excellence/ACE-Methodology.

13. Ibid.

14. Craig A. Lockard, *Societies, Networks, and Transitions: A Global History* (Boston: Houghton Mifflin, 2008).

15. World Bank's Railway Database (2013), http://go.worldbank.org/ AS6SFABKJ0.

16. J. Andrew Peterson and V. Kumar, "Can Product Returns Make You Money?" *MIT Sloan Management Review* 51(no. 3): 85–89, 2013.

17. Ibid.

Chapter 5

1. Dean S. Ammer, "Is Your Purchasing Department a Good Buy?" *Harvard Business Review*, March-April 1974, 36–59.

2. G. Tomas M. Hult, William M. Pride, and O. C. Ferrell, *Marketing* (Mason, OH: South-Western Cengage Learning, 2013).

3. Ibid.

4. Institute for Supply Management (2010), http://www.ism.ws/content.cfm ?ItemNumber=5558.

5. Robert M. Monczka, Robert B. Handfield, Larry C. Guinipero, and James L. Patterson, *Purchasing and Supply Chain Management* (Mason, OH: South-Western Cengage Learning, 2011).

6. Robert J. Trent and Robert M. Monczka, "Achieving Excellence in Global Sourcing," *MIT Sloan Management Review* 47(no. 1): 24–32, 2005.

7. Masaaki Kotabe and Kristiaan Helsen, *Global Marketing Management* (Hoboken, NJ: John Wiley & Sons, 2010).

8. George S. Yip and G. Tomas M. Hult, *Total Global Strategy* (Upper Saddle River, NJ: Pearson, 2012).

9. Kenneth Karel Boyer, Markham T. Frolich, and G. Tomas M. Hult, *Extending the Supply Chain: How Cutting-Edge Companies Bridge the Critical Last Mile into Customers' Homes* (New York: AMACOM, 2005).

Chapter 6

1. Lee J. Krajewski, Larry P. Ritzman, and Manoj K. Malhotra, *Operations Management: Processes and Supply Chains* (Boston: Pearson, 2013).

2. Kasra Ferdows, "Making the Most of Foreign Factories," in *World View*, ed. Jeffrey E. Garten (Boston: Harvard Business School Press, 2000).

3. George S. Yip and G. Tomas M. Hult, *Total Global Strategy* (Upper Saddle River, NJ: Pearson, 2012).

4. G. Tomas M. Hult, David J. Ketchen, Jr., S. Tamer Cavusgil, and Roger Calantone, "Knowledge as a Strategic Resource in Supply Chains," *Journal of Operations Management* 24 (no. 5): 458–475, 2006.

5. Michael E. Porter, *Competitive Strategy: Techniques for Analyzing Industries and Competitors* (New York: Free Press, 1980).

6. Robert B. Handfield and Ernest L. Nichols, Jr., *Supply Chain Redesign: Transforming Supply Chains into Integrated Value Systems* (Upper Saddle River, NJ: Pearson Prentice Hall, 2002).

7. Krajewski et al., *Operations Management*.

8. Ibid.

Chapter 7

1. Kenneth Karel Boyer, Markham T. Frolich, and G. Tomas M. Hult, *Extending the Supply Chain: How Cutting-Edge Companies Bridge the Critical Last Mile into Customers' Homes* (New York: AMACOM, 2005).

2. G. Tomas M. Hult, William M. Pride, and O. C. Ferrell, *Marketing*, 17th International Edition (Mason, OH: South-Western Cengage Learning, 2013).

3. Boyer et al., *Extending the Supply Chain*.

4. Rajendra K. Srivastava, Tasadduq A. Shervani, and Liam Fahey, "Marketing, Business Processes, and Shareholder Value: An Organizationally Embedded View of Marketing Activities and the Discipline of Marketing," *Journal of Marketing* 63 (Special Issue): 168–179, 1999.

5. Ibid.

6. G. Tomas M. Hult, William M. Pride, and O. C. Ferrell, *Marketing* (Mason, OH: South-Western Cengage Learning, 2013).

7. Ibid.

8. Ibid.

9. *A Basic Guide to Exporting: The Official Government Resource for Small and Medium-Sized Businesse*s (Washington, DC: U.S. Department of Commerce, International Trade Administration, U.S. Commercial Service, 2012).

10. Ibid.

11. Hult et al., *Marketing*.

Chapter 8

1. George S. Yip and G. Tomas M. Hult, *Total Global Strategy* (Upper Saddle River, NJ: Pearson, 2012).

2. Charles Kenny, "Give Sam Walton the Nobel Prize," *Foreign Policy*, May/June 2013, pp. 22–23.

3. C. K. Prahalad, *The Fortune at the Bottom of the Pyramid: Eradicating Poverty Through Profits* (Upper Saddle River, NJ: Pearson Prentice Hall, 2005).

4. Donald J. Bowersox, David J. Closs, M. Bixby Cooper, and John C. Bowersox, *Supply Chain Logistics Management* (Boston: McGraw-Hill Companies, 2012).

5. Ibid.

6. G. Tomas M. Hult, *An International Organizational Learning Study of the Internal Marketing System* (Memphis: University of Memphis, 1995).

7. Hakan Hakansson and Jan Johansson, "A Model of Industrial Networks," in *Industrial Networks—a New View of Reality*, ed. B. Axelsson and G. Easton, (London: Routledge, 1984).

8. James C. Anderson, James A. Narus, and Wouter van Rossum, "Customer Value Propositions in Business Markets," *Harvard Business Review*, March 2006, 1–10.

9. G. Tomas M. Hult, Jeannette A. Mena, O.C. Ferrell, and Linda Ferrell, "Stakeholder Marketing: A Definition and Conceptual Framework," *AMS Review*, 1 (1), 44–65, 2011.

10. Donald J. Bowersox, David J. Closs, M. Bixby Cooper, and John C. Bowersox, *Supply Chain Logistics Management* (Boston: McGraw-Hill Companies, 2012).

Index

About the Authors

Tomas Hult is Professor, Byington Endowed Chair, and Director of the International Business Center in the Eli Broad College of Business at Michigan State University. He is also Executive Director of the Academy of International Business (AIB), President of the AIB Foundation, and President of the Sheth Foundation. Dr. Hult is one of the world's leading authorities on global strategy, operations, and supply chain management.

David Closs is Professor, McConnell Endowed Chair, and Chairperson of the Department of Supply Chain Management in the Eli Broad College of Business at Michigan State University. He is executive editor of *Logistics Quarterly* and former editor of *Journal of Business Logistics*. Dr. Closs is one of the world's leading authorities on global logistics and supply chain management.

David Frayer is Director of Executive Development Programs in the Eli Broad College of Business at Michigan State University, where he leads a group responsible for world-renowned executive education programs in supply chain management, strategy, leadership, and other key business disciplines. Dr. Frayer is known for his applied knowledge and skills in global purchasing and supply chain management.